A PATH THROUGH GENESIS

A PATH
THROUGH
GENESIS

by Bruce Vawter, C.M.

SHEED & WARD—NEW YORK

92514

FOR MONSIGNOR

ERNEST LANGENHORST

Tu se' lo mio maestro, e il mio autore . . .

FOREWORD

Some of the material of this informal commentary has appeared previously as a series of articles on Genesis in the *Saint Louis Register*. Its kindly reception there has provoked the present book. I must thank those who have urged this publication and who have contributed to it their suggestions and criticisms.

What I have tried to do in this book I think will be clear enough from the Introduction. It is, I hope, popular in both its form and content. Since popularizations are designed for the educated nonprofessional, I have made no studied effort to insult the reader's intelligence while explaining those things he has the right to find explained. In purely technical matters such as the transcription of Hebrew words, where this has been necessary, I have admitted no rule of consistency but only of convenience for the better illustration of the text.

The text of Genesis reproduced in this book is from *The Holy Bible, translated from the original languages . . . by members of the Catholic Biblical Association of America* (Paterson, New Jersey: St. Anthony Guild Press, 1952), and appears through the permission of the copyright owner, the Confraternity of Christian Doctrine. Other quotations from the Old Testament are either from this version or are my own translation. The New Testament is cited from the Confraternity of Christian Doctrine edition of 1941.

The maps and other drawings are the work of Mr. James Hogan.

ILLUSTRATIONS

CONTENTS

A PATH THROUGH GENESIS

(1) Why This Book Was Written

For some curious reason unpleasant beliefs like purgatory, and hellfire, and a personal devil, and unpleasant practices like auricular confession, are said to have been the inventions of priestcraft to command more surely the simple faithful's fear and obedience. One wonders at the naïveté that could imagine such a change in human nature, since the charlatans whose business it is to know human nature have always borne down rather heavily on the themes of sweetness and light and the certainty of salvation, rather than enticed a following by offering them a chance at damnation. Anyone who has sat in a confessional box the size of a coffin during the long hours of a hot summer afternoon knows that, whoever invented the Sacrament of Penance, it was not a parish priest.

There is a similar *non causa pro causa* that accounts for the marked reluctance of Catholics to read the Bible. Why the private reading of the Bible has all but disappeared among us in recent centuries, is not readily evident. There are probably many historical and social reasons which historians and sociologists, who are not much interested in the matter, have not bothered to follow up for us. The reason, however, is certainly not lack of encouragement on the part of modern popes and of our bishops, whose efforts to restore the Bible as a household book have been resisted with such high success. It is true, in the years immediately following the Reformation ecclesiastical authority at least in theory laid some rather heavy restrictions on the use of the Bible. One gets the impression, somehow, that the restrictions were as superfluous then as they would be today. Those were, in any event, times of tension and suspense, when churchmen were still seeking the wherewith to cope

3

with the unheard-of thing that had happened in Christendom. **And** those times are long past.

Since the rise of the mediaeval heresies in the twelfth century down to the present, bishops and popes have condemned one or another Bible translation which had been made to serve the alien purposes of a sect. This was to strengthen, not to weaken the cause of the Bible. A man does not insist on his copyright because he wants his book to have a narrow circulation, but because he wants a controlled circulation and a text that is not for every journeyman printer to tamper with. Nor is it evident that any contrary intention was ever widespread. The number of blithe spirits prepared to jettison, because it has been misused, either Bible or Constitution, has fortunately been small in every generation.

For whatever reason, with whatever excuse, the average Catholic is today about as familiar with the pages of Holy Writ, except for a few snippets acquired second-hand, as he is with the *Bhagavad Gita*. That is the shame.

Now one can be a good Catholic without knowing the Bible, but he cannot be an informed Catholic. Goodness is a thing of the will, not, as some of the Greek philosophers thought, of the mind, and that is why a very ignorant person can be a saint and a tremendous theologian can go to hell. But the Church has never held up the ignorant saint as an ideal, rather with a kind of wonder at "what hath God wrought." The will works with what the mind has to offer it, and if that is very little, it sometimes does a very good job all the same. To be *willingly* ignorant of intelligence intended for one's spiritual welfare, however, is to leave the climate of good faith in which alone the will can pretend to good. To be willingly ignorant of what can make one better is not to remain good but to become bad. It is to reject the grace of God.

The Bible is one of such graces, and a chief one. This is a conclusion from the Catholic doctrine of *inspiration*.

"From thy infancy thou hast known the Sacred Writings, which are able to instruct thee unto salvation by the faith which is in Christ Jesus. All Scripture is inspired by God and useful for teaching, for reproving, for correcting, for instructing in justice; that the man of God may be perfect, equipped for every good work" (2 Tim. 3:15f.).

If we believe this, that the Scripture is inspired by God, that He is therefore its Author, and that He has inspired it that we may be taught, reproved, corrected, instructed, for our perfection in good works, we must believe that we have a duty to the Scripture. True, God has given other means to these same ends, even if none is so apt as His own written word. But who is so rich in means that he may disregard any one of them?

We do not withdraw what we said before, that one can be a good Catholic without knowing the Bible. He can be, but only if he has never really understood this duty that follows on one of the Church's dearest teachings. This amounts again to saying that without a knowledge of the Bible he is not an informed Catholic.

"All Scripture is inspired by God," said St. Paul. As it happens, he was speaking of the Old Testament, the sacred writings which Timothy had known from his infancy. This brings us to the question, why this book was written.

I think there is no better way to discourage Bible reading than by the oft-repeated advice to "read the New Testament first, then the Old." This is one of those witless axioms supposedly based on experience, but in reality pure untested theory. I wish that priests who are so handy with this advice would recall their feeling of futility each Fourth Sunday in Lent as they stand in the pulpit to read the passage from Galatians which begins: "It is written that Abraham had two sons, the one by a slave-girl and the other by a free woman." By the time they have informed their people that "Sinai is a mountain in Arabia, which corresponds to the present Jerusalem, and is in slavery with her children," they are conscious of the silent reproach of their uncomprehending audience and must hurry through the rest of it in the hope that the Gospel story will make some amends.

Just what is anyone supposed to make of this beautiful allegory who knows nothing of the story of Abraham, Agar and Sara, Isaac and Ismael? Just how sensible is it to tell him to read the New Testament first if he is going to meet this sort of thing at every turn?

And he does meet it at every turn. He can follow the bare historical facts of the Gospel, just as a man ignorant of Catholic theology can tell that the *Divine Comedy* is a chronicle of rather remarkable adventures, or a person who knows nothing of Rembrandt can see that *The Night Watch* is a painting of soldiers. But what the evangelist *did* with these facts, and what they meant to him, will be one with Babylon and Tyre and the two wives of Abraham. Will he see the point of Matthew's insistence that it was on a mountain top that our Lord delivered the epitome of His New Law? Or why the Jews wanted to stone Him when He said, "I am"? These are not frivolous details, they are the keystones of the Gospel. Granted that a commentary is needed for a real appreciation of the Gospel, the commentary can only refer the reader to the Old Testament. Can we seriously expect anyone to make sense of Paul, of the race of Israel, of the tribe of Benjamin, a Hebrew of Hebrews, as regards the Law a Pharisee, apart from the one Book that was Paul's literature and religion and history and morality and culture? Or to follow John through an Apocalypse that is a tissue of Old Testament allusions?

The New Testament is the end of the Old, that is Christian dogma. What we do not sufficiently stress is that this is true not only as the New Testament is religious fulfilment, but as it is religious literature. Throughout the entire history of the Christian canon of the Scripture the Old Testament has been set at the beginning of a Book that was held to be basically one. Today when both Catholic and Protestant scholars are bringing forth arguments old and new to prove the harmony of the two Testaments, it seems to me that we cannot do better than reaffirm this ancient order. The Old Testament is, if you wish, the preface to the New, but, unlike most prefaces, it was really written first.

This book has therefore been written on the premise that it may just be possible to help restore Bible reading by guiding the reader through the part which should be read first in any worthwhile book, the beginning. Therefore this is a commentary on Genesis, not on Matthew's Gospel.

There are other reasons, of course. One of them certainly is the fascination which the Book of Genesis holds for the author. Genesis is sometimes thought of as the most difficult book of the Bible. I am sure this is not true. It has nothing of the profundity and subtlety of John or Paul, its text is not almost hopelessly disorganized like Osee's, it does not conceal its historical origins as Ezechiel does or ask a question that is still unanswered, as does Job. Yet probably no other book can challenge its reader in so many different ways. No other book is quite so fundamental as Genesis, nor hews so close to the simple truths according to which men live and for which they are prepared to die. No other book is so universal in its appeal, yet so uncompromisingly dogmatic. Genesis is surely the inevitable beginning of the Bible.

The Bible is the record of what God has done, "the book," wrote Victor Hugo, "in which God is made visible." Genesis is the beginning of that record. This is why Genesis is a fundamental book, and why it is fundamental to us.

Christianity, like Judaism of which it is the fulfilment, is an *historical religion*. Its roots are in the records of history, and those records are in the Bible. Significantly enough, it is the Christians and Jews whom the Moslems call "peoples of the Book." An historical religion worships a God who has revealed Himself to men in human history, who has done certain things that are facts of history, who has made known His will in the matter of moral conduct. Because of the foundation on which it rests, the morality of revealed religion is universal and unchanging however human *mores* may change.

Thus the essential cleavage between historical religion and paganism, which has always coexisted with it. Paganism is divorced from history, for it has no God who stands outside history and who can intervene in history. It finds its gods in the here and now, in the crude personalizing of natural forces, as with the Chanaanites among whom Israel settled with its transcendent God, or in the more refined mystique of Humanity or Democracy or Freedom. From this religion set in time, no timeless morality can derive. Really pagan morality, which has sometimes been of a very high order, has always been the possession of the few with the mind and leisure to discover some permanent values in the world about them.

We need to remind ourselves constantly that we are people of the Book. We need to return to our origins often that we may be mindful what manner of men we are. "If Christ has not risen, vain is your faith, for you are still in your sins." The Resurrection is the historical fact, the thing which God has done, that underlies Christianity. If the Resurrection is not true, then Christianity is a sham and Christian morality is an idle and vain pursuit. The New

Testament is the witness to the resurrected Christ. "You have seen for yourselves how I treated the Egyptians and how I bore you up on eagle wings and brought you here to myself. Therefore, if you hearken to my voice and keep my covenant, you shall be my special possession, dearer to me than all other people, though all the earth is mine." If God did not covenant with Israel, neither did the God of Abraham and Isaac and Jacob raise Jesus from the dead, for there is no fulfilment without a promise. The Old Testament is the witness to the Covenant, and Genesis is its beginning.

There is a final, rather special purpose to this book on Genesis, as concerns the first few chapters which we shall read in Part One. These chapters are perhaps what has given Genesis the reputation of a difficult book, for what they say seems to clash with what the world at large now commonly admits as proved scientific fact with regard to the nature of the universe and of man and their beginnings. I deem it a most particular obligation to face up squarely to the problems that these chapters occasion. We have said so often that there is and can be no real conflict between faith and reason when both are properly understood, we have the right to see this demonstrated in the Book of Genesis.

As much as possible I have tried to make this a guide through Genesis and not a book about Genesis. A guide's role is to introduce, and the best sort of guide tries to keep explanations to the minimum, confident that, if the introduction was worth the effort, the object will have its own message for the subject. Neither can even the best guide hope to explain everything. For further information on a number of topics with which this guide is not directly concerned, but which of themselves are of the utmost importance, the reader must be referred elsewhere. The articles on the Inspiration and Inerrancy of the Scripture, and on the Languages, Texts, and Versions of the Bible in the *Catholic Commentary on Holy Scripture*[1] may be especially recommended.

(2) Why Genesis Was Written

Those who are eager to begin the reading of Genesis may prefer to omit this division for the moment. It will be better, though, if

[1] *A Catholic Commentary on Holy Scripture*, edited by Dom Bernard Orchard, et al. (London and New York: Thomas Nelson and Sons, 1953).

they read it now, together with the following section which should on no account be omitted. The following section, as a matter of fact, should be reread more than once during the course of Genesis.

What is usually called the special introduction to a biblical text, that is, the discussion of its author, its historical and literary qualities, and the like, is not the most popular department of Bible study, as anyone knows who has tried to teach it. There is the tendency to regard such matters as the peculiar province of scholars, who contradict one another anyway and leave the case so muddled it is better left alone by the ordinary reader who wants to avoid confusion. When we try to extend this attitude to other literature, however, we begin to see that it is not at all reasonable and that it credits the ordinary reader with very little concern for the truth. It does matter, after all, whether the leader article in *The Morning Blast* was really written by the foreign correspondent who witnessed the street fighting in Belgravia which it describes, or was put together by a copy boy in the editor's office. It matters, that is, if we are interested in what it says, not merely in the level of its prose. *I, Claudius* is an account of Rome in the days of the Caesars done, as the title indicates, in the first person singular. It considerably helps in the interpretation of this book to know that it is an historical novel written by Mr. Robert Graves at a time rather later than that of the Emperor who expelled the Jews. If the title page of our copy had been lost, we would not think it tedious to have these facts pointed out to us. The Bible is a work of writing as these others are, produced by determined authors at determined times. Although I have agreed that we must try to keep these questions down to the minimum in this book, therefore, it is plain that we cannot ignore them altogether if we plan to learn very much about Genesis.

What disposes us to think differently of the Bible than of other books is, of course, the Bible's sacred character. It is God's word. God is its Author. Does not the word of our God endure for ever, and are not its spiritual values permanent, independent of place and time? Does an inspired text intended for godly men have a meaning that can be unlocked only through scholarly paraphernalia for which they have neither taste nor talent? Is the Bible not read best of all with the eye of faith, which can find within the living word, if not the sense that scholars will allow, at least one that is meaningful to the spirit?

It is easy to be put on the defensive by this kind of protest, for in opposing it one seems to be drawing a line against piety, which is of far greater importance than scholarship. Yet there is a fatal flaw in this line of thinking. The good people who reason in this fashion are really asking to be left in peace to a rather selfish *use* of the Bible, and not to be forced to recognize in it a purpose that far transcends their personal spiritual needs. I would be far from suggesting that the Bible does not make admirable spiritual reading; the contrary has been proved in both Jewish and Christian history. But this is a use of the Bible quite incidental to its character as the inspired word of God delivered to His saints. The same end is served equally well, and much more continuously, by the *Imitation of Christ* or by one of Father Leen's remarkable books. On the other hand, it is a safe assumption that the seekers of spiritual food of this kind will find very little in the census lists of the Book of Numbers, in the catalogues of cities and villages of Josue, or in Leviticus' careful distinctions between leprosy and eczema. If they have never conceived of the Bible as having any other purpose than this, they are apt to conclude, without actually saying so, that passages like these are rather worthless, though they are every bit as inspired as the Sermon on the Mount or the Twenty-second Psalm. This idea of the Bible turns it from an inspired Book into an anthology of inspiring texts interleaved with great areas of valueless stuff.

Only when we read the Bible to find what its inspired authors meant to put in it are we reading it as the message of God to His people. The Bible was not written in a vacuum, but by men of highly individualized personalities whose powers of mind and spirit were separate creations of God. Inspiration did not change, it accepted these men. Their writings bear the impress of themselves, of their times, of their capabilities and limitations. If we would know the meaning of the Bible, then, we must take it for what it is, the noblest work of human endeavor. In this context we can see the sense of all the Bible, not just its purple passages. This means, I fear, that the Bible must be studied, not simply read. For this study, however, there is no substitute. It will not prevent, rather it will encourage our using the Bible in other, more personal ways, but these must never conceal from us what the Bible is as an objective fact.

I have said above that *the Bible is the record of what God has done*. In a most especial way this description is true of the first major section of the Old Testament, to which Genesis belongs, called by us the *Pentateuch* and by the Jews the *Torah*, "the Law."

It is interesting that such a thoroughly Hebrew work as the Pentateuch we call by a Greco-Latin name, just as we do Genesis, Exodus, Leviticus, Numbers, and Deuteronomy, the books that make it up. The titles of these books come from the Greek translation of the third century B.C. in which the Old Testament became known to the Western world.[2] Later on in Christian times when the Bible was put into Latin these names were simply carried over and by this means have passed into our modern languages.

The word *pentateuchos* untechnically translated means "the five scrolls" of the Law. When the Pentateuch was translated into Greek it had already been divided—presumably for convenience' sake—into its present five parts. Originally, however, we can see that it was conceived as a single book. Who made the divisions, and when, are among the many questions to which we as yet have no answer.

Why the Pentateuch was written we can see from its contents. It is the record of God's dealing with the Hebrew people, from their dimmest origins to the eve of their installation in a Promised Land given them in fulfilment of His Covenant made on Mount Sinai, by which He chose them for His special possession. The Covenant is the unity of the Pentateuch, for in Hebrew eyes all their history was either its preparation or its consequence. It was the unique divine act that had made them like none of the other peoples of the earth, an act filled with the goodness and mercy and mystery of a God who gives life to the dead and calls into existence things that were not.

---

[2] This translation, called the *Septuagint* after its seventy(-two) traditional authors, is of considerable importance in the study of the Bible. Since it was made when the Hebrew text was better preserved than it now is, it is useful in restoring parts of the Hebrew that have become corrupted. Countless of its translations of obscure Hebrew words have been followed by all later versions of the Old Testament. It is usually given the abbreviation LXX, as in this book.

Basic in the Pentateuch is the consciousness of *election*, the conviction that the Jewish people are the chosen of God. There have been later Jews who have tried to repudiate this fact which alone gives meaning to the Jewish past and present. Having seen their people suffer more than once the horrors set loose by a brutish *Herrenvolk* myth, they have perhaps imagined that Israel itself helped set the pattern of these unholy ideologies through its doctrine of exclusivism. Nothing could be less true. This is not to say that no Jew ever abused the idea of the Covenant, just as it has not been unknown for Christians at times to anticipate the separation of the sheep from the goats. But when the Prophet Amos spoke in God's name,

> "Only you have I known of all the families of the earth,
> hence I visit upon you all your iniquities,"

he voiced the authentic Jewish notion of election. Election is *for* something, it does not have its end in itself. Election supposes obligation, and the Jews remembered this more often than they forgot it. It is not for nothing, I think, that they gave the Pentateuch a name which said nothing of their glory, but only of their duty: the Law.

"I will give you as a light to the Gentiles, that my salvation may extend to the ends of the earth" (Is. 49:6). The Covenant was made that salvation might come from the Jews, and of this we see the fulfilment only in the New Testament. But the Covenant was made as well that salvation might be seen in the Jews, that they should be a light to all the nations of the world, who might perceive in their history the goodness of the God who had chosen them, His willingness to forgive, His desire to save. Thus Israel is the story of all man. Thus Genesis, which describes Israel's earliest beginnings, is especially the story of all man. It is part of the divine paradox that only through a religion of the strictest exclusivism—in the Old Testament and in the New—is universal salvation made possible. That a Book intended to strengthen this exclusivism and directed to one of the tiniest nations of the earth should become the heritage of all mankind, is only in keeping with the larger mystery of which it is the written record.

The Pentateuch was an act of faith in response to the oldest of all challenges, the call to conformity. The Israelites entered Chanaan in the thirteenth century B.C. as conquerors, but conquerors so little to the manner born that their success, if we did not know it before, would convince us that their destiny was not wholly of their own devising. "I know that the LORD has given you the land," said the harlot Rahab, apparently with unconscious irony, to the spies sent to reconnoiter Jericho, who seem to have succeeded only in thoroughly alerting the city against attack. In everything that is humane and cultivated they were the inferiors of the peoples whom they destroyed or enslaved, painfully, over a period of two centuries. Archaeologists have learned to detect the signs of the Israelite conquest in the burnt and broken masonry of skilled workmanship which lies beneath the crude and slavish imitation laid by later hands. Whoever is unduly sensitive to a spectacle of this sort will not regard the Israelite invasion as much different from the pillage of Rome by the barbarians from the North.

Yet the Israelites brought with them something far more precious than anything they destroyed. Both ancient and modern, not to say contemporary, history have familiarized us with peoples whose brilliant material culture goes hand in hand with a decadent morality and a religion of vain observance. So it was with the Chanaanites. The land into which Israel came with its God of promise and command was the home of Baal and Ashera, Anath and Kadesh, deities in whose service every conceivable lust and vice had been sanctified. Magic, superstition, debauchery, ritual prostitution, human sacrifice, little children burnt alive as offerings to a god called the King, the aged and useless slain to lie beneath the threshold and ward off demons: these were the folkways of Chanaan.

In Chanaan the Israelites had to learn the virtues of a settled people; it was far easier, and much more pleasant, to learn their unsettling vices. They who had known little of the arts and crafts, agriculture, and proprietorship, found models and teachers ready at hand, but they felt too the tug of Chanaan in many other devious directions. If the Chanaanites had so much to offer, if Chanaan was a land flowing with milk and honey, it was because the gods of the land had made it so. This was the argument of the day, and it was a powerful one. The stern moral code observed in a past that had been put away forever, fitted to a world whose horizons did not extend far beyond the family tentpole, became a felt restraint to spirits eager for the new ideas and opportunities that had before been denied them. It was easy, too, to be ashamed of the crudities of their ancestors who had had none of these good things of life. All this is a common enough picture, which has appeared again and again in human history. It could have meant the end of Israel, but it did not. Instead, it brought forth the Pentateuch, for it is in this age of decision, of seething loyalties and counter-loyalties, that we must find the origins of this book of testimony.

The teachers of Israel reached back into their traditions—some dimly remembered and some with dazzling clarity—into the chronicles of their forefathers and the utterances of divine revelation which they had preserved as a holy trust, and from this material emerged the document which ever after was to tell their people who they were, why they were and must remain different from all other nations, and how great and unique were their God and their sacred laws and customs. The Pentateuch was not the work of a day, nor of a single hand. It is in every sense the work of Israel, a work lovingly reshaped and expanded by its inspired writers and editors throughout its long history. It is, in the end, a product of religious development that reached its climax probably in the fifth century B.C.

Both Jewish and Christian tradition have consistently attributed the Pentateuch to Moses, the liberator, lawgiver, and mediator with God. In 1906 the Biblical Commission[3] ruled that critical arguments to the contrary had not been of sufficient weight to shake this traditional "substantial Mosaic authorship." This deci-

[3] The *Pontifical Biblical Commission* was founded in 1902 by Pope Leo XIII to encourage biblical studies by granting academic degrees in scriptural science and to decide questions submitted for judgment, both of which it still does. The instructions and rulings of the Commission express the mind of the Church and must be accepted by Catholics; they are not, of course, infallible, and they may be revoked. The Commission should not be confused with the *Pontifical Biblical Institute,* a Roman college established by Pius X in 1909, which accepts students for graduate work in scriptural and allied fields, and, like the Commission, grants degrees. The text of the Biblical Commission's decrees and of the papal documents cited throughout this book may be found conveniently gathered in English translation in *Rome and the Study of the Scripture* (St. Meinrad, Indiana: Grail Publications), fifth edition, 1953.

sion was not nearly as purely negative and conservative as its opponents—and, it must be added, not a few Catholics—thought it to be. Already serious misgivings had begun to form in the minds of independent scholars about the truth of the conclusions that had been reached in Old Testament studies during the past century. In all that time the scientific study of the Bible had been dominated by the German critics, who were largely of a rationalist persuasion. These were honest men, but obviously not much disposed to attach any great value to traditional views. Neither had they been given much reason to do so by any argument from the Catholic side. The scientific age had caught the champions of orthodoxy unprepared, and, with brilliant exceptions, they had fled the field of debate and tried to ignore rather than interpret the real points that had been scored against traditional formulas which they continued to repeat in a loud, clear voice. It is not surprising that they in turn were ignored by the scholarly world, which had to its own satisfaction proved the Pentateuch to be a collection of Jewish legend and pious fiction composed at a late date, edifying but hardly historical. The reaction to this radical reversal had already begun when the Commission spoke. Scholars had begun to suspect that the critics had applied to the Pentateuch standards that went very well in nineteenth-century German literature, but not at all in that of the ancient Near East, of which they were generally quite ignorant. Then too, the first trickles from what was later to become a flood of new information from archaeology and the study of long-lost literatures of the ancient world had started to undermine the wall of their assurance. It appeared that the Pentateuch was after all historical, down to many surprising details, which could not be the fabrication of later writers.

The Commission's decision, which did not insist that the evidence proved Mosaic authorship, but simply that it did not disprove it, has now been vindicated to the satisfaction of a great many authorities. The old criticism has been replaced by one which has learned to respect the mentality and to understand better the intentions of the biblical authors. An important school of Scandinavian scholars has helped call attention to the tremendous influence and tenacity of oral tradition in the ancient Semitic world, a factor almost entirely overlooked by the nineteenth-century critics. Nowadays vast sections of the laws and narratives of the Pentateuch are ascribed on purely critical grounds to the Mosaic age. Professor W. F. Albright sums up the new spirit very well in his statement that "it is sheer hypercriticism to deny the substantial Mosaic character of the Pentateuchal tradition."[4] We shall have occasion to return to some of these developments in the commentary on Genesis.

It is pleasant to know that since the rebirth of positive biblical study in the time of Leo XIII Catholic scholars have played their full part in the new criticism. What is less fortunate is how little known among Catholics their contribution has been, and the results that it has had in revising traditional attitudes and interpretations. These are better understood at the present time in Germany and France than among English-speaking Catholics.

Perhaps the most important single fact established by criticism is the existence of *sources* in the Pentateuch. How this affects our interpretation of Genesis I shall try to show in the following section. That false historical and religious assumptions were attached to this recognition of sources by many of the older critics must not blind us to the existence of the sources themselves, nor relieve us of the debt of gratitude we owe their discoverers. The Biblical Commission agreed in 1906 that Moses could have used oral or written sources in compiling the Pentateuch, and that there could have been inspired additions to the text after Moses' time. Returning to the question in 1948 it stated that "no one today doubts the existence of these sources or rejects a gradual increase of Mosaic laws due to the social and religious conditions of later times, a process manifest also in the historical narratives." These words of the Commission show the modification that has occurred in Catholic thinking on the subject of the "substantial Mosaic authorship" of the Pentateuch.

Now it is doubtful that anyone ever thought that Moses himself wrote every word of the Pentateuch, including Dt. 34, the moving description of the great prophet's death. Probably few thought that he had prepared the detailed legislation for the Israelite monarchy two hundred years before Israel had a king. These post-

[4] W. F. Albright, *The Archaeology of Palestine* (Baltimore: Penguin Books, 1949), p. 224.

Mosaic elements, as we can call them, were evident to everyone. St. Jerome had proposed the theory that while Moses was the author, Esdras the Scribe in the fifth (or fourth) century B.C. may have been the revisor of the Pentateuch. (Jerome was following a Jewish tradition; the theory may not be too far from the mark.) Besides this, it was plain enough that there are numerous repetitions in the Pentateuch, and various viewpoints and styles that point to a variety of authors. It was from these data that the critics worked out the distinction of the sources.

As we shall see, it is generally admitted that at least four major sources were used in compiling the Pentateuch. Three of these sources only were used in Genesis. Each source has its distinctive vocabulary, attitudes and viewpoints, indications of the age and environment which helped to shape it. One seems to reflect the background of northern Israel, another that of the tribes of the south. A third source is filled with the spirit of the age of Esdras, while a fourth (chiefly the Book of Deuteronomy) has a language and method all its own. At the same time, all these sources contain laws and narratives which at least in part, as we have seen, present-day scholars are prepared to trace back to the Mosaic age. What then of Mosaic authorship?

We have not yet reached the point when we can give a wholly satisfactory answer to this question. The prevailing opinion today, however, is that while each of the sources is Mosaic, stemming from Moses' activity in gathering together his people's historical traditions and codifying and enacting their laws under divine inspiration, each has taken on its own distinctive form derived from the people among whom it was handed down as well as from the particular purpose it was fitted to serve. Therefore Moses is the author of the substance of the Pentateuch, but the Pentateuch is also the work of other inspired writers and editors who have developed its laws and narratives, gathered its sources into one, and given it its present form. This is what Father Joseph Chaine in his commentary on Genesis (1951) called the "substantial or mediate authorship" of Moses.[5] More at length, the late Father M. J. Lagrange surmised in 1938 that the Biblical Commission was "less

---

[5] Joseph Chaine, *Le livre de la Genèse* (Paris: Éditions du Cerf), p. 492.

interested in Moses' literary authorship than in his substantial authorship. Such authorship is what would result, moreover, in the additions made after his death in his same spirit. In the same way, a teaching which cannot be found in so many words in St. Thomas' works, but which is considered by his disciples to be in harmony with his thought, is called by Thomists a teaching of St. Thomas."[6] The Biblical Commission seems to have agreed with this interpretation in 1948 when it invited Catholic scholars to study the problem of Mosaic authorship "with an open mind in the light of sound criticism and of the results of other sciences which have their part in these matters," confident that "such study will without doubt establish the large share and the deep influence of Moses both as author and lawgiver." In other words, substantial Mosaic authorship may be seen to be rather of the order of quality than of quantity.

It would be presumptuous to try to determine the matter any further in these brief notes. The reader can find more detailed surveys of modern Catholic criticism in Father Robert Dyson's article, "Some recent Catholic viewpoints on the Pentateuchal question," in the *Catholic Commentary,* and in Father Moriarty's excellent little *Foreword to the Old Testament Books.*[7]

I hope I have made it clear that our critical acceptance of Mosaic authorship does not affect the inspiration of the books of the Pentateuch. Moses the original author was certainly inspired. The Pentateuch as we at present have it in the Bible we know from the definition of the Council of Trent is inspired as a whole and in all its parts. It follows from this, as Canon Clamer points out in his commentary on Genesis (1953), that "the final editor who compiled the different sources and added his own work to theirs certainly enjoyed the grace of inspiration."[8] Until we know more of the handing down of the sources from Moses and of the changes they underwent, we cannot be precise concerning other inspired authors and editors, nor can we be sure which parts of the sources

[6] "L'authenticité Mosaïque de la Genèse et la théorie des documents," *Revue biblique* 47 (1938) 164.

[7] Frederick L. Moriarty, S. J., *Foreword to the Old Testament Books* (Weston, Massachusetts: Weston College Press, 1954), pp. 6–11.

[8] Albert Clamer, *Genèse* (Paris: Letouzey et Ané), p. 57.

were inspired and which were not before they were adopted by the compiler. In this book when I refer to "the author of Genesis" the reader will understand the need of this vagueness, since we cannot tell whether a given passage or development should be attributed to Moses, to the compiler who may have been the great Esdras, or to another anonymous author. In any case there is such unity of purpose in Genesis that we find it easy to take these several possible authors as one.

That unity, I have already said, is *the religious aim of the Pentateuch*, which is likewise the most essential key to its interpretation. The late Albert Einstein once wrote that "the man who regards his own life and that of his fellow creatures as meaningless, is not merely unfortunate but almost disqualified for life." This was a conviction profoundly shared by the men who wrote the Old Testament. The determination of the Sorokins and Toynbees to find meanings and patterns in human history is nothing new, for the Hebrew authors were resolved that a history that did not show the hand of God was no true history. In *The Book of Books* Rabbi Solomon Goldman has admirably summed up what these men tried to do:

"Theologians generally treat divine grace, salvation, or human perfection as intellectual concepts and expound them in rigid and definitive terms. The Hebrew Bible, the fount of grace, spoke another language. Its inspired authors . . . wrote history instead of theology or philosophy, and dramatized the destiny of all mankind in the career of a people."[9]

The Germans, who have a no-nonsense language and the knack for using it properly, call this kind of history *Heilsgeschichte*. A pallid English equivalent is sometimes found in "sacred history," but, besides sounding like a Sunday school lesson, this term does not grasp the idea at all. "Sacred history" evokes sacred themes, edifying people doing edifying things, the *acta martyrum*, Walter and the patient Grisilde. *Heilsgeschichte*, however, is as much at home with the scabrous and the depraved in human conduct as with the noble and exalted. God, after all, has an interest in sin as well as in virtue, and a far greater interest than He has in merely

---

[9] *The Book of Books: an Introduction* (New York: Harper & Brothers, 1948), p. 10.

innocuous respectability. The ways of God with men and of men with God are not all light, but darkness too, yet somehow God pervades the whole. History is the record of His presence and His purposes, sometimes thwarted but always there, often more apparent against the black of contrast than in the white of fulfilment. A *theology of history* is what the Hebrew authors set out to write, of all men the most convinced that life is not a collection of casual facts that disappear into a brainless void. To the Hebrew mind it was a primal blasphemy to suggest that anything had ever just "happened."

Whoever reads Genesis therefore with the idea that its author gathered together the bits of the past only as so many statistics has missed the point of the book. Whoever, indeed, thinks that the author's primary intention in writing his book was to tell history is invariably going to arrive at some very wrong conclusions about the meaning of Genesis. Genesis is an historical book, but not everything in it is history, and the history that is in it is history with a purpose. The author certainly did not fancy himself an historian in any modern sense of the word, and he used his sources in ways that no modern historian would dream of. What are today esteemed as essentials in historical method—exact chronologies, tracking down discrepancies, separating the kernel of fact from popular exaggeration, and the like—did not interest him at all, for they presuppose that history has an end in itself, and this he did not believe. Our first principle in reading Genesis must be to discover how the author *used* history, for in this lies the meaning of Genesis.

The fact that the author of Genesis used history for a purpose did not diminish its value as history. If the hand of God was to be found in the record of the past, after all, it had to be a real record. He respected the sources on which he depended, the written or oral traditions through which history had come down to him, and our modern studies are day by day increasing in us a healthy respect for the accuracy of these traditions. Our commentary will, I think, make this very plain. "This process of handing down the ancient tradition by word of mouth from generation to generation led to the omission of many details which would have interested a modern historian," Professor Albright has written, "but it also brought about a recasting of tradition in more dramatic form, emphasizing its religious and pedagogical values. Our gain is thus far greater than any possible loss."[10]

It remains now to explain

(3) How To Read Genesis

which could also be entitled "how Genesis was written." The knowledge of the one gives us the answer to the other.

We have seen above that the criticism of the nineteenth century (and late eighteenth) which was dominated by the great names of Eichhorn, Ilgen, Riehm, Graf, and above all, Julius Wellhausen, built up an elaborate theory of the origin of the Pentateuch based on the distinction of the four sources that had been used in its composition. We have said all that we intend to say about the problem that these sources raise concerning the authorship of the Pentateuch. What is of far greater importance is to see how they will affect our interpretation of Genesis.

The *fact* that sources have been used, whatever their origins may have been, can hardly be questioned. This is simply a conclusion from the literary examination of the text, and no one today would dream of trying to explain Genesis without taking this fact into account. We may quarrel occasionally over details, and here or there one may find a source that others refuse to recognize, but it is plain enough to all that the Pentateuch as a whole and as now constituted is a work of *composition*. In the introduction to his translation of Genesis (1951) for *La Sainte Bible de Jérusalem,* Father Roland de Vaux has summed up the evidence rather well:

These are the undeniable facts. One after another in the Pentateuch we discover doublets, repetitions, and discordances. Genesis begins with two juxtaposed accounts of creation. There are two genealogies of Cain (4:17 f. and 5:12–17). Chapters 6–8 contain two stories of the flood, in which the cataclysm is produced by different means and has a different duration, and in which Noe takes a different number of animals into the ark. Twice Abraham risks Sara's honor in making her pass for his sister (12:13 ff. and 20:1 ff.), and the same adventure is told of Isaac and Rebecca in 26:7 ff. The kidnaping of Joseph is told in two ways (by the Madianites, with the intervention of Ruben; by the Ismaelites, with the intervention of Juda: 37:18–35), as is the story of his intro-

[10] Albright, op. cit., p. 236.

duction into Egypt (with Phutiphar, who entrusts prisoners to him;
with an anonymous Egyptian, who puts him into prison: 39), and
similarly the story of the second journey of Jacob's sons to Egypt
(Ruben, then Juda goes surety for Benjamin: 42:37 and 43:9).
Moses' father-in-law is sometimes called Raguel (Ex. 2:18, Num.
10:29), sometimes Jethro (Ex. 3:1). Moses receives the divine
vocation twice (Ex. 3 and 6), and the name of Jahweh is revealed
to him twice, while according to Gen. 4:26 this name had already
been known before the flood. There are several different versions
of the story of the plagues of Egypt in Ex. 6–12. Twice there is the
incident of the waters of Meriba, where the Israelites resisted
Jahweh: Ex. 17:7 and Num. 20:13. And countless other analogous
cases.

One may say—and it has been said—that it is not unheard-of that
the same fact should be written twice, that oral accounts delight in
repetition, that the primitive mentality is not bound by our logic.
But these explanations are insufficient. These parallel accounts are
the very constitution of the narrative; they differ in style, vocabulary, and in the way they represent God and His relation to men
. . . They fall into groups by their affinities of language, manner,
concepts, their "constants," which determine the parallel lines
pursued in the Pentateuch.[11]

The groups which emerge from this analysis are our four
sources. One of them, called "J" by the critics because of its
affection for the ancient Hebrew proper name for God, *Jahweh*
(translated LORD in this book), is more "primitive" than the
others in its theology, using language which the other sources may
have deliberately avoided lest it be misunderstood. In "J" the
LORD walks in the garden of Eden in the cool of an evening,
bargains with Abraham for the lives of the Sodomites, and wrestles
with Jacob beyond the Jordan. Yet for all its rugged simplicity,
this picture of a God who stands face to face with His creatures is
a truer portrait than any of the Gentiles, of whatever age, was able
to fashion. This source evidences what some may feel is a regrettable habit of making puns on the sound of Hebrew names. Some
of the most colorful and gripping passages of Genesis derive from
"J." The second source, called "E" because it favors the divine
name *Elohim* (which means simply "God"), is staider than "J,"
more interested in details, and more inclined to give explanations

[11] Roland de Vaux, *La Genèse* (Paris: Éditions du Cerf), p. 13 f.

where "J" would let the facts speak for themselves. These two traditions run parallel throughout Genesis, except that "E" either contained nothing about the time before Abraham, or, if it did, it was not used by the compiler. The third source is called "P" because it reflects the concerns of the priestly element of the people of Israel. It likes to stress religious values and to trace the origins of worship and law in antiquity. It is much subtler than the other two traditions. In particular, "P" has worked out a fascinating symbolism of numbers which we shall have to discuss at the proper time. A fourth source of the Pentateuch, "D" (for Deuteronomy), has not been used in Genesis.

Having given these sources their names, we shall not make it a point of identifying them as we go through Genesis. It will be enough for us to know at a given time that we are reading a passage that has been compiled from two or more of these sources.

The particular traits, what Father de Vaux has called the "constants," of these sources were of course acquired by them in the various circles among which they were handed down after the time of Moses. At the same time they acquired variations in detail. We all know the process. Our own family archivists—and we must bear in mind that the narratives of Genesis are essentially family history—can often disagree rather heatedly in their versions of the family annals which are invariably retold when a wedding or a funeral has drawn the scattered brothers and sisters and cousins back to the once common hearth. What Happened to Grandfather at the Columbian Exposition may be a "J" version of What Happened to Grandfather at the St. Louis World's Fair in "E," while "P" may insist that it did not happen to Grandfather in any case, but to Granduncle John. Stories vary with the telling, there is no helping it, and traditions handed down separately are going to differ in details.

This is the kind of material the compiler of Genesis had to work with when he combined the Mosaic traditions into a single narrative. Any historian, of course, is confronted with varying accounts of the same event which he must try to sift down to get at the original story or else give the job up as hopeless. Juries have to do the same often enough with the testimony of "eyewitnesses." In Genesis, however, something was done that is very surprising to us, and which shows how different is our idea of history from that of the ancient Near East. *All* the traditions were used, with their variations, either in part, when they could be welded together into a single story, or entirely, when they were simply used to form parallel accounts. This explains why the same action, described in meticulous detail, can be ascribed in one place to Abraham, in another to Isaac. This is the reasonable explanation. We are no longer obliged to attribute such a long arm to coincidence as were some of the older commentators who were unaware of the sources used in Genesis. This explains why Genesis can apparently contradict itself in matters of trivial moment. The discrepancies come from the discordant sources.

I just said that this method of using source material is quite surprising to us. *We* would not do such a thing—and how often the undeniable "we would not" somehow gets confused in our minds with the unproved "no one would." Yet someone did. That the Semitic mentality differs from the Anglo-Saxon may be a pity, but differ it does. In 1906 Father Ignazio Guidi published a study of the Semitic historical method in which he showed from various examples that it consists in laying parallel versions of the same story side by side or editing them into a single whole, retaining the original thoughts and expressions even though they may conflict. Cardinal Tisserant, the famous orientologist, published a similar study, with the same results, in 1921. These authors have their proofs in works whose sources still exist: it is not necessary to reason to their existence as we must do in Genesis. These proofs confirm what we have seen in the preceding paragraphs on the use of sources in Genesis, for, in Father Guidi's words, "this is the characteristic of Semitic historical method."[12] In recognizing it and conforming to it our interpretation we are heeding the sound direction of our present Holy Father's encyclical *Divino afflante Spiritu* (1943): "It is absolutely necessary for the interpreter to go back in spirit to those remote centuries of the East, making proper use of the help afforded by history, archaeology, ethnology, and other sciences, in order to discover what literary forms the writers of that early age intended to use and did in fact employ."

[12] Ignazio Guidi, "L'historiographie chez les Sémites," *Revue biblique* 3 (1906) 519.

But what does this do to the Bible as the inspired word of God, and to its resulting inerrancy? If we make Genesis say in one breath that Abraham did a certain thing, and in another that it was Isaac, are we not saying that Genesis is wrong at least once? Family traditions about Grandfather are all well and good, but family traditions about Grandfather are not God's inspired word.

But neither were the sources of Genesis God's inspired word. True, they doubtless contained words that had been written under divine inspiration. Moses, whom both tradition and critical judgment bid us acknowledge the ultimate author of these traditions, was an inspired man, and particularly in much of the law that has been handed down in these traditions we can believe that the actual words of the text go back to Mosaic times. As I said above, however, until we know more of the handing down of the sources from Moses and of the changes they underwent, we cannot be precise concerning other inspired authors and editors, nor can we be sure which parts of the sources were inspired and which were not before they were adopted by the inspired compiler. We can only be very sure that where there were any real contradictions in the sources, the error, wherever it may have lain, was not part of an inspired text but had been introduced through the frailty to which all that is human is heir. As such, therefore, as completed traditions with all their modifications and changes, the sources of Genesis were not the inspired word of God. We can echo Canon Clamer, then, in saying that "the doctrine of inspiration does not authorize us to consider J, E, P, and their successive editions, as Scripture."[13]

They became the inspired word of God, that is, those parts of them that were used, when the inspired writer who gave the Pentateuch its present form gathered them into his text. Inspiration is not revelation. Revelation is a divine communication of knowledge in which the words and ideas come wholly from God. Some of the inspired authors of the Bible also received revelation, and the Bible contains revelation, as for example in the teaching of Jesus and the oracles of the Prophets. But inspiration of itself is entirely independent of revelation. In inspiration God moves the will and enlightens the mind of the human writer with the result that the written word is not man's only but also God's. By reason of

[13] Clamer, op. cit., p. 57.

this grace of inspiration the biblical author's judgments are also God's judgments, and as a consequence what the biblical author has judged to be true, must be true. During the entire process the biblical author may be—probably generally was—unaware of the presence of this grace. He writes a book as a man would normally write a book, drawing on his own experiences or on the work of others for his material. He may copy another's words verbatim. In the biblical text these words are inspired and have all the guarantees of inspiration, but this is not true of the words in their previous context. The author of 2 Maccabees states explicitly that his book is a condensation of a longer, five-volume work of another writer. 2 Maccabees is Scripture and its author's judgments were without error. The volumes that he used were not Scripture and may have had a mistake on every page as far as we know.

Am I trying to say that we can lay the blame for the errors of Genesis on the author's uninspired sources rather than on the inspired author himself? Not a bit of it. I am only pointing out that the discrepancies on various points of fact that undeniably occur in Genesis arose from causes having nothing to do with inspiration. They are in Genesis now because the author of Genesis took them from his sources without change. To say that they are errors of Genesis is something else altogether.

What is Genesis? Like any other book, it is the expression of its author's mind. If that author is inspired, then the expression is of a mind enlightened by grace which will therefore be unerring. How did the author of Genesis intend to express his mind in including the "doublets, repetitions, and discordances" of his sources in the book which he produced? He was as well aware as we that it was not likely that a striking event which "E" had associated with Abraham had taken place once more down to the last detail with Isaac, as "J" had it. Neither was he in any better position than we to decide which version was correct. What is more important is that he could not have cared less. The fact that he included both versions, not only here but countless other times, is eloquent testimony that verifying details of this sort was of no concern to him whatever. If he has included rival traditions that clash over the "who" or the "when," he could not have told us better that to him the "who" and the "when" were unimportant, and that he had a purpose that transcended these trivialities. What that purpose was, we must try to find when we read Genesis. All we need say for the moment is that it is this *use* of his sources, this *purpose* that he had, that is the expression of the author's mind. It is this, therefore, that is the inspired meaning of Genesis, and whatever is foreign to this purpose is not the meaning of Genesis. *What the author intended to teach* is the meaning of Genesis; this is the word of God which is free from error. We can say, therefore, that while Genesis undoubtedly contains errors, it teaches none.

"The fool has said in his heart, 'There is no God'" (Ps. *13*:1). Are the words, "there is no God," inspired? Most assuredly; Catholic teaching has consistently upheld the verbal inspiration of Scripture. Are they therefore guaranteed free from error? In the context and purpose with which the author used them, yes; and that purpose he has made plain enough by putting them on the lips of a fool. Separated from his context and purpose they are a fundamental lie. We have to use this same principle in reading Genesis, separating the author's meaning from his sources, or rather, finding his meaning in his use of the sources. Admittedly, it is easy to see how the Psalmist above used his "source," and it is not always easy in Genesis. But then, that is part of the fascination of Genesis. Besides, if it were not so, there would be very little market for a book like this.

I shall have to come back to this question shortly for some special remarks that apply to the first chapters of Genesis. There are several other notations that could be made at this time on the peculiarities of our author's source material, but I think they will be better appreciated if we take them up as we come to them. This book is intended above all to be a guide through Genesis, not a handy substitute for it.

One final word. As I have no desire, however unintended, that this little vessel should sail under false colors, I must emphasize that what it contains is, in the final analysis, my personal opinion as to the meaning of Genesis. It is an opinion, however, which I think is fairly shared by the recognized Catholic biblical scholars of our day; and since for the most part it has been shamelessly borrowed from them, there is little wonder. It represents the interpretation of Catholics, not of the Catholic Church, except in the sense that it is in harmony with her teachings, which could not be otherwise if it is to be a true interpretation of God's word. "The rules and laws laid down by the Church are concerned with the teaching of faith and morals, and among the many matters set forth in the legal, historical, sapiential, and prophetical books of the Bible there are only a few whose sense has been defined by the authority of the Church, and equally few about which the opinion of the Holy Fathers is unanimous" (*Divino afflante Spiritu*). Subject always to the rule of faith of the Christian revelation, on the considered principle that truth is one and not contradictory, the Church leaves us free to our interpretation honestly arrived at, and to this end urges on us every means of modern knowledge.

No "traditional Catholic interpretation" of any word of Genesis is opposed in these pages. Not a few of the interpretations of earlier Catholics, however, have been abandoned in favor of explanations which some readers will find quite new. This is to be expected. The interpreters of the past, saints and humble men of learning that so many of them were, would not have us do other than build higher on the foundation which they laid. We must hope in turn that later generations will find many of our interpretations obsolete, in the light of a greater knowledge that has not been vouchsafed us.

"This true freedom of the sons of God," the Pope has said, "loyally maintaining the doctrine of the Church and at the same time gratefully accepting as God's gift and exploiting every contribution afforded by secular knowledge, must be vindicated and zealously upheld by all, for it is the condition and source of any real success and any solid progress in Catholic science."

PART ONE:
THE MEETING OF GOD AND MAN

PART ONE: THE MEETING OF GOD AND MAN

The first eleven chapters of Genesis are to Genesis what Genesis is to the rest of the Pentateuch. They are its introduction. Genesis begins the history of God's Covenant with Israel with the story of Abraham, Israel's first ancestor in Chanaan and the father of all the Jews. As far as the author of Genesis was concerned, history in a real sense, the only history in which he took an interest, at any rate, had begun with Abraham. At the same time, Israel had to be fitted into its place in the larger family of man if it was to understand its unique destiny. The mercy of God to Abraham would have made no impact unless Israel were shown what the world was like before Abraham. If history had begun with Abraham, God had not, for the God who covenanted with Israel was the God of all mankind. Therefore to begin the fundamental book which is Genesis, the author reached back to the ultimate fundamental and began *In the beginning*.

It should be obvious from this that these introductory chapters have not merely the same religious character as the rest of Genesis, they have it to a surpassing degree. It is vital to bear this in mind, for at one time or another they have been taken as an encyclopedia of practically every useful or useless science known to man, and they have been made to say many amazing things about which the author of Genesis had neither knowledge nor concern.

In our sense of the word, these chapters will not be called history. They relate events that took place before the dawn of history, by anyone's calculation of history, that is. To some of what they relate there was no human witness, and without witnesses you hardly have history. In the sense, however, that we use "history" to distinguish fact from fancy, the true from the imaginary, these chapters can be called historical. What they teach is not myth or fable, but reality.

To give a complete history of mankind from the first year of creation was not only a simple impossibility, it was the farthest thing from the author's mind. What these chapters were intended to do, as the Biblical Commission wrote in 1948, was to "relate *in simple and figurative language,* adapted to the understanding of a less developed people, *the fundamental truths underlying the divine plan of salvation,* as well as the *popular* description of the origin of the human race and of the chosen people." I have underscored the words to which we ought to give special attention. But first, we should ask ourselves where the author got his information for these chapters.

We have already seen how the recognition of the sources used in compiling Genesis has clarified and changed our interpretation of many a passage. This is more than ever true in the first eleven chapters. Centuries before 1753, however, when Jean d'Astruc, physician to the King of France, published a brochure that was to lead later scholars into the determination of the source material of the Pentateuch, it had been seen that the peculiar nature of these chapters demanded some rather special accounting.

Genesis begins, for example, with a description of creation. But who, besides God, witnessed creation? If Genesis describes what only God could know, it was concluded, then God must have *revealed* these words to Moses fairly as they stand. This erroneous notion, in fact, that all or much of Genesis was simply the dictation of the Almighty, has made inroads into the thinking of some who are quite unconscious of its presence. It explains their attempts to read Genesis *1* as a blow-by-blow account of earth's first waking moments, or, failing that impossibility, to find an elaborate symbolism beneath the obvious meaning of the words. Mechanical dictation, however, is not the traditional Christian idea of inspiration. It does little credit to reason and is hardly respectful to God, upon whom it unloads the responsibility for grammatical blunders and a frequently tepid style, to name only the least faults. There is revelation in Genesis, of course, but we have no right to assume that the inspired writer was exempt from any of the ordinary rules when he sat down to compose this book. Before invoking the highly extraordinary (and, incidentally, unworkable) explanation of personal revelation to account for the words of Genesis, we must see if there is not a more obvious solution in the normal processes in which God usually deals with man.

Failing direct revelation, could not the facts described in the beginning of Genesis have come down to the author in an unbroken line of tradition? Thus the argument ran, as Father Lagrange exposed its shortcomings in 1903: "Moses was easily a much earlier writer than any other, and well-informed too, for his witnesses went back to the first days of mankind in an unbroken line ... 'Sem who saw Lamech, who saw Adam, at least saw Abraham, who saw Jacob, who saw those who beheld Moses.'" And Adam, of course, spoke with God. (The inner quotation is from Pascal.) This argument, Father Lagrange continued, was once tenable and seemed secure, "but now unexpected witnesses have emerged from the shadows where they were thought to have been buried forever."[1] These witnesses were the fossil remains which proved the tremendous age of the world and of man, and the newly discovered literatures of ancient Egypt and Mesopotamia, far older than Moses. Israel was a newcomer among the nations of man, and its traditions could not be very old. (Some historians still begin "ancient history" with the Greeks, who in comparison are of yesterday.) Traditions can be preserved with astounding accuracy of detail even over centuries, as the Pentateuch makes clear, but who could imagine a tradition kept intact for hundreds of thousands, a half million, or more years? For the life of man upon earth, we now know, is no less than this.

What, then, are these first chapters of Genesis, if they are neither revelation nor historical tradition? They are what the Biblical Commission called them, a catalogue of the fundamental truths of faith which underlie the Jewish and Christian revelations, and a popular description of the origins of men, done in the simple and figurative language that is proper to primitive peoples. The author had certain truths which had been made known to his people through revelation: There is one God, Creator of the universe by the act of His will, who created man in His image and likeness, raised him to

[1] M. J. Lagrange, *La méthode historique* (Paris: Victor Lecoffre), p. 120 f.

a level above his created state and endowed him with gifts which he forfeited through sin, who promised man an eventual redemption from this sin. These and other truths are taught in the poetic imagery of Genesis' first three chapters, great songs of faith fashioned by the religious teachers of Israel. After these, to span the mighty chasm between creation and the time of Abraham, the author had to draw on popular narratives, folk literature, some proper to Israel, most of them inherited by Israel from more remote ancestors, which told of man's early life and development on earth. Some of these stories turn up in other ancient literatures, and it is always interesting to compare them with the Bible to see how Israel transmuted the most unlikely material into chapters of a great religious document. "A strict history was impossible," writes Father Lagrange, "yet it was necessary to show in a continuous chain the unity of the history of salvation. The Bible avoided stories that were absurd and unfitting. It did not pretend that sin does not exist, but it showed sin punished, not glorified as though its nature could change when it became the privilege of the hero. The Bible even refrained from pointless stories. It seized on the tangible, on existing institutions, spoke of their origins and progress, and left them in a twilight which does not even pretend to be a documented history."[2]

These stories do contain some historical facts, "reminiscences" Father Chaine calls them,[3] for they are not simply myths or fables. Their historical content is far higher than most of the earlier critics dreamed. But it is folk history, not circumstantial history, which means that historical and legendary elements frequently and inevitably appear side by side. Note that I do not say Genesis teaches legend, but Genesis has used a partly legendary history to teach enduring truths.

What the inspired author intended to teach, that is the meaning of the Bible. I have stressed this before, and it cannot be repeated too often. Our Lord used purely fictitious tales, the parables, to teach the word of life in Galilee. Joatham in Judges 9:7 ff. used a fable of talking trees to bring the men of Sichem to their senses. The author of Genesis has done the same. This is what the biblical

---

[2] *La méthode historique*, p. 212 f.
[3] Chaine, op. cit., p. 57.

scholars mean when they speak of the author's "literary form" according to which his meaning must be seen. The literary form is the particular type of writing that has been chosen to convey the author's meaning, and that form may be fact or fiction, popular or scientific. We all presume on this commonsense principle of interpretation in daily life. If I praise the sunset over the Grand Canyon, would he not be three times a fool who would think I had denied the discoveries of Copernicus? "But you *said* the sun *set* . . ." I must be allowed the literary form of popular description. The author of Genesis deserves the same courtesy. "But the Bible *says* . . ." is not the interpretation of Scripture.

The literary forms of Genesis are not those of modern literature. Again, what *we* would do or say or mean is not the sufficient criterion of what Genesis did or said or meant. "These literary forms do not correspond to any of our classical categories and cannot be judged in the light of the Greco-Latin or modern literary types," the Biblical Commission has affirmed. I cannot pretend that what I have outlined above in regard to the formation of these chapters has removed every obstacle to their interpretation, for, the Commission continues, "known scientific facts do not allow a *positive* solution of all the problems which they present." We still need to know much more about the literary methods of the ancient Orient, its psychology and notion of historical truth, before we can finally solve these problems.

What we have already learned, however, has been enough to revolutionize our approach to Genesis, and the interpretation we now give it is vastly different from that of a generation or so ago. "During the past fifty years the conditions of biblical studies and their subsidiaries have greatly changed," writes Pius XII, and adds that "much light has been derived from these explorations for the more correct and fuller understanding of the Sacred Books." We must today interpret the Bible in the light of knowledge that was denied our ancestors. Any interpretation of Scripture that contradicts a known fact of science we may be very sure is no true interpretation. This principle was established fifteen hundred years ago by St. Augustine, who in his *De Genesi ad litteram* attacked the problems of Genesis in the light of the knowledge of his age. We can do no better than imitate his spirit.

"Fundamentalism" or "literalism" has never had a home in the Catholic Church. It is regrettable, however, that some Catholics have felt that the fundamentalists are "on our side" in their reverence for the letter of God's word amid a world that has so largely gone over to unbelief. Fundamentalism is not born of respect for the Bible. It is born of contempt for man's God-given intellect. It has failed the most elementary task of religion, which is the rational service of God.

*1:*1 In the beginning God created the heavens and the earth;
2 the earth was waste and void; darkness covered the abyss,
and the spirit of God was stirring above the waters.

BERESHÍTH BARA ELOHÍM
ETH HASHAMÁYIM W'ETH HAÁRETS . . .

No translation can capture the assonance and the rugged beauty
of these inspired lines, but the beauty of their thought is inescapable in any language. "In the beginning God created the
heavens and the earth." The Old Testament Jews were probably
among the least speculative people known to history. The concrete earthiness with which they speak of sacred things can sometimes shock us. But there is a wisdom in these few words for which
all other races of man sought in vain. The Greeks, perhaps the
most speculative people of history, thought much about God and
His nature and attributes. They did not know, however, that He
is a Person to be prayed to, a God who cares, whose goodness and
love had burst forth into creative act. This knowledge was God's
gift to Israel, and Israel's gift to the world.

Before creation, there was only God. No one save God saw the
origin of all things. It is plain, therefore, that the story we are reading is an artist's conception of this truth about God's relation to
the world. Michelangelo was to paint it in the Sistine Chapel, and
Rodin was to carve it in stone. The author of Genesis wrote it in
words.

He had no word for "universe," and had to make do with "the heavens and the earth"; but it is very clear that he knew that God had made it all. He pictures the world in the dawn of creation as an unformed mass, for God is to be shown not only as one who makes, but who disposes and orders. In this first instant of time all is darkness and chaos, and above the earth and covering it are the surging waters of a primordial deep. Yet above all, and distinct from it all, is the spirit of God. In the author's Hebrew the word "spirit" means also "breath" and "wind." The idea of God's spirit or breath as life-giving is quite common in the Old Testament, and St. Paul thought in similar terms when he spoke of Christ as the life-giving spirit of our supernatural life. We see a scene, therefore, in which the breath of God soars overhead like a mighty wind prepared to bring forth life.

These, of course, are all word-images. But as Dietrich Bonhoeffer has beautifully said, "Images are not lies: they point to reality, and let the reality appear through them. Images differ: those of a child are not an adult's, and those of an inhabitant of the desert are different from the city-dweller's. Nevertheless they remain true, just as human speech and ideas remain true, to the extent that God remains in them."[1]

> 1:3 God said, "Let there be light," and there was light, God saw
>   4 that the light was good./ God separated the light from the
>   5 darkness,/ calling the light Day and the darkness Night.
>   And there was evening and morning, the first day.

The author of Genesis was undoubtedly acquainted with the creation-myths of the polytheistic religions of Egypt and Babylon; there are enough indications in Genesis to suggest that the author was consciously opposing his account to the Babylonian story. According to the myth, matter already existed at the beginning of time in the person of the first gods, from whom were fashioned the earth and the heavens, and who gave birth to the other gods. The world became the battleground of rival deities, and out of their struggle, as a kind of by-product, living creatures were formed, and finally man to be the slave of the gods.

---

[1] *Schöpfung und Fall* (München: Kaiser Verlag, 1955), p. 57.

In Genesis there are not many gods; there is one only. He is not part of the world, differing from creatures only in degree; He exists before all things and has caused all things. He has simply willed that a thing should be, and it is. And He has seen that His creation is good. There is behind the universe not only an almighty Power, but an all-pervading Goodness who has willed to express Himself in creation. What is, is for a purpose, and it is good because God willed it to be.

1:6 Then God said, "Let there be a firmament in the midst of the
   7 waters to divide the waters." And so it was./ God made the firmament, dividing the waters that were below the firma-
   8 ment from those that were above it./ God called the firmament Heaven. And there was evening and morning, the second day.
   9 Then God said, "Let the waters below the heavens be gathered into one place and let the dry land appear." And so it
  10 was./ God called the dry land Earth and the assembled wa-
  11 ters Seas. And God saw that it was good./ Then God said, "Let the earth bring forth vegetation: seed-bearing plants and all kinds of fruit trees that bear fruit containing their
  12 seed." And so it was./ The earth brought forth vegetation, every kind of seed-bearing plant and all kinds of trees that bear fruit containing their seed. God saw that it was good.
  13 And there was evening and morning, the third day.

Having made the simple statement that God created all things, the author proceeds to itemize one by one the most important elements of his world, calling the roll of all that God had made. Light, that most blessed gift, he named first. Only when we think back to a time when the darkness of night with all its hidden and unseen terrors was unbroken except by the most primitive lighting, do we realize what the light of day meant to ancient man. Light and life were almost the same thing. After light, the earth is formed in its present state. Then come all the adornments of creation, the sun, the moon and the stars, as he will go on to list them, creeping, crawling, and swimming creatures, and last of all the most important, man.

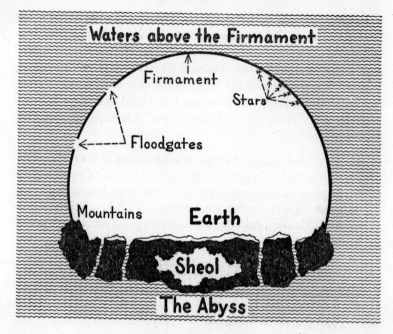

Semitic Cosmogony

If you will look at the illustration above, you will see how an ancient Semite thought of the world in which he lived, and understand therefore the description of v. 6 ff. The earth was of course flat, with a mountain here or there and some rather large ones at the end of the earth. The sky was a firmament, a solid bowl set over the earth. It had to be solid: how else would the waters above it fail to pour down and entirely flood the earth? That there were waters above this solid firmament was an easy deduction: how else explain the rain, which happened when water made its way through windows in the firmament (the "floodgates of the heavens" in 8:2) to fall on the earth? The rim of the firmament joined the extremities of the earth tidily and kept the land dry. Underneath the earth, however, were more waters, which pushed through the earth's surface to form the seas and rivers and springs. The firmament served the further purpose, we see in v. 14 ff., of a resting place for the sun, moon, and stars, which moved about its surface as they shed light on the earth and measured the seasons. Because of these ideas the author has pictured the beginning of the world as the separation of waters by means of the great firmament which God has raised above the earth.

Scientifically speaking, this is obviously a pathetic notion of the universe. As we can see, it is based entirely on appearances. The earth does *look* flat, it does *appear* to meet the sky at the horizon. The sky does *seem* like an inverted blue bowl overhead. All this was enough for the Hebrew, who never thought it worthwhile to enquire much further, even if he had had the means of doing so.

This erroneous conception of the universe, however, is no more part of the author's teaching than is the faulty science included in the "sunset," "celestial sphere," or "four winds of heaven" of our everyday speech. Genesis is less interested in teaching natural science than the catechism in teaching geometry. Everything the author intended to tell us is true. God did create the sky, the seas, and the dry land, He did bring forth life. The sky is not a solid bowl, as the author believed, but it looks like one, and that is all he has said. We have been able to find out many things about the world that he did not know, but we have never been able to improve on what he has told us.

1:14 And God said, "Let there be lights in the firmament of the heavens to separate day from night; let them serve as signs
15 and for the fixing of seasons, days and years;/ let them serve as lights in the firmament of the heavens to shed light upon
16 the earth." So it was./ God made the two great lights, the greater light to rule the day and the smaller one to rule the
17 night, and he made the stars./ God set them in the firma-
18 ment of the heavens to shed light upon the earth,/ to rule the day and the night and to separate the light from the
19 darkness. God saw that it was good./ And there was evening and morning, the fourth day.

The Gentiles worshipped the stars as gods; we still preserve their names, through successive transformations, Venus, Saturn, Jupiter, and the rest. In Egypt the sun was supreme, and anyone who has lived in that land of cloudless skies and unending heat will understand how to a pagan mentality the sun became lord, the

giver and taker of life. In the Semitic world it was rather the moon-
god who was above all venerated. The Babylonian creation-myth
Enuma elish, which I said before was doubtless known to the author of Genesis, made the stars play a large role in the story of the
world's beginnings, assigning them as residences and centres of
power for various of the gods.

To the author of Genesis the heavenly bodies are merely items
of God's creation. Perhaps it was to insist that they are in no sense
lords or rulers that he did not even permit them to be the causes of
light, whose creation he placed on the first day. Here again we
have the non-scientific mind at work, of course, which did not
necessarily see a causal connection between the sun and daylight,
and which certainly was unaware that the light of the moon was a
reflection, and that there is a difference of the same kind between
the planets and the stars. Possibly much of the success of the moon-
god in Semitic mythology was due to the thought that the moon
was of greater value than the sun, since it shone at night when
light was needed rather than in the day when it was not. It is hard
to be sure, therefore, but it is still quite likely that the man whose
pagan ancestors had called these luminaries gods was very deliberate in making them functional creatures, signs of the times and
distributors of the light which God had made.

1:20 Then God said, "Let the waters abound with life, and above
        the earth let winged creatures fly below the firmament of
21   the heavens." And so it was./ God created the great sea mon-
        sters, all kinds of living, swimming creatures with which the
        waters abound and all kinds of winged birds. God saw that
22   it was good,/ and God blessed them, saying, "Be fruitful,
        multiply, and fill the waters of the seas; and let the birds
23   multiply on the earth."/ And there was evening and morn-
24   ing, the fifth day./ God said, "Let the earth bring forth all
        kinds of living creatures: cattle, crawling creatures and wild
25   animals." And so it was./ God made all kinds of wild beasts,
        every kind of cattle, and every kind of creature crawling on
        the ground. And God saw that it was good.

We still speak of "the heavens" as a plural. In the Semitic cosmos
there were three heavens, the watery heaven above the firmament,

the firmament itself, and the air. Because the firmame[nt]
separator of the waters, it was natural to speak of the cre[ation of]
denizens of air and water in a single breath. There [were]
reasons as well. Primitive man thought that the birds l[ived in the]
sea, since he saw them apparently disappear into it [as they]
flew out to the horizon. Even in the scientific age, the botanist
Charles Linnaeus believed that swallows hibernated in lakes.

The author of Genesis had a special interest with the sea creatures, however. In Chanaanite mythology, and Babylonian as well,
sea monsters, the *tanninim*, figured as primaeval rivals of the gods
who ruled the earth. They are not rivals of God, says Genesis. How
could they be? If the sea swarms with their life it is by His command, and upon them rests the divine benediction to be fruitful
and multiply. They are His creatures, just as the living things of
the land, the domesticated cattle, serpent life, and the wild animals.

1:26 God said, "Let us make mankind in our image and likeness;
and let them have dominion over the fish of the sea, the
birds of the air, the cattle, over all the wild animals and
every creature that crawls on the earth."
27 God created man in his image.
In the image of God he created him.
Male and female he created them.
28 Then God blessed them and said to them, "Be fruitful and
multiply; fill the earth and subdue it. Have dominion over
the fish of the sea, the birds of the air, the cattle and all the
animals that crawl on the earth."

The pagan myths presented man as the plaything of the gods,
made to serve their whims with labor the gods were too lazy to
bear. For the author of Genesis man has an incredible dignity,
made in the image and likeness of God, not as a slave, but to have
dominion over the earth.

The creation of man he has reserved to the very last, the place of
greatest emphasis. Man, too, like the other creatures, comes into
existence simply at God's command. Yet here, for the first and
only time, God deliberates before He creates. Before proceeding
to this supreme act of creation, He takes counsel: "Let us make...."
These words have always troubled commentators. Why does God

say, "Let *us*"? Is this an indication that this story was once told by polytheists, such as the author's ancestors had been, and that he neglected to change the plural to a singular when he made it the account of a single Creator? The whole idea is fantastic. The story shows in its every line that it could have been written only by a monotheist, and besides, the author of Genesis was not stupid enough to leave a glaring betrayal of this kind in his work. What then? Did he put on God's lips the plural used by oriental monarchs and still employed by popes, kings, and newspaper editors? Strange though it seems, this practice was apparently unknown in Hebrew. Father Lagrange, as so often, has given the best answer: "If God used the plural, it is because He has such a fulness of being that He can deliberate with Himself in the same way that several persons deliberate among themselves."[2] The Hebrew was no philosopher. He knew that between the Being of God and that of creatures there was a vast difference. But he had no words or ideas like "quality" or "analogy" to express the difference; in this sense he did not have even the word "being." He did the best he could to show the difference by using the plural, confident that he would not be misunderstood, as indeed he never was by his own people.

What is the meaning of the "image and likeness" of God in which man was created? For some authors the two words mean the same thing. It is true that Hebrew writers like double-barrel expressions of this kind, but this does not seem to be one of them. Nowhere else in the Bible is anything said to be the image and likeness of anything else. An "image" to the Hebrew was a picture or statue which, the artist at least hoped, was an exact reproduction. It is possible that the author, having used this term of man, suddenly caught himself up with the realization that nothing after all can be exactly like God, and therefore added "likeness," which can indicate mere similarity. Having made his point he uses either word indifferently thereafter.

But in what does this image and likeness consist? This is a more difficult question. Perhaps the author himself was not quite sure, or at least would have been unable to put it into words. It means, of course, that man is entirely apart from the rest of visible crea-

[2] M. J. Lagrange, "Hexaméron," *Revue biblique* 5 (1896) 387.

tion. It means that what distinguishes man from these other creatures is shared with God, that man's dignity is his Godlikeness. It
certainly does not mean that man's external form is God's image
and likeness; in the first place, man's body is too uncomfortably
like many of the other animals', and in the second place the idea
that God could be externally represented in any fashion is foreign
to the Old Testament. In Christian language we say that man has a
spiritual soul with the powers of intellect and free will, and in
these he is like God. These conclusions, however, have come to us
after much religious thinking and have been aided by Greek philosophy, of which the Hebrew author was ignorant. It is very
likely that he saw man's similarity to God at least partially fulfilled
in his having been created to rule over the earth: just as God is
sovereign over all, man was intended to share in this dominion by
God's will. But there is no reason to think that he completely com-
prehended the mystery of man any more than we do. At any rate,
he knew that man was somehow like God, that he had in him a
spark of the divine, and knowing this he had a considerable advantage over not a few modern people to whom man is just a few
pounds of chemicals, another biped whose mating habits can be
judged by the same standards as, say, those of wasps.

1:29 God also said, "See, I give you every seed-bearing plant on
the earth and every tree which has seed-bearing fruit to be
30 your food./ To every wild animal of the earth, to every bird
of the air, and to every creature that crawls on the earth and
has the breath of life, I give the green plants for food." And
31 so it was./ God saw that all he had made was very good.
And there was evening and morning, the sixth day.

There was an old notion, which is found also in Greek and Latin
mythology, that man in his first state, in a long-lost golden age,
had lived exclusively from the fruits of the earth, and only after he
had become corrupted did he begin to eat meat. This theme of the
golden age may itself be a half-remembered echo of the primitive
innocence and later fall of man which are part of the revelation
taught by Genesis. This notion has been adopted by the author
of Genesis, though it is not pursued throughout the entire book as
we now have it. It turns up again in 9:3, in a part of the flood-epic

which belongs to the same source from which this creation story was taken, when God is shown giving fallen man permission to eat flesh. This does not mean, of course, that Genesis has set up vegetarianism as an ideal. We are dealing here with a symbol pure and simple, by which the author signified the perfect harmony in which God first created the world. He had made man the ruler of this world, and it was a rule that was accepted by creation. How better picture this than by imagining man and beast living side by side, not preying on one another? The prophets of Israel took up the same symbol in speaking of the golden age of the future, the time of the Messias, when the harmony God had intended for the world would be restored: "The wolf shall dwell with the lamb, and the leopard shall lie down with the kid; the calf and the lion's cub shall pasture together, and a little child shall be their shepherd. The cow will pasture with the bear, and their young shall lie down together; the lion will eat straw like the ox" (Is. *11*:6 f.).

> 2:1 Thus the heavens and the earth were finished and all their
> 2 array./ On the sixth day God finished the work he had been
> doing. And he rested on the seventh day from all the work
> 3 he had done./ God blessed the seventh day and made it holy
> because on it he rested from all his work of creation.

As we finish this creation story, we see clearly for the first time why the author has used an outline of successive days to divide his account (undisturbed by the fact that while each day has had its evening and morning, he allowed the sun to be created only on the fourth day). On the seventh day, "God rested." The seventh day was the sacred Sabbath of the Jews, when they set aside their daily toil to honor God.

Now the author knew full well that God does not rest as human beings do. Yet it is often easier to think of God in human terms, the terms that we know best of all, which are part of our own experience. We do this when we dread "God's anger," though God has no emotions, or "wound God" through sin, though we cannot injure Him. We have invented for this the word *anthropomorphism*, which, if we used English the way the Germans use German, would come out "manlikeness." In this superficial sense, the scoffer's word is true, that we have made God over in our own image and likeness. But we have to do so to some extent if we are to think of Him at all.

Thus the author of Genesis has done, representing God as the good laborer who does his full week's work and on the Sabbath takes his rest.

Having determined the outline of his story by this religious motive, the author proceeded to use it very interestingly. If we examine the six days of creation carefully we find how neatly they have been tied together. There are really two series of three days in which the first, second, and third of each series correspond one to the other. The first day light is made, and on the fourth are created the sun and moon and stars to govern the light. The second day the waters are divided by the firmament of heaven, and on the fifth day are made the water-creatures and the birds of the air. The third day there are two works, the separation of the dry land and the creation of plantlife. Correspondingly, the sixth day sees two works, the creation of land-creatures and of man, who is to feed upon the plants.

But this is far from being all. Father Anton Deimel's commentary[3] on the creation story points out that in the description of God's eight works (two on the third and sixth days, one on each of the others) the author has used seven different literary elements (the sacred number). These are (1) the introductory, "God said," (2) the word of creation, "Let there be," (3) the statement of fulfilment, "And so it was," (4) a description of the particular act of creation, (5) God's naming or blessing the creature, (6) the divine satisfaction, "God saw that it was good," and (7) the conclusion, "There was evening and morning." Not all these elements have been used to describe each work, but if we count them up in order we see that they have been interlocked in this fashion:

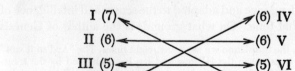

I (7)   (6) IV
II (6)   (6) V
III (5)   (5) VI
(6)   (7)

[3] *"Enuma elish" und Hexaëmeron* (Rome: Pontifical Biblical Institute, 1934), pp. 77–80.

In particular, seven times occurs the fulfilment of God's creative word, "And so it was,"[4] seven times the act of creation is described, and seven times God expresses satisfaction with His creation.

There is no need to labor the conclusion that these complicated arrangements are not accidental. The author has worked out a highly artistic scheme that entailed an artificial disposition of material. Aside from the poetic symmetry of the thing, it served as a memory device. The creation story was handed down orally long before it was put in writing, and even after it had been written down, it was in a world that knew few books. Memory was the means by which most would know the text.

It is therefore apparent that we should not be seeking a concord between the poetry of Genesis and the scientifically established data on the development of the universe. Ever so often, however, we run into well-meaning attempts in that direction, as the following:

Most educated Catholics now take the word *yom* (day) of the first chapter of Genesis to mean a certain undefined period of time, an interpretation which incidentally fits very well with the evidence of historical geology concerning the sequence of different forms of plant and animal life and the length of time, perhaps millions of years, often estimated to be necessary for this development to have taken place.[5]

This sally into bad science and bad interpretation surely does not represent the belief of most educated Catholics. It was written in 1943, but already in 1909 the Biblical Commission had affirmed: "It was not the intention of the sacred author in composing the first chapter of Genesis to give scientific teaching about the internal constitution of visible things and the entire order of creation, but rather to communicate to his people a popular notion in accord with current language and adapted to the senses and intelligence of the men of that time." On what grounds is the author of Genesis

---

[4] Actually, in the translation we are using, eight times. The "And so it was" of *1*:20, however, is not in the Hebrew and has been supplied by the translators from the LXX. The above scheme suggests that the Hebrew text has been preserved correctly and that the LXX has added to it.

[5] Raymond W. Murray, *Man's Unknown Ancestors* (Milwaukee: Bruce, 1943), p. 348. Cited by Edward F. Siegman, C. PP. S., "Not Geological Periods, but Real Days," in *The Priest* (July 1945), 21.

presumed to have anticipated the discovery of the geological ages (which in any case are four, not six)? He would have needed divine revelation, which he did not have; and to what purpose would God reveal such an inconsequential thing?

The creation story of Genesis neither affirms nor denies our scientific knowledge of the universe; it disregards it. The author has used his story to teach that there is one transcendent God who is Creator of all things, who has created by His almighty will for a purpose of His own, and who has set over His visible creation the man whom He made in His image and likeness. Positive science knows nothing of this, just as he knew nothing of positive science.

We now know that the world we live in was millions of years developing. But no matter how long and how complicated and through how many stages was the work of God's creation, it is still His act. If the author of Genesis had known what we know, would he have written otherwise than he did? Dante Gabriel Rossetti wrote in the age of modern science, but he could not improve on the language Genesis used when he wanted to say what Genesis said:

"If the light is,
It is because God said, 'Let there be light.'"

CHAPTER II: THE CREATURE MAN

How little the author of Genesis regarded the account in 1:1–2:3 as anything other than an artist's conception of God as Creator, can be seen from the fact that beginning with 2:4 he has told the entire story of creation afresh, using another source that has its own distinct vocabulary, a different order of events, and its own way of speaking of God. Why he has given us this second story is clear enough from its contents. It is almost exclusively concerned with man, in whom the author of Genesis was quite interested, and it includes, in chapter 3, the revealed fact of man's fall from original grace. Each of the two creation stories had its own virtues which caused it to be preserved for the completed text of Genesis. They fit together nicely, yet it is easy to see that they were once independent narratives.

2:4 This is the story of the heavens and the earth at their creation. When the LORD God made the earth and the heav-
5 ens,/ there was not yet any field shrub on the earth nor had the plants of the field sprung up, for the LORD God had sent no rain on the earth and there was no man to till the
6 soil;/ but the mist rose from the earth and watered all the
7 surface of the ground./ Then the LORD God formed man out of the dust of the ground and breathed into his nostrils the breath of life, and man became a living being.

Here there is no primaeval chaos and no successive days of creation. The earth is not at all covered by water, rather it is dry and arid. At least it is dry in v. 5; v. 6 speaks of its being watered by something like a "mist" (the meaning of the word is not certain).

50

The obscurity of these verses has led some to think that behind this story lie even earlier sources that have been combined into one. While in the first creation story man was created only after the plants and the animals, here we have first the creation of man and later on (v. 9) plantlife and (v. 19) the animals, birds and beasts together. In the first story mankind was created at once, both male and female (1:27), but here the creation of woman comes only at the end of the account (v. 22).

This story is much more anthropomorphic than the former. God, now consistently called the LORD God, is not pictured as simply willing things to be, but he "forms" man (the verb is the one used of the fashioning of a craftsman) and "plants" a garden (v. 8) He is represented as shaping man's body from the clay of the earth and blowing breath into his nostrils to transform him into a living being.

There has been a temptation here for some who are over eager to defend the author's progressiveness, who have wanted to think that he was hinting at or symbolizing, ages before Darwin, the idea that man's body has been derived from some lower form of existence, as the theory of biological evolution holds. It is as futile to try to find an argument in favor of evolution from Genesis as it is to seek one against it. The author of Genesis undoubtedly believed, for he had no reason to believe otherwise, that man had been created directly and immediately by God. This notion of the mode of creation, however, no more forms part of his teaching than does his notion that the sky was a solid something or other that held back the superior waters.

Whether evolution is a fact or not, I am certainly incompetent to say. It is my non-professional opinion, as one who takes his science from the scientists, that the connection of man's bodily organism with the lower animals and a certain development in the human structure itself have been established with all the certitude we can expect when direct evidence is lacking, namely as a plausible hypothesis. I think we must imitate the good sense of Pius XII who in his encyclical *Humani generis* (1950) outlines the conditions under which Catholics mindful of revealed truth may accept the theory of evolution, and insists that the question must be left open to free discussion which is necessary for any advance in human knowledge. By no means can we assert that it has been proved beyond all doubt. On the other hand, we cannot simply dismiss it as "an unproved hypothesis," as though the evidence in its favor and the apparently unanimous consent of the scientific world counted for nothing. In this sense, nuclear fission remains "unproved," but we know that we have to live with the atom.

At any rate, the question of evolution must not be made a false issue in this or any other passage of Genesis. The author has not told us *how* man was created, but the fact that he was. It does not affect this fact one particle whether God created man's body directly or through an evolutionary process. What makes a man what he is, his spiritual soul as we say, both sound philosophy and religion tell us could be the result only of God's direct creation. The author of Genesis has already taught that man exists in God's image and likeness, therefore distinct from the beasts as sharing something in common with God, and that because of God's creative will. When we hold to these truths, which no positive science is in any position to deny, from then on the question of the mode of creation becomes largely one of historical biology.

It is no more permitted us to overextend the boundaries of revelation to the detriment of free scientific pursuit than it is permitted science to question what only revelation can tell us about man. Modern scientists are aware of their own limitations, if we can judge from a recent reiteration, with approval, of the judgment of one of the greatest of their number:

We are driven to the conclusion that in his large and well-developed brain [man] possesses an organ quite disproportionate to his actual requirements, an organ that seems prepared in advance only to be fully utilized as he progresses in civilization ... The brain of prehistoric and of savage man seems to me to prove the existence of some power distinct from that which has guided the lower animals.[1]

We must likewise admit that the biblical sources of revelation have not traced for us man's possible ancestry among the primates, nor excluded it.

[1] Quotation of the biologist Alfred Russel Wallace (1823–1913) in "Fossil Man," by Loren C. Eiseley, *Scientific American* 189/6 (December 1943), 65–72.

The author of Genesis has used, and extended, a Hebrew meta-phor found frequently in the Bible, which calls flesh "dust." He was helped by the coincidence that in Hebrew *adam* means "man" and *adamah* is "the ground." The "breath of life" which God breathes into man's nostrils does not signify man's spiritual soul. For the author's teaching on man's distinctive dignity we must seek elsewhere. This means only what it says, breath, the outward manifestation of animate existence which man shares with the animals. Our passage tells us, then, that man is God's creation, nothing more.

2: 8 The LORD God planted a garden in Eden, to the east, and
   9 he put there the man he had formed./ The LORD God made to grow out of the ground all kinds of trees pleasant to the sight and good for food, the tree of life also in the midst of the garden, and the tree of the knowledge of good and evil.

It is now that the second creation story begins to make its special contribution to the history of man. The LORD God *took* the man, *adam*, who was of the earth, earthy, *adamah*, and *put* him in a garden in Eden, to the east. Man's life in this garden, in other words, relates to his existence in a state over and above his mere creation.

The story of the garden seems to be the elaborate symbol of a revelation that only Israel had preserved intact, if indeed it had ever been known to other peoples. This is the fact of man's primi-tive elevation to a state above his nature, and, as told in chapter 3, his fall from this state through sin. I call it an elaborate symbol because the author, whether or not he believed that man had actu-ally lived in a real garden, certainly did not consider the garden as such to be important. Rather, what went on in the garden is im-portant, the state of man as he is described living in the garden.

Actually it is difficult to say whether the author has tried to locate the garden for his readers. It was, he says, in Eden. Now Eden is not a Hebrew word, but an ancient name which Israel had inherited from the past, which may have meant to the Israelite something of what Utopia or Erewhon signify to us. It was "to the east," he adds. The East was to the ancients, as it still is to us, the remote land, the land of mystery.

The Tree of Life on an Assyrian Seal

The "tree of life" without question tells us that we are in the realm of symbols. The author has borrowed this figure of speech from Mesopotamian literature where it frequently occurs as a legendary plant conferring immortality. A representation of the "tree of life" may be seen on this page, taken from an Assyrian seal. Of this tree man was free to eat while he was in the garden (v. 16). We know, then, one gift that was part of man's privilege in the state to which God had raised him above creation: he would not die. What the "tree of the knowledge of good and evil" was, we shall see in a moment.

 2:10 A river rose in Eden watering the garden; and from there, it
11 separated into four branches./ The name of the first is Phi-

son, which encircles all the land of Hevila where there is
12 gold./ And the gold of that land is good; bdellium and onyx
13 are there./ The name of the second river is Gihon, which en-
14 circles all the land of Chus. /The name of the third river is
Tigris, which flows east of Assur. And the fourth river is the
15 Euphrates./ The LORD God took the man and placed him
16 in the garden of Eden to till it and to keep it./ And the
LORD God commanded the man thus, "From every tree of
17 the garden you may eat;/ but from the tree of the knowledge of good and evil you must not eat; for the day you eat
of it, you must die."

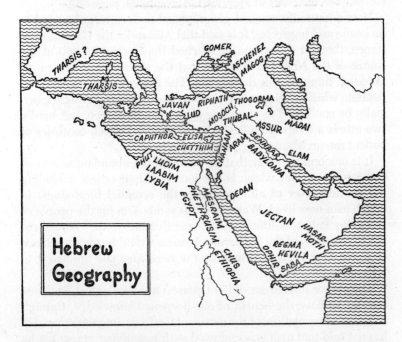

What again suggests that the author was hardly concerned with
Eden as a physical place is the extraordinary geography he has
proposed in v. 10 ff. It is true, we are not absolutely sure of all these
names, but we know enough to be fairly convinced that no place
on earth could correspond to his description. He represents Eden

watered by a huge river which is the source of four other rivers. The location of two of these rivers is certain enough, the Tigris, which as the author mentions flows east of Assur, and the Euphrates, which he needed only to name, since to the Hebrews it was *the* great river of the world. (See the map of the Near East on page 57.) The other two names cannot be identified with any known rivers. The Phison, however, the author says encircles Hevila, which is the Hebrew name for part of Arabia, the land of gold, spice, and precious stones. The Gihon, on the other hand, encircles Chus, and if Chus means what it does everywhere else in the Old Testament, it is Nubia or Ethiopia, to the south of Egypt. (See the chart of Hebrew Geography on page 55.)

Now admittedly, ancient geographical notions were inclined to be vague and imprecise. It is said that Alexander the Great, for instance, thought that when he reached the Ganges he was at the source of the Nile. But it seems that the author has deliberately muddled things in this description. The two great rivers of Mesopotamia which originate in the mountains of Armenia might poetically be conceived as springing from a single source, but hardly two others a thousand miles or more removed which centuries of patient research have been powerless to locate.

It is much more likely that he intended the abundant waters of the garden—a river which is the source of four others, including the greatest river of all!—to signify the essential blessedness in which man now lived. Water had this symbolism for the people of water-shy Palestine; the prophets said that one of the characteristics of the reign of the redeeming Messias would be an abundance of water. Our Lord later took up the same idea and applied it to Himself in John 4:10 ff.

The author of Genesis did not possess our theological language nor did he have the benefit of our deepened knowledge, through subsequent revelation, of the nature of God's dealing with man. He has not said that man was endowed with sanctifying grace. Yet he has given us, in a primitive and even naïve way, to be sure, all the elements which we sum up in this term for the supernatural life. Man, he says, was removed from the status of a simple creature into a sphere of life where he enjoyed God's superabundant blessings. He was in God's friendship, and lived with Him familiarly.

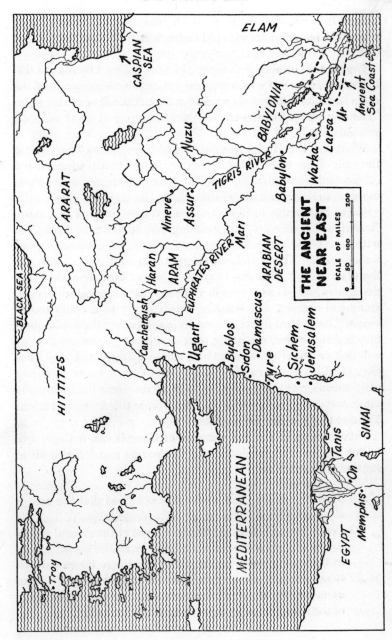

ELAM

CASPIAN SEA

ARARAT

Nuzu

BABYLONIA

Ancient Sea Coast

Ur

Larsa

Warka

Babylon

TIGRIS RIVER

Nineveh

Assur

Mari

ARABIAN DESERT

THE ANCIENT NEAR EAST

SCALE OF MILES

0 50 100 200

BLACK SEA

Carchemish

Haran

ARAM

EUPHRATES RIVER

Ugarit

Byblos

Sidon

Damascus

Tyre

Sichem

Jerusalem

HITTITES

MEDITERRANEAN

SINAI

Tanis

On

EGYPT

Memphis

Troy

This will be shown best in contrast, after man's fall from grace, when "the man and his wife hid themselves from the LORD God" (3:8).

He has told us also of the special favors enjoyed by man in this blessed state, one of which was immortality. Now he speaks of the divine condition imposed on man for the permanence of this state: "The day you eat of the tree of the knowledge of good and evil, you must die."

What was this "forbidden fruit," which is quite as figurative as the fruit of the tree of life? The "knowledge" that is meant is not intellectual knowledge, but the knowledge of experience. Man was innocent in doing, not in understanding. The Hebrews customarily spoke of knowledge in this way, as when they referred to a man's "knowing" his wife (cf. 4:1), meaning that he had sexual relations with her. "Good and evil" is not good *or* evil, but good-and-evil as a single unity. This is Hebrew idiom for an act that demonstrates the cleavage between good and evil, just as binding-and-loosing designates judicial sentences in general, and entering-and-leaving, going-and-coming, and the like, refer simply to a man's movements. The context in every case decides whether the act in question is good *or* evil, a binding over *or* a loosing from penalty, an entering *or* a leaving, a going *or* a coming. Translated very literally, Deut. 1:39 speaks of "children who do not know good and evil," meaning that they are innocent of sin. Here the idea is the same, and consequently we could paraphrase the divine condition: *The day that you sin, you shall die.*

Philosophers, of which the author of Genesis was not one, will tell us that such a prohibition was not purely negative. To avoid sin, one must practise good.

2: 18 Then the LORD God said, "It is not good that the man is alone; I will make him a helper like himself."

19 When the LORD God had formed out of the ground all the beasts of the field and the birds of the air, he brought them to the man to see what he would call them; for that which

20 the man called each of them would be its name./ The man named all the cattle, all the birds of the air and all the beasts of the field; but he found no helper like himself.

21 The LORD God cast the man into a deep sleep and, while
   he slept, took one of his ribs and closed up its place with
22 flesh./ And the rib which the LORD God took from the man,
23 he made into a woman, and brought her to him./ Then the
   man said,

> "She is now bone of my bone,
>   and flesh of my flesh;
> She shall be called Woman,
>   for from man she has been taken."

24 For this reason a man leaves his father and mother, and
   clings to his wife, and the two become one flesh.

This engaging picture of the animals being passed in review
before man had at least two purposes. In the mind of the ancients,
naming and ownership were synonymous. We therefore see a
teaching which the first creation story presented more bluntly,
that man was made to rule over the other creatures of the earth.

The other purpose was to tell something quite new about man.
It is, perhaps, a commonplace to us, but only because the Old
Testament has made it so.

In a society where physical strength was arbiter, women were
at best an inferior caste. Even under the Law of Moses a woman
was in theory at least the chattel of her husband or father, though
in her customary way she usually found ample means at hand to
equalize the situation. The Gentiles accepted this social fact with
enthusiasm and justified it with legends proving that woman was
the cause of human ills (Pandora's box is one such story) and, in
any case, was a lower type creature than man. If the world was a
man's world, it was because nature had made it so. Before we are
enviously awed at the success of this male propaganda, I think we
should seriously question whether it was ever really successful.
The legends were made by men for male consumption; there is no
evidence that any woman believed them.

The author of Genesis took a more realistic view. Women's social inferiority was a fact (3:16), but only because this was not the
best of all possible worlds. It was not so intended from the beginning. It was just another of the imperfections of an imperfect
world that man had made for himself.

We see now why the second creation story separated the account of woman's creation from that of man, and why it inserted the creation of the animals between the two. In all the procession of birds and beasts, says the author, man found no helper like himself. This is the lesson of the first story, that mankind is unique in creation, distinct from the animals because he is made in the image and likeness of God. But it is more besides. The author makes man himself acknowledge it: woman is bone of his bone and flesh of his flesh. They have the same nature and the same prerogatives. Woman is as man, for good or for evil.

Therefore this very primitive story of woman's origin, as the Biblical Commission insisted in 1909, represents a true historical fact. Woman is really formed from man, not that she has been literally taken from his flesh and blood (the word translated "rib" may mean something vaguer), but she has received his nature. Man is the exemplary cause of woman, in the language of Thomistic thought.[2] Woman is the glory of man, said St. Paul, as man is the glory of God.

Because of this the author knew that the love of man for woman is a holy thing, rooted in his nature and blessed by God, as different from the coupling of animals as man himself is different. He knew what the Jews for a time forgot, that only in a society built on monogamy does woman have the deserved safeguard of her dignity, under the protection of a husband who cherishes her as his own flesh. "For this reason a man leaves his father and mother, and clings to his wife, and the two become one flesh." Our Lord made this interpretation His own, when he repudiated divorce (Matt. *19*:4 ff.).

In v. 23 occurs the first of an interminable series of folk etymologies that will plague us throughout Genesis. "She shall be called Woman (*ishshah*), for from man (*ish*) she has been taken." Lin-

[2] This is the interpretation of Father H. Lusseau (*Précis d'histoire biblique*, p. 55 f.), who does not deny that the text may mean more than this: we are in many respects still groping towards the fulness of Genesis. I cite Father Lusseau from Charles Hauret's *Origines* (Paris: Gabalda & Cie, 1952), p. 119. The English translation of this fine discursive commentary on the first three chapters of Genesis is now available (*Beginnings, Genesis and Modern Science*, translated by E. P. Emmans, O.P. [Dubuque: The Priory Press, 1955]). The reader can find there a much more extensive treatment of all the problems raised by these chapters than can be ventured in this guide.

guistically, as it happens, the two words have no real connection, but they were associated in the popular mind by reason of their similarity of sound and meaning, just as today "sorry" is thought to derive from "sorrow," though it does not really, and "sovereign" has picked up its strange spelling from a fancied connection with "reign." The Oriental mind highly relished these word-plays. Before we dismiss them as exotic vagaries, however, let us remember that the prime offenders in folk etymology have belonged to the Western world. St. Isidore of Seville explained *aqua*, "water," as coming from *aequus*, "level," because water seeks its own. And of course the mediaeval *lucus*, "forest," from *non lucendum*, "no light," is classic. It is a tendency men have never been able to resist. It is part of Genesis' essential humanity.

2:25 Both the man and his wife were naked, but they felt no shame.

Thus the second creation story is brought to a close with the mention of another gift, no less wonderful than the others, which man enjoyed in his primitive state of innocence. Man and woman had no cause to feel shame; they had no uncontrolled emotions, the powers of their body and soul were properly related, with their mind and will in full charge. They were free, in other words, from what we call and know to our sorrow as concupiscence.

CHAPTER III: THE FALL

From now on we may as well call the man and woman in our story by the traditional names of our first parents, Adam and Eve, since we have to do with what historically happened to these historically determined persons, though it is told in a continuation of the imagery of the second creation narrative.

Whether the author of Genesis believed that the human race *began* with only one man and one woman, we do not know. He probably did. However, it cannot be shown that this forms part of the teaching of Genesis. The first account of creation, in fact, speaks of the origin of *"mankind . . . let them* have dominion . . . male and female he created *them . . ."* While the second account describes one man and one woman, it does not insist on their individuality as creatures. As we have seen, *adam* in Hebrew means simply "man." The word *hawwah*, which we have simplified to "Eve," probably meant something like "living one" (cf. 3:20). What is taught of the man and woman in this story as pertains to their human nature and qualities applies to all men and women, not to two only.

But Genesis most certainly teaches that one man and one woman were raised by God to a state above their nature, and that it is from this one man and one woman that the present human race is descended. That is the obvious sense of the following few chapters. Pius XII was only being faithful to the Scripture when he decreed in *Humani generis* that "the faithful cannot embrace that opinion called 'polygenism' which maintains either that after Adam there existed on this earth true men who did not take their origin through natural generation from him as from the first parent of all, or that

Adam represents a certain number of first parents," because "it is in no way apparent how such an opinion can be reconciled with that which the sources of revealed truth and the documents of the teaching authority of the Church propose with regard to original sin, which proceeds from a sin actually committed by an individual Adam and which through generation is passed on to all and is in everyone as his own."

The precise machinery of the creation of man is, as we have concluded, outside the scope of Genesis as not part of the author's concern. The historical unity of the human race, its possession of a common human nature, its descent from a common pair of ancestors from whom original sin has been transmitted, are, on the other hand, fundamental religious truths which are at the base of both the Old and the New Testaments. As a matter of fact, what is sometimes called polygenism in scientific literature is not in every case what the Holy Father has ruled out above. If science distinguishes *homo sapiens*, "true" man, from various prehistoric types of men whom it does not classify as "true," it is for structural and purely physical reasons which do not touch on the religious notion of man at all. What science may divide into several species on the basis of these criteria, in other words, may not necessarily conflict with what Christian tradition upholds as the oneness of "the human species." What makes a man a man is his rational and immortal soul. Prehistoric men may have differed from us in the size of their brain-pans, the slope of their foreheads, or the shape of their noses, but they were men for a' that. There are hardly less extravagant differences among the different races and types of modern man, but in Catholic language they are differences in accidentals. If scientists try to go farther, saying that these differences demand separate origins and that there is more than one human race, they go beyond what their premises allow.

The story of chapter 3, then, is the story of man's fall from grace through the sin of our first parents. It is another of Israel's gifts to the world, this priceless knowledge of man's historical nature.

Chesterton once wrote that when the doctrine of original sin had been explained to him it was as though the pieces of a Chinese puzzle began to click into place in his mind. The mystery of man,

capable of angelic good and diabolical evil, the reconciliation of
the two and their explanation, man the eternal contradiction—it is
to these problems that we find the answer in chapter 3. Destined
for the highest things, with a yearning for them in his soul, at the
same time "the inclination of man's heart is evil from his youth"
(8:21).

3:1 Now the serpent was more cunning than any beast of the
field which the LORD God had made. He said to the woman, "Did God say, 'You shall not eat of any tree of the gar-
2 den'?"/ The woman answered the serpent, "Of the fruit of
3 all the trees in the garden we may eat; /but 'Of the fruit of
the tree in the middle of the garden,' God said, 'you shall
not eat, neither shall you touch it, lest you die.' "
4 But the serpent said to the woman, "No, you shall not die;
5 for God knows that when you eat of it, your eyes will be
opened and you will be like God, knowing good and evil."
6 Now the woman saw that the tree was good for food, pleas-
ing to the eyes, and desirable for the knowledge it would
give. She took of its fruit and ate it, and also gave some to
her husband and he ate.

Jewish and Christian interpretation have always seen in "the
serpent" the ancient enemy of man whom later Jewish writers
called Satan and who has been identified in Christian revelation as
a fallen angel. This is certainly the only possible meaning. He
figures in this story as a rational being of considerable craft, far
more cunning than man who is no match for his wiles. Probably
the reason that the author chose the symbol of a serpent was the
serpent-worship common among the Chanaanites and other Gentile peoples, on which he wished to vent his contempt. A picture of
one of the serpent-gods, from Egypt, appears on page 65.

The author has given a good commentary on the psychology of
temptation, which has not changed much with the years. First
comes the distortion of the divine command, the misrepresentation
of the law: "Did God say, 'You shall not eat of *any* tree of the
garden'?" This the woman is able to resist, for she correctly re-
states what God had required of them. But she is not prepared to

cope with the father of lies. "No, you shall not die"; though God had decreed the penalty of death. What is Satan's allurement to sin, his interpretation of the knowledge of good and evil? *You will be like God!*

Egyptian Form of a Serpent-god

To be like God: there is the root of sin. To acknowledge no dependence, to be a law to oneself, this is the vulgar idea of being like God. Man was made in God's image, intended to be like God, but in God's way and with God's means. Satan counted on enticing man to adopt his own means, and he won.

What precisely was the sin that Adam and Eve committed, we shall probably never know. In all likelihood the author of Genesis was quite as ignorant of it as we. We can be very sure that the sin was not the normal use of their sexual faculties, contrary to the curious interpretation made infrequently in the past, which shows a strange notion of the meaning of sex and marriage. The author of Genesis included in his first creation story God's blessing on the human race, with the injunction that it was to be fruitful and multiply, and the second story extols marriage as of divine institution and in accordance with the nature of man and woman.

The sin could not have been of sensuality, for our first parents were free of concupiscence. It was not something to which they could be tempted of themselves, but the temptation had to be insinuated from without. Their sin was certainly at bottom one of pride, but how it was manifested, and in regard to what object, we cannot know. It is not too important that we should know. What is important is that man did eat of the "tree." He transgressed God's command, and he had to suffer the consequences.

3:7 Then the eyes of both were opened, and they realized that they were naked; so they sewed fig-leaves together and
8 made themselves coverings./ When they heard the sound of the LORD God walking in the garden in the cool of the day, the man and his wife hid themselves from the LORD God
9 among the trees of the garden./ But the LORD God called
10 the man and said to him, "Where are you?"/ And he said, "I heard you in the garden, and I was afraid because I was
11 naked; and I hid."/ Then he said, "Who told you that you were naked? You have eaten then of the tree of which I com-
12 manded you not to eat."/ The man said, "The woman you placed at my side gave me fruit from the tree and I ate."
13 Then the LORD God said to the woman, "Why have you done this?" The woman said, "The serpent deceived me and I ate."

The author has been extremely clever in his portrait of man after he had sinned. The whole picture has an uncomfortably familiar look to it, and if we peer closely enough we shall see ourselves. For, in fact, after they had sinned, our first parents were quite like ourselves. Gone was their innocence: hereafter their own bodies would be at them to draw them to evil. Gone was their intimacy with God, who was now rather someone to be dreaded. In a very true way, sin can be called its own punishment.

How characteristically the man tries to shift the blame to his wife's shoulders, not so much in the hope of really succeeding as in maliciously returning insolence for God's goodness in giving him a mate. Sin breeds sin. How typically the woman finds fault with the tempter first, with herself secondarily. "I did wrong (if you say so), but only because . . ." Our first parents are very much like ourselves.

> 3: 14 Then the LORD God said to the serpent:
> "Because you have done this,
> cursed are you among all animals,
> and among all beasts of the field;
> On your belly shall you crawl,
> dust shall you eat,
> all the days of your life.
>
> 15 I will put enmity between you and the woman,
> between your seed and her seed;
> He shall crush your head,
> and you shall lie in wait for his heel."

Sentence must now be passed on the sinners; yet first of all God turns to the tempter. If Genesis had done nothing but explain the mystery of man, which is seen in his fall and its consequences, it would have done more than all the other literature of antiquity was capable of doing. But Genesis has done more. It has also pointed to man's future hope and glory.

In the condemnation of the serpent the author is playing a tune on a Hebrew idiom. Having used the serpent to symbolize the evil one, he adheres to the figure in putting on God's lips words which obviously refer to the way a serpent has of slithering about the earth. But Satan, not the "serpent," is the intended reality and the basis of the word-play. "Crawling on the belly" and "eating dust" were expressions signifying contempt and loathing. "They shall lick the dust like serpents," says the Prophet Micheas of the enemies of God, "like the creeping things of the earth" (7:17). The sense of the divine condemnation of the serpent is, then, a prophecy of Satan's defeat. It is the corollary of mankind's hope.

God puts enmity between Satan and the woman, between Satan's seed and the woman's. We should see, first of all, that this enmity is no mere repugnance, no simple hostility—it is an enmity which God *puts* there of deliberate act, an enmity in which God plays a part. If Satan had thought to win man to himself through the fall which he had brought about—and of course, for the moment he had won—it is not to be an everlasting victory.

Rather there will be incessant war waged between Satan's "seed," that is, his lineage, the diabolic order, and the "seed" of Eve, that is, the human race. Man will struggle to break the bonds that tie him to the father of evil; and the struggle will be successful! He —the woman's seed, the human race—will eventually crush Satan's head. The author carries his imagery through to the end, and we see the picture of a man grinding the head of a serpent into the soil. The serpent's fangs, however, are fixed in the man's heel. "You shall lie in wait for his heel" less freely translated is "you shall wound his heel."

These last words are mysterious. How did the author think of them in terms of the divine prophecy which he was telling? Perhaps he referred to nothing more than the weapons of evil with which Satan would constantly belabor the race of man.

But he knew that the victory would be man's: the figure of the serpent's crushed head shows us this much. It was enough that he should know this, enough to permit him to interpret God's dealing with man in the light of a great plan of redemption, in which his own people had been chosen to serve as the means by which victory would be achieved.

In later times Israel's knowledge of the future victory broadened. By degrees it was made known that it would be the work of a single person, a descendant of the great King David, who would suffer and die for the sins of man. We know, in the fulness of Christianity, that this person was Jesus Christ.

Because the Bible is not a merely human book, but has God for its ultimate Author, we have no difficulty in seeing Christ intended in this prophecy from the very beginning, though the human author was unaware of the full significance of what he wrote. Similarly, our blessed Lady is necessarily to be joined to her divine Son. By "the woman" in 3:15 the author meant Eve, and by her "seed" the human race which would conquer Satan. But as the final fulfilment of the prophecy of the "seed" is verified only in Christ, so "the woman" who bore the seed is finally fulfilled in the Blessed Virgin.

3:16 To the woman he said:
    "I will make great your distress in childbearing;
        in pain shall you bring forth children;
    For your husband shall be your longing,
        though he have dominion over you."

17 And to Adam he said, "Because you have listened to your wife, and have eaten of the tree of which I commanded you not to eat:
    "Cursed be the ground because of you;
        in toil shall you eat of it all the days of your life;
18   Thorns and thistles shall it bring forth to you,
        and you shall eat the plants of the field.
19   In the sweat of your brow shall you eat bread,
        till you return to the ground,
    Since out of it you were taken;
        for dust you are and unto dust you shall return."

20 [And the man called his wife Eve because she was the mother of all the living.]

The great hope promised the human race would be many ages in fulfilment. Meanwhile God must impose sentence on man's disobedience. Death He had threatened, and death was to be man's lot henceforth. Gone was the grace by which man had been elevated above his nature. Once more he is of the earth, earthy, whose lot is to return to the elements from which he sprang.

With death comes pain and suffering, which for womankind is epitomized in the travails of childbirth. A society in which violence and selfishness have replaced the order of reason will inevitably accord a minor place to its weaker members.

Mankind is not cursed by the Almighty. Rather, it is the earth that is cursed because of man. Man had been made to rule over this earth, but henceforth the earth will be restive under his rule and will yield itself to his uses only reluctantly and through his strenuous toil. Original sin did not make man a depraved creature and a mass of corruption. If we speak of a "weakened will" and a "clouded intellect," Catholic theology has always understood these terms to imply the external difficulties that beset these faculties rather than any intrinsic change in them. Man had been intended for a destiny to which he would always aspire, yet now was bereft of the divine grace which alone made it a possible destiny. Thus the tragedy of man in his fallen state.

In the biblical text above v. 20 has been bracketed by the translators because to some authors it seems to be out of place as it stands. Yet I think it is appropriate that the biblical author, with a kind of grim irony, after describing the sorry state to which all man is subject should now name her who helped make it so "the mother of all the living."

3: 21 The LORD God made garments of skin for Adam and his
    22 wife and clothed them./ And he said, "Indeed! the man has become like one of us, knowing good and evil! And now perhaps he will put forth his hand and take also from the
    23 tree of life and eat, and live forever!"/ Therefore the LORD God put him out of the garden of Eden to till the ground
    24 from which he was taken./ He drove out the man; and at the east of the garden of Eden he placed the Cherubim, and the flaming sword, which turned every way, to guard the way to the tree of life.

These verses write a fitting conclusion to the story of man's fall. The easiest way to understand the LORD's words is according to the interpretation usually given, that they are ironical, even sarcastic, contrasting the promise Satan had made with what in fact had occurred. Far from being like God, man is now banished from the garden of God's presence.

The author stresses the finality of man's exclusion in the picture of the Cherubim and the flaming sword set to guard the entrance to the garden. The Cherubim are not the fat little cupids that fill the canvases of Renaissance painters. On page 71 you can see the form of an authentic cherub. These awesome beasts, symbols of divine protection, were quite as mythical as Alice's Cheshire cat, of course, though no more so than the simpering winged things that sometimes pass for angels in our art. The author is thinking of the Assyrian and Babylonian temples and palaces whose gates were flanked by these carved creatures; between them is a fiery sword with a twisted blade, the conventional sign of a thunderbolt, also a divine symbol. It was only much later, through a transfer of ideas, that the Jews began to call the members of the angelic court by the name cherubim.

An Assyro-Babylonian Cherub

In Romans 5:12 ff. we have the prophetic completion and fulfilment of the story found in Genesis 3. Here St. Paul develops, in the fulness of time, the religious thinking of Israel strengthened by later revelation, in which the whole significance of Adam's fall is seen in relation to all subsequent sin and to the salvation of Christ. The fulness of the New Testament teaching would, of course, be incomprehensible without the revelation handed on by Genesis. The author of Genesis, too, knew that the sin of Adam and Eve was not theirs only, but had somehow infected the entire human race that descends from them. How he taught this is the burden of chapter 4.

4:1 The man knew Eve his wife, and she conceived and bore
Cain, saying, "I have given birth to a man-child with the
2 help of the LORD."/ Later, she bore his brother Abel. Now
3 Abel was a keeper of flocks and Cain a tiller of the soil./ In
the course of time Cain brought to the LORD an offering of
4 the fruit of the ground./ Abel also brought some of the first-
lings of his flock with their fat portions. The LORD was
5 pleased with Abel and his offerings;/ but for Cain and his
offering he had no regard. Cain was very angry and down-
6 cast./ The LORD said to Cain, "Why are you angry and
7 why are you downcast?/ If you do well, will you not be accepted; but if you do not do well, will not sin crouch at the
door! Its desire is for you, but you must master it."

The author of Genesis knew very little of the long and painful
process through which man gradually developed his material culture. His portrayal of Adam and Eve and their immediate descendants makes them hardly distinguishable as men and women from
the men and women he knew in his day.

As we have seen, a strict history of the past was altogether impossible. Neither was the author interested in writing a strict history; his purpose throughout was religious. He had no well-
thought-out explanation to account for the fact that mankind was
sinful because of Adam's sin, but the fact itself he did know, and
this he intended to teach by means of the following stories.

There were no authentic historical records of the goings and
comings of the first men and women on earth; how could there be?
They were buried in a past so remote that in comparison the time
that separates us from the author of Genesis is hardly a day. The

names given to the men and women in Genesis 4 and 5 are all good Hebrew, and as we have seen Hebrew is a relatively late language in the world. The material of these chapters is, therefore, comparatively recent traditions, containing some historical recollections, but amassed almost exclusively for their religious value.

The original story of Cain and Abel, we can easily see, was not about human beings in the second generation of world history. It is a story which reflects the social conditions of a much more advanced age. Shepherding and agriculture already exist (v. 2), and regular ritual worship has been established (v. 3 f.); the world is obviously populated, since later on Cain fears death at the hands of other men (v. 14), and the fact that he took his brother out into a field (v. 8) is accounted for evidently by his desire for seclusion. The story has been joined to that of the fall, then, to bring out the religious lesson which we shall see. The original story itself, how God favored a good shepherd over his wicked farmer brother, is precisely the kind that would have been treasured by a pastoral people like the Hebrews.

The names in the story have been chosen for their sound, as is brought out in Eve's exclamation, "I have given birth" (*canithi*) to Cain. Abel (in Hebrew *Habel*) sounds like the word *hebel*, meaning "breath," and reflects the transitory appearance and disappearance of Abel in history. Similarly, "the land of Nod" where Cain goes to dwell in v. 16 is certainly related to *nad*, "wanderer," even as Cain is to be "a fugitive and a wanderer on the earth" (v. 14).

Because the story had a later origin, we can understand why "Cain was a tiller of the soil" (v. 2), despite the fact that Genesis uses another tradition further on which names Noe the first husbandman (9:20). This also explains why this story makes no effort to account for Cain's easy discovery of a wife (v. 17). The author of Genesis would have said, had he been asked, that in the initial propagation of the human race from a single pair of first parents there must have been considerable intermarriage of very close relatives, even of brothers and sisters. Such marriages, in fact, continued down into historical times among various peoples, such as the Egyptians. But Genesis is unconcerned with the theory or the history of genetics.

The religious purpose of the story as used by Genesis begins in
v. 6 f., in the LORD's words to Cain. The exact translation of these
verses is not assured, but their general sense is plain enough. Sin has
been let loose in the world through Adam's fall, and man must be
on his guard against it. Cain, who belongs to the race of Adam, is
subject to the same consequences that Adam brought upon himself by disobedience.

4:8 Cain said to his brother Abel, "Let us go out into the field."
Now when they were in the field, Cain turned against his
9 brother Abel and slew him./ Then the LORD said to Cain,
"Where is your brother Abel?" He answered, "I do not
10 know. Am I my brother's keeper?"/ And the LORD said,
"What have you done? The voice of your brother's blood
11 cries to me from the ground./ And now cursed are you in
the soil which has opened its mouth to receive your brother's
12 blood from your hand./ When you till the soil, it shall not
give its fruit to you; a fugitive and a wanderer shall you be
13 on the earth."/ Cain said to the LORD, "My punishment is
14 too great to bear./ You are driving me today from the soil;
and from your face I shall be hidden. And I shall be a fugitive and a wanderer on the earth, and whoever finds me will
15 kill me."/ But the LORD said to him, "Not so! Whoever
kills Cain shall be punished sevenfold." Then the LORD
gave Cain a token so that no one finding him should kill
16 him./ And Cain went out from the presence of the LORD
and dwelt in the land of Nod, to the east of Eden.

Adam had sinned against God's command. Cain's sin is also
against his fellowman. In the wake of original sin enters murder,
cruel, calculated, contemptuous. Adam had excused his sin; Cain
denies his. Adam had feared God's presence, but Cain throws in
God's face the primal repudiation of responsibility and dependence, the rejection of God's fatherhood: "Am I my brother's
keeper?"

And murder multiplies murder. "Whoever kills Cain shall be
punished sevenfold," confirms the LORD, driving Cain from His
presence. Most commentators today see in this a reference to the
blood-vengeance exacted during early man's lawless days. When
man was a wanderer without an established government and

agencies of law and order to mete out justice, the terrible and multiple vengeance which a family or tribe would demand for the slaying of one of its members was the only deterent to complete anarchy. Perhaps this is the meaning, too, of the "token" or sign which God gives Cain to preserve him from death, the mark of tribal membership. This is Father de Vaux's[1] understanding of the passage, but admittedly it is quite obscure. The Jews were still living in a society characterized by blood-vengeance when they entered Chanaan. They recognized as an evidence of God's mercy the Law of Moses which mitigated the policy of the old days by establishing courts and restricting reprisals to the limits of strict justice: "Life for life, eye for eye, tooth for tooth. . . ." (Ex. 21:24).

Cain had polluted the ground by the slaying of his brother. Therefore he was not allowed to till the soil but was sent forth to wander upon the face of the earth. So, too, before God had given them their Promised Land, the Israelites had been nomadic wanderers. All this, the author says, was not so intended from the beginning. Man was not meant to live in fear and hatred of his brother, and in isolation from him. All this was man's sad state in the sin which he had sinned.

4:17 Cain knew his wife, and she conceived and bore Henoch; Cain was the founder of a city which he named after his son
18 Henoch./ To Henoch was born Irad, and Irad became the father of Mahujael, and Mahujael the father of Mathusael,
19 and Mathusael the father of Lamech. /Lamech took two
20 wives, the one named Ada and the other Sella./ Ada bore Jabel; he was the forerunner of those who dwell in tents and
21 have flocks. His brother's name was Jubal;/ he was the fore-
22 runner of all who play the harp and flute./ It was Sella who bore Thubalcain, the forerunner of those who forge vessels of bronze and iron. The sister of Thubalcain was Noema.

This old genealogy which, as we shall see, is a companion piece to the one in chapter 5, was originally not closely connected with the preceding story. Above, the origin of the nomadic life was seen in Cain, but here he is the founder of a city. It was appropriate that the Hebrews would attribute city-life to Cain, for they never wholly approved of cities, which to them were characterized by

[1] *Genèse*, p. 51.

sinful ways. In Genesis city-dwellers are more than once contrasted unfavorably with those who follow the pastoral life. Also in the above story shepherding already existed, while in the genealogy (v. 20) it begins seven generations later. The seven generations of the genealogy are, of course, no accident; seven is an ideal Hebraic "round" number.

The genealogy has preserved some historical recollections: that shepherding and the use of metals had developed in later times, for example. Probably the fact that bronze is mentioned before iron in v. 22 indicates that the Hebrews knew of the long period (the Bronze Age of the archaeologists) which preceded the discovery of iron.

The names, however, are Hebrew, and have been made to fit their context. The first city was named Henoch because Cain founded (*hanach*) the city for his son. Jabel was the forerunner of those who shepherd (*jabal*) flocks, and his brother Jubal of those who play the harp and flute (*jobel*). Thubalcain is the forerunner of the blacksmith (*cain*).

Perhaps the author also intended to give his opinion of polygamy in naming Lamech, whose character is described sufficiently in the next passage, as the first to take two wives. At least in the ideal the Hebrews favored monogamy, though a plurality of wives was tolerated. The author knew that this, too, had not been so in the beginning according to the divine intention; it was part of man's present sinful state.

4:23 Lamech said to his wives:
> "Ada and Sella, hear my voice,
>> wives of Lamech, give ear to my speech:
>> I kill a man for wounding me,
>> a youth for bruising me.

24 > If Cain shall be avenged sevenfold,
>> Lamech seventy times sevenfold."

25 Adam knew his wife again and she bore a son and called him Seth, saying, "God has given me another child in place
26 of Abel whom Cain slew."/ Seth also had a son whom he called Enos. At that time men began to call on the name of the LORD.

The author has not yet finished his graphic portrayal of the evil state of man that is the result of Adam's sin. Lamech out-Cains his ancestor Cain; he slays a man simply for an injury done him, and demands not merely sevenfold vengeance, but seventy times sevenfold. Again the Law of Moses was a first redemption from this terror, when it decreed that for a wound only a wound in kind could be given, nothing more. Our Lord, however, who destroyed the reign of sin, gave the final redemption in His law expressed to Peter: "*Forgive*, not seven times, but seventy times seven" (Matt. 18:22).

The picture is ended with the birth of Seth, with whom the LORD replaced (*sath*) the murdered Abel. In the time of Seth and his son Enos, the author says, "men began to call on the name of the LORD." Thus mankind was not hopeless: there were good people in the world. This is, in fact, the beginning of a theme that will be followed through the next few chapters, the opposition of good and evil men, whom the author derives from Seth and Cain respectively. It is part of the true image of fallen man, that bundle of contradictions, created for good but tending to evil.

Having arrived at this point of development, the author of Genesis retraces his steps for the moment. To understand chapters 4 and 5 properly, we must realize what sort of outline the author has used in composing his religious impression of man's prehistory. He has divided the story of man from creation to Abraham into two parts: the period from Adam to the flood, and the period from the flood to Abraham. The religious significance which he saw in the flood, we shall note later. Chapter 4, which we have just seen, represents the history from Adam to the flood as it appeared in one of his sources. (Noe, the hero of the flood story, probably originally appeared in the genealogy of chapter 4.) Chapter 5 is another version of the same history, consisting in a genealogy from Adam to Noe. The author wanted to keep both these sections because each had its own precious religious teaching. Therefore he laid them side by side, just as he laid the two creation stories side by side for the same reason. And here, too, the final result has been harmonious enough.

5:1 This is the record of the descendants of Adam. When God
2 created man, he made him in the likeness of God./ Male and

female he created them, and he blessed them and called them Man when they were created.

Here we have the language and viewpoint of the first creation story, of which this is the continuation. Chapters 3 and 4, as we saw, continued the second creation story.

5: 3 When Adam was one hundred and thirty years old, he be- came the father of a son in his own likeness, after his image, and he called him Seth.

4 Adam lived eight hundred years after the birth of Seth, and
5 had other sons and daughters./ The whole lifetime of Adam was nine hundred and thirty years; then he died.

6 When Seth was one hundred and five years old, he became the father of Enos.

7 Seth lived eight hundred and seven years after the birth of
8 Enos, and had other sons and daughters./ The whole life- time of Seth was nine hundred and twelve years; then he died.

9 When Enos was ninety years old, he became the father of
10 Cainan./ Enos lived eight hundred and fifteen years after
11 the birth of Cainan, and had other sons and daughters./ The whole lifetime of Enos was nine hundred and five years; then he died.

12 When Cainan was seventy years old, he became the father
13 of Malaleel./ Cainan lived eight hundred and forty years after the birth of Malaleel, and had other sons and daugh-
14 ters./ The whole lifetime of Cainan was nine hundred and ten years; then he died.

15 When Malaleel was sixty-five years old he became the father
16 of Jared./ Malaleel lived eight hundred and thirty years after the birth of Jared, and had other sons and daughters.
17 The whole lifetime of Malaleel was eight hundred and ninety-five years; then he died.

18 When Jared was one hundred and sixty-two years old, he
19 became the father of Henoch./ Jared lived eight hundred years after the birth of Henoch, and had other sons and
20 daughters./ The whole lifetime of Jared was nine hundred and sixty-two years; then he died.

21 When Henoch was sixty-five years old, he became the father
22 of Mathusale./ Henoch walked with God three hundred
years after the birth of Mathusale, and had other sons and
23 daughters./ The whole lifetime of Henoch was three hun-
24 dred and sixty-five years./ Henoch walked with God; and
he was seen no more because God took him.
25 When Mathusale was one hundred and eighty-seven years
26 old, he became the father of Lamech./ Mathusale lived
seven hundred and eighty-two years after the birth of La-
27 mech, and had other sons and daughters./ The whole lifetime of Mathusale was nine hundred and sixty-nine years;
then he died.
28 When Lamech was one hundred and eighty-two years old,
he became the father of a son, and called him Noe, saying,
29 "This one shall bring us comfort from our work and from the
toil of our hands in the ground which the LORD cursed."
30 Lamech lived five hundred and ninety-five years after the
31 birth of Noe, and had other sons and daughters./ The whole
lifetime of Lamech was seven hundred and seventy-seven
years; then he died.
32 When Noe was five hundred years old, he became the father of Sem, Ham and Japheth.

This genealogy is symmetrically arranged with the repetition
of set phrases, like the seven-day division of the first creation story.
The only verse that really breaks the rhythm of the whole is v. 29,
and most critics today think that it originally belonged in chapter
4. It uses the name LORD, as does the second creation story, the
story of the fall, and chapter 4, it makes a play of words on Noe's
name (*naham*, "bring comfort") as these chapters are accustomed
to do, and it speaks of the cursing of the ground which is told by
the second creation story. I mentioned above that Noe's name probably originally stood somewhere in the genealogy of chapter 4.

The first thing the commentators would have us do is compare
the similarities which we find in the lists of chapters 4 and 5.

Adam		Adam
Cain	Seth	Seth
Henoch	Enos	Enos
Irad		Cainan

Mahujael		Malaleel
Mathusael		Jared
Lamech	(Noe?)	Henoch
		Mathusale
		Lamech
		Noe

The spelling has altered in a few names and their order has been freely adapted, but we can hardly disagree when Canon Clamer concludes that "the two genealogies have used common traditional data for different ends," and that "the presence of these identical names in such short lists once more confirms the artificial and symbolic character of these lists."[2] We have already seen the teaching of chapter 4; now we shall see to what use chapter 5 put the list of names that it had derived from the same ultimate source.

It contains ten generations, which was the original number. (Chapter 4, we noted, separated the list in two to bring out the distinction between good and bad men.) In employing the round number ten the author of the tradition was following a recognized literary form of the time. This we have learned from the discovery of the ancient Babylonian literature. The Babylonians shared with the Hebrews the tradition of a great flood which had devastated civilization; before and after the flood they counted a token ten generations to signify the time that had passed. When we see that the author of Genesis in 11:10 ff. (which is from the same source as chapter 5) again shows ten generations between the flood and Abraham, we see that the numbers were intended as nothing more than generalizations.

The Babylonian parallels likewise clarify what Genesis means by the fantastic ages which it has attributed to the persons which it has listed in chapters 5 and 11:10 ff. Both the Hebrews and Babylonians knew that many more than ten generations had elapsed during these periods. To bridge over the enormous gaps in time, therefore, both of them assigned tremendous ages to the few names that they possessed. While the Babylonians simply set down astronomical figures, however, none of them under twenty thousand years, the Hebrew author has been comparatively moderate, and, above all, he made his ten generations serve a religious purpose.

All commentators agree today that these inflated figures are not

2 *Genèse*, p. 172.

historical and were never intended to be. Anthropology has shown that, if anything, early man's lifespan was shorter, not longer than it is today. That the figures were known to be symbolic and nothing more is demonstrated by the freedom with which they were altered in one or another of the three versions in which they have come down to us: the present Hebrew text, the LXX, and the Samaritan Pentateuch.[3] It is, in fact, instructive to compare the figures as they appear in these three versions.

	Hebrew		*SP*		*LXX*	
Adam	130	930	130	930	230	930
Seth	105	912	105	912	205	912
Enos	90	905	90	905	190	905
Cainan	70	910	70	910	170	910
Malaleel	65	895	65	895	165	895
Jared	162	962	62	847	162	962
Henoch	65	365	65	365	165	365
Mathusale	187	969	67	720	187	969
Lamech	182	777	53	653	188	753
Noe	500		500		500	
	100	950	100	950	100	950
	1656		1307		2262	

In each case the numbers in the first column represent the ages of the patriarchs at the time the next generation began, while the second column gives the whole lifespan of each patriarch. By totaling the numbers in the first column, adding the hundred years between the birth of Noe's sons and the flood (7:6), we have the number of years that were counted between creation and the flood.

Which of the versions has best kept the author's original text can be debated. It is generally agreed, however, that the LXX has deliberately altered some of the numbers in the interest of harmony.

All the commentators agree that the numbers have a symbolic meaning. Just how the symbolism was worked out, however, is not certain. We have time for only a couple of opinions.

[3] The Samaritans, racially the result of intermarriage of Jews and various Gentile peoples, became a separate religious sect in the fourth century B.C., of which a tiny remnant still exists in Palestine. Since they handed down the Pentateuch independently of the Jews, the SP is another testimony to the primitive biblical text which it may sometimes have better preserved than the present Hebrew.

Father Edmund Sutcliffe, in his introduction to Genesis in the *Catholic Commentary,* thinks that

The original numbers are probably those of the Samaritan text, according to which the ages of the antediluvian patriarchs gradually diminished with almost complete regularity in each successive generation from Adam to Lamech: 930; 912; 905; 910; 895; 847; 365 (Enoch); 720; 653. This fits with the ancient conceptions that wisdom comes with years, that wisdom was the special prerogative of the ancients, and that its fountain-head was to be found in the first generation, Job 15:7. According to this scheme Noe, the second father of the stock whence sprang the Hebrew people, must have a life as long as the first father and indeed longer as Adam had incurred the divine displeasure whereas Noe had not. Accordingly Noe lived for 950 years, and after him the ages descend again, much more rapidly now that the list approaches historical times.[4]

In other words, the author of this tradition has spelled out in a much more complicated fashion the teaching of the second creation story and the fall, that through Adam's sin man was deprived of immortality, and that in succeeding generations the sin begun by Adam remained and increased. He has also brought out, though not so obviously, the distinction that chapter 4 made between good men and bad. It is also this consideration that accounts for Henoch's spectacularly short life of 365 years.[5] The number, of course, is another "round" one, the total of the days of a solar year. Henoch formed an exception to the rule because he "walked with God" (the same is said of Noe in 6:10); "and he was seen no more because God took him."

In his *Vom Geheimnis des Gotteswortes* (1950),[6] Father Johannes Schildenberger approaches the problem differently. He thinks the Hebrew numbers are correct and that the symbolism is in the first column. From Adam these ages drop progressively till they reach sixty-five, that is, half Adam's age of one hundred thirty; this also marks the end of the first half of the list. These first five numbers are all divisible by five. Jared begins the second half with one hundred sixty-two years, thirty-two more than Adam; and

---

[4] P. 181.

[5] We should note that Henoch has been put seventh in this list.

[6] Heidelberg: Kerle Verlag, p. 267 f.

thirty-two is just half the sixty-five years of Malaleel and Henoch on either side (a half year is not counted). Henoch, the traditional holy man of the period, has been used as the basis of the whole series: his lifespan is the symbol of an age, and his year at begetting has been simply doubled to give Adam the number that began the series. Skipping over Henoch, the second half of the series advances Jared's number by twenty-five to give Mathusale's, and by twenty to give Lamech's; these two numbers are again divisible by five, and their product is five hundred, which is Noe's age in this list. Jared and Adam, the beginners of the two halves of the series, each live eight hundred years after begetting the following generation. Without attempting to analyse the symbolism further than this, it is evident that the list has been worked out with deep artifice.

Both chapters 4 and 5, each in its own way, have filled in the gap between creation and flood with what Father de Vaux calls "the corrupted remains of ancient traditions."[7] Each in its own way has brought out basically the same religious truths. Each had something distinctive to contribute. It remains to be noted that the symbolic ages of the patriarchs are pursued all the way through Genesis, as we shall later see.

Again we are impressed by the vast difference between our notion of how history should be written and the author's. A modern historian confronted by the same problems would have to say: "A long period of time now intervened. How long, we do not know. Our knowledge of the period is practically nil. We have a few traditional names, but there are conflicts in our sources, and we do not know their precise relationship." But Genesis had an audience that expected more than this, and its author gave them more.

There is very little history in these chapters, because history in our sense of the word was impossible. Yet who can deny that what the author of Genesis has taught us is true? The sin unleashed by Adam did increase in his children. Civilization did develop, during those uncounted ages. The rest is silence, but we should be rather thankful that the author's concept of history did not permit it to be all silence.

[7] *Genèse,* p. 53.

CHAPTER V: THE FLOOD

6: 1 When men began to multiply on the earth, and had daugh-
   2 ters born to them,/ the sons of God saw that the daughters
     of men were fair, and they took wives for themselves as
   3 many as they wished./ Then the LORD said, "My spirit
     shall not remain in man forever, since he is flesh. His lifetime
     shall be one hundred and twenty years."
   4 There were giants on the earth in those days, and also
     afterward, when the sons of God had relations with the
     daughters of men, who bore children to them. These were
     the mighty men who were of old, the men of renown.
   5 When the LORD saw that the wickedness of man on the
     earth was great, and that man's every thought and all the in-
   6 clination of his heart were only evil,/ he regretted that he
     had made man on the earth and was grieved to the heart.
   7 Then the LORD said, "I will wipe from the earth man whom
     I have created—man and beast, crawling creature and bird
   8 of the air as well—for I regret that I made them." But Noe
     found favor with the LORD.

What the author wanted to tell us in these verses is plain enough.
His teaching is found in vv. 5 ff., where he pictures God so distressed at the sinfulness of man that He is resolved to destroy both
man and the world He had created for man.

But the first four verses, which are evidently an introduction to
this theme, are among the most obscure in the entire Bible. They
are, says Solomon Goldman, "despite the painstaking labors of
ancient, mediaeval and modern commentators, an enigma."[1]

[1] *In the Beginning* (New York: Harper & Brothers, 1949), p. 756.

Who are the "sons of God" who took wives for themselves from the daughters of men? "Daughters of men," as seems obvious from v. 1, is simply the wordy Hebrew way of saying "women." Some commentators think that "sons of God" means *good* men, and that we must accordingly look on the "daughters of men" as *evil* women. Now I do not think it at all unlikely, in view of the distinction made in chapter 4, that the author intended "sons of God" in his narrative to stand for the good people of the earth, symbolized by the descendants of Seth, and "daughters of men" to refer to the evil people, symbolized by the descendants of Cain. Thus he would be telling us that the good were corrupted by the evil and man as a whole was worthy of destruction.

But though this may be true enough as an interpretation, it does not account for the singular terms used in the text, nor does it explain how the union of good men and evil women was supposed to have produced a race of giants.

It is very probable that the passage had a different meaning before it was adopted by Genesis. In Job 1:6, 2:1, and elsewhere in the Bible, "sons of God" means "angels" (either good or bad). It was a common persuasion in ancient times that giants had once existed on the earth, to whom a superhuman origin was ascribed. The pagans considered these mythical giants to have been the offspring of gods who had mated with mortal women (we remember the Titans of Greek mythology). The Hebrews, of course, believed in only one God. If they had adopted this legend, therefore, they would have looked on the superhuman parents of the giants as angels, not gods.

So this passage was interpreted commonly in former times. The Jews before the time of Christ believed it, and the LXX translated "sons of God" by "angels." Many of the Fathers of the Church adopted this interpretation, and it was a general belief of the Middle Ages. Numerous modern Catholic commentators are convinced that this was the original sense of the passage.

Our developed knowledge of angels as purely spiritual beings who do not marry or have children tells us that in any case the story could be nothing more than a legend. Whether the author of Genesis believed in the possibility of the thing, is immaterial. He passed the story on not to explain the origin of alleged giants, who do not figure elsewhere in his text, but to illustrate the kind of lawlessness that made God regret that He had created man. A made-up story is just as good as a true one for this purpose, and he could have used it as a parable of corruption even as our Lord used fictitious stories to teach divine truths. Anyway, as I suggested before, he may have intended to work the story into the development of chapter 4 with a different meaning, in which case the legend has been transformed into historical fact.

While the explanation given above which modern Catholic interpreters attach to the "sons of God" episode is, I think, very likely, it is far from certain. Quite recently (1955) Father A. Jamme has published some ancient Semitic inscriptions which speak of "daughters of God,"[2] apparently meaning girls who had been dedicated in some fashion to the service of a deity. This is new knowledge which may have a bearing on the interpretation of Genesis. We must be content to say that while the author's religious teaching is clear enough, the details of the text remain as they have been characterized, an enigma.

The "hundred and twenty years" that God allows man in v. 3, according to many commentators, signifies a period of time given the human race for repentance before God would bring down the punishment of the flood. Others take it to mean another symbolic shortening of the individual lifespan. It is from another source than that used in chapter 5 and 11:10 ff.

And so we are brought to the story of the flood. The author has shown God's justice, His impatience with sin, His holiness that cannot tolerate corruption. The flood will be the great object-lesson of these facts, but of others as well. For there is another side to God's dealing with men. He is merciful: He will not destroy the innocent with the guilty. He allows time for repentance, and He does not condemn all indiscriminately, even when sin characterizes the vast majority.

> 6: 9 This is the story of Noe. Noe was a just man, blameless
> 10 among the men of his day./ He walked with God. Noe became the father of three sons, Sem, Ham and Japheth.

<hr>

[2] "Some Qatabanian Inscriptions Dedicating 'Daughters of God,'" *Bulletin of the American Schools of Oriental Research* 138 (April 1955) 39–47.

11 The earth was corrupt in the sight of God, and it was filled
12 with violence./ God saw that the earth was corrupt; for all
13 men lived corruptly on the earth./ And God said to Noe,
    "The end of all creatures of flesh is in my mind; the earth is
    full of violence because of them. I will destroy them with
    the earth.

14 "Make an ark of resin-wood; make it tight with fibre and
    cover it with pitch inside and out.

15 "This is how you shall make it: the length of the ark three
    hundred cubits, its width fifty cubits, and its height thirty
16 cubits./ Make an opening for the ark and finish it a cubit
    from the top. Set a door in the side of the ark; make it with
17 a bottom, second and third level./ For in truth I will bring
    the flood upon the earth to destroy from under heaven all
    flesh in which there is the breath of life. All that are on the
18 earth shall die./ But I will establish my covenant with you;
    you shall go into the ark, you, your sons, your wife and your
19 sons' wives with you./ Of every sort of living creature of all
    flesh you shall bring two into the ark, to keep them alive
20 with you; they shall be male and female./ Of birds accord-
    ing to their kind and of cattle according to their kind, of
    every kind of creature moving over the ground, two of each
21 shall enter with you to be kept alive./ Take with you also
    every kind of food that can be eaten and store it up with
22 you, and it shall serve as food for you and for them."/ And
    Noe did all that God commanded him.

Other ancient oriental peoples besides the Hebrews have preserved the tradition of a great flood that took place in a dim age of
the past. Several versions of a Babylonian account have come down
to us which parallel Genesis often in striking detail. Genesis has
not copied from the Babylonian stories, nor have the Babylonian
stories from Genesis; the accounts have a common, more remote
source. Where there is so much traditional evidence, it is plain that
there was really an historical fact behind the traditions, an outstanding cataclysm that impressed itself on the memory of ancient
man. (Sir Leonard Woolley once thought that he had found phys-

ical evidence of the flood in southern Mesopotamia, but further study has shown that this conclusion was unfounded.)

If the flood is an historical fact, we must nevertheless recognize that our information about it has come to us only through folk history; consequently we cannot determine the exact nature and extent of the happening that gave rise to these traditions. Popular history had exaggerated the flood into a universal inundation that had covered the whole earth: a thing conceivable when the world was thought to be quite small, but which we now know is simply impossible. That enough water should have been created out of nothing to cover the highest mountains of the earth, that Noe should have been able to gather together specimens of the mere 519,000 distinct species of living creatures and feed and house them in an ark of whatever dimensions, would have required a series of unheard-of miracles. These embellishments grew up in an age when life was thought to be much simpler than we now know it is.

The traditional sources which the author of Genesis used in telling the story of the flood were part of this popular history. They took it for granted that the flood had been world-wide. Even if we try to read the words of the text against their obvious sense and restrict the universality of the flood to the inhabited earth, we have solved nothing. The same physical impossibilities exist. The world was always larger than the Old Testament Hebrews thought it to be; there were people scattered over the face of the earth about whom they knew nothing, and among whom there has never been discovered the slightest trace of a flood-tradition. The solution to the problems presented by this part of Genesis does not lie in trying to wrest a concordism between primitive traditions and scientifically established facts of which they were entirely ignorant. This is just as artificial and unconvincing as to pretend that the six days of the first creation story are really geological ages.

The solution, as always, lies in determining the use that the author made of his source material. The flood story in chapters 6-9 speaks of a catastrophe that engulfed the entire earth, just as the first creation story speaks of the sky as a solid upturned bowl. But was the author of Genesis interested in teaching natural history any more than he was in teaching physics?

He was interested in teaching religious truths, using material that was at least basically historical. What he intended to bring out by means of this story is the inspired meaning of the Bible, and nothing else is its meaning.

With the same genius wherewith he transmuted the dry statistics of chapter 5 into religious doctrine, he has converted the story of Noe and his ark into a drama of God's ways with men. In this consists the great difference between the flood story in Genesis and its Babylonian parallels, which are simply childish and superstitious.

First of all, he saw the flood as the divine chastisement of human wickedness. To us it is a commonplace that God hates and punishes sin. It was not so to the ancients. Among the peoples of their time, only the Hebrews had a religion which dictated a morality. Only they had a God who called men to account according to fixed moral laws. The gods of the Gentiles were governed only by caprice—as the Babylonian flood story makes the flood a capricious act of the gods—and their conduct was frequently more reprehensible than men's.

The moral God of the Hebrews is, at the same time, a most merciful God. Because "Noe was a just man, blameless among the men of his day," God is good to him. Again, we take it for granted that a man is to account for his own sins, and that the good are not to be destroyed with the wicked. But in Genesis' time there was little idea of personal responsibility. The individual was submerged in the mass, the people, the state, or the king. Genesis' teaching that a man could rise above his evil generation to stand blameless in the sight of a loving God shattered pagan thinking with a mighty voice of contradiction. In the Babylonian story of the flood, one man and his family were saved only by accident when one of the gods revealed to him the plan which the gods had agreed upon to destroy all men, good, bad, and indifferent (and nearly destroyed themselves in the process).

These were the teachings of the author of Genesis; there were others, as we shall see. That he was unconcerned with the factual details of the story will be brought out more clearly below.

The religious purpose of the author is brought out from the beginning, however, in his description of the ark. He makes it a box of fabulous size: four hundred fifty feet long, seventy-five feet wide, forty-five feet high. (The cubit was the measure of the elbow to the fingertips, about a foot and a half.) This would fit nicely in St. Peter's, which has a length of 619 feet, but it would have been a tremendous wood-structure for that day. More interesting is the name he gives it, which we traditionally translate by "ark." He calls it the *tebah*, a word found otherwise in the Bible only in Exodus 2:3,5, where it is used for the basket (which was also daubed with pitch) in which the infant Moses escaped the fury of the Egyptian executioners. The parallel is apparent; the ark is in very fact the symbol of God's protection. This significance was not lost upon the early Christians who filled the catacombs with representations of the box-like ark in which they saw a foreshadowing of the Church.

7:1 Then the LORD said to Noe, "Go into the ark, you and all your household; for you, in this generation, I have found

2 just in my sight./ Of all clean animals take with you seven pairs, a male and its mate; and of the unclean animals two, a

3 male and its mate;/ of the birds of the air also, seven pairs, male and female, that they may raise up offspring over all

4 the earth./ For after seven days I will send rain on the earth for forty days and forty nights, and I will wipe from the ground every living thing that I have made."

5.6 Noe did all that God commanded him. He was six hundred

7 years old when the flood came upon the earth./ Noe and his sons, his wife and his sons' wives went together into the ark

8 to escape the waters of the flood./ Of clean animals and the unclean, of birds and of every creature crawling on the

9 ground,/ pairs, male and female, entered the ark with Noe,

10 as God had commanded him./ And after the seven days the waters of the flood came upon the earth.

11 In the six hundredth year of Noe's life, on the seventeenth day of the second month, on that very day all the fountains of the great deep burst forth, and the floodgates of the

12 heavens were opened./ And rain fell on the earth forty days

13 and forty nights./ On the very same day Noe and his sons, Sem, Ham and Japheth, Noe's wife and the three wives of

14 Noe's sons entered the ark together:/ they and every kind
   of wild animal, every kind of cattle, every kind of reptile
   crawling on the earth and every kind of bird, every kind of
15 winged creature./ Pairs of all flesh in which there was the
16 breath of life entered the ark with Noe./ And they that entered were male and female of all flesh as God had commanded him; and the Lord shut him in.
17 The flood continued forty days upon the earth. The waters
   increased and bore up the ark and it rose above the earth.
18 The waters rose higher and increased greatly on the earth;
19 but the ark floated on the surface of the waters. The waters
   rose higher and higher on the earth so that all the highest
   mountains everywhere under the heavens were covered.
20 The waters rose fifteen cubits above the mountains so that
21 they were covered. All flesh that moved on the earth died:
   birds, cattle, wild animals, all creatures that creep on the
22 earth, and all men. All that were on the dry land in whose
23 nostrils was the breath of life, died./ And every living
   thing on the earth was wiped out, from man to beast, from
   reptile to bird of the air; they were wiped from the earth.
24 Only Noe and those with him in the ark were left./ The
   waters rose on the earth one hundred and fifty days.
8:1 Then God remembered Noe, and all the wild animals and all
   the cattle that were with him in the ark. And God sent a
 2 wind over the earth and the waters subsided./ The fountains
   of the deep and the floodgates of the heavens were closed.
 3 The rain from the heavens was withheld./ The waters
   steadily receded from the earth. They subsided at the end of
 4 one hundred and fifty days./ And in the seventh month, on
   the seventeenth day of the month, the ark rested on the
 5 mountains of Ararat./ The waters continued to recede until
   the tenth month; on the first day of the tenth month the tops
   of the mountains appeared.
 6 At the end of forty days, Noe opened the window which he
 7 had made in the ark,/ and released a raven. It flew to and
 8 fro until the waters had dried off the earth./ Then he sent a
   dove to see if the waters had abated from the surface of the

9 ground./ But the dove found no place to alight, so she returned to him in the ark; for the water covered the whole
earth. He put forth his hand and caught her and drew her to
him in the ark.

10 He waited another seven days, and again sent forth the dove
11 from the ark. The dove came back to him in the evening,
and there in her mouth was a green olive leaf! So Noe knew
12 that the waters had abated from the earth./ Then he waited
another seven days, and sent forth the dove; but she did not
return to him any more.

13 Now in the six hundred and first year, in the first month, on
the first day of the month, the waters were dried off the
earth. Noe removed the covering of the ark and saw that the
14 surface of the ground had dried. In the second month, on the
15 twenty-seventh day of the month, the earth was dry. Then
16 God said to Noe,/ "'Go out of the ark, you and your wife and
17 your sons and your sons' wives with you./ Bring out with you
every living thing you have of all flesh: birds, cattle, and
every creature crawling on the earth, that they may abound
18 on the earth and be fruitful and multiply on the earth."/ Noe
went forth with his sons and his wife and his sons' wives.
19 All wild animals, all cattle, all birds and all creatures crawling on the earth: according to their kinds they went out of
the ark.

In this long and circumstanced account, much of which in broad
outline agrees closely with the Babylonian stories, we are struck by
the more than ordinary repetitiveness of our author. It is true that
Semitic writing favors repetition and recapitulation, but not to the
extent of telling the same story over twice. Yet that is what we
have in the text: twice God observes the malice of men (6:5, 6:12),
twice He predicts the flood (6:13, 17 and 7:4), twice He orders
Noe to enter the ark (6:18 ff., 7:1 ff.), twice Noe obeys (6:22, 7:5),
twice he enters (7:7, 7:13), twice the flood begins (7:10, 7:11),
twice the waters increase and raise the ark (7:17, 7:18), twice all
livings things die (7:21, 7:22 f.), twice the waters abate (8:1a, 8:3a),
and so on. So many coincidences are hardly accidental.

The story of the flood was brought from Mesopotamia, the Hebrews' ancestral home, by Abraham when he moved into Palestine, probably in the nineteenth century B.C. It is from Mesopotamia also that the other non-Hebrew parallels to the story derive. Among the Hebrews the story was told and retold and acquired various forms. At least two versions of the tradition have been combined by the author of Genesis to make up the narrative as we now have it.

Previously we have seen the author lay parallel traditions side by side, when each had distinctive traits that he wished to preserve. Here, however, he has mingled the two, to an extent that it is frequently difficult if not impossible to separate them.

He did not bother to remove the conflicting details in the two versions of the story. It may be as well to note just a few of these. In 6:19 f. and 7:15 f., from one tradition, Noe is said to have taken a pair of *every* kind of living creature with him into the ark. In 7:2 f., the other tradition followed a different calculation based on Jewish dietary laws which distinguished between "clean" and "unclean" animals. Likewise the duration of the flood was different in the two traditions. In one, it was a flood of forty days and forty nights, while in the other the flood lasted one hundred and fifty days.

In fact, an entirely diverse system of counting is used throughout the whole story. According to one tradition, after the rain of forty days and forty nights (7:4,12) Noe waited forty days before opening the windows of the ark to release a raven (8:6 f.). Then he waited seven days (cf. 8:10, "*another* seven days") before he released the dove for the first time (8:8), followed by another seven days, and still another seven after the dove returned with the olive leaf (8:12). There is, therefore, a period of sixty-one days during which the waters recede, and all together the catastrophe lasted one hundred and one days. But in the other tradition the floodgates of heaven and the sources of the deep were open one hundred and fifty days (7:24, 8:2a, 3b) before the waters began to descend. In the six hundred and first year of Noe, the first month, the first day of the month, the waters had dried off the earth (8:13). Since the flood began in the six hundredth year of Noe, the second month, the seventeenth day (7:11), the recession of the waters and the flood together lasted about ten and a half months. A month and twenty-seven days later the earth was dry (8:14). Many additional discrepancies can be discerned in the text, but we need not labor the point further.

It is true that the author has harmonized the two accounts as best he could in order to bring them into a single narrative: any writer would do the same. The fact, however, that he did not hesitate to join together such conflicting data is the best possible evidence that the factual nature of the details of either tradition was of little interest to him. He could not, and did not intend to warrant their historical accuracy; neither, therefore, did the Holy Spirit who inspired his writing. To him, the history of the flood was a parable of God's justice and mercy.

8:20 Then Noe built an altar to the LORD; he took of every clean animal and of every clean bird, and offered holo-
21 causts on the altar./ When the LORD smelled the sweet odor he said to himself, "I will never again curse the ground on account of man, for the inclination of man's heart is evil from his youth; I will never again destroy
22 every living creature, as I have done./ As long as the earth shall last, seedtime and harvest, cold and heat, summer and winter, day and night, shall not cease."

9:1 God blessed Noe and his sons and said to them, "Be fruitful
2 and multiply, and fill the earth. The fear and dread of you shall be upon all the wild animals of the earth and upon every bird of the air, upon all creatures that crawl on the ground, and all the fish of the sea; into your power they are
3 delivered. Every creature that moves and lives shall be food for you; as I gave you the green plants, I give you every-
4 thing./ But flesh with its life—that is, its blood—you shall not
5 eat./ Surely I will require an account of your life's blood; from every beast I will require it, and from man; from every man I will require the life of his fellow.

6   "Whoever sheds the blood of man,
              by man shall his blood be shed;
           For in the image of God man was made.
7   But you, be fruitful and multiply;
              abound on the earth and subdue it."

8.9 Then God said to Noe and to his sons with him, "I will establish my covenant with you, and with your descendants
10 after you; and with every living creature that is with you,
the birds, the cattle, and every wild animal with you; all
that came out of the ark, even the wild animals. I will es-
11 tablish my covenant with you./ Never again shall all flesh
be destroyed by the waters of the flood; never again shall
12 there be a flood to destroy the earth."/ And God said, "This
is the token of the covenant; I set it between me and you and
every living creature that is with you, for all generations
13 to come./ I will set my bow in the clouds and it shall be a
14 token of the covenant between me and the earth./ When I
bring clouds over the earth, and the bow appears in the
15 clouds, I will remember my covenant which is between me
and you and every living creature of all flesh. Never again
16 shall the waters become a flood to destroy all flesh./ When
the bow is in the clouds, I will look upon it and recall the
perpetual covenant between God and every living creature
17 of all flesh that is on the earth."/ And God said to Noe, "This
is the token of the covenant which I will establish between
me and all flesh that is on the earth."
18 The sons of Noe who went out of the ark were Sem, Ham
19 and Japheth. [Ham is the father of Chanaan.]/ These three
were the sons of Noe and from these the whole earth was
peopled.

With the conclusion of the flood story we are again fully in the
realm of Israel: no parallels to these religious teachings are found
in the Babylonian traditions.

God accepts Noe's sacrifice in words that show that He has, so
to speak, reconciled Himself to living with man. He will abide
man's wickedness, for "the inclination of man's heart is wicked
from his youth." We must not look, says Genesis, to see God visit
upon man the full consequences of his crimes. If He did so, the
world would be forever blotted out. "That there was a deluge
once," wrote Sir Thomas Browne, "seems not to me so great a
miracle as that there is not one always." Yet God is sometimes
more lenient in His judgment of man than is man of himself. He is

merciful and long-suffering; He takes man's weakness into account.

As Genesis has taken the flood as a symbol of God's perennial dealing with man, His justice in punishing, His mercy in sparing, and His willingness to give man a second chance, the first few verses of chapter 9 characteristically describe humanity after the flood as a new creation, in the language of the first creation story.

Once more the earth and its fulness are delivered into man's charge, yet now with a difference. Creation is now subject to man not willingly, but in fear. God's agreement to take man as he is, is at the same time an avowal of man's sinful state and the consequences which this sin has wrought in the perfect world that God had planned. The world is and will remain far from perfect. In the first creation story we saw the author dramatize the peace and harmony of the world as God intended it to be by depicting man restricting himself to the plantlife for food. The prophets repeated the same figure in their confident prediction of the redeemed world of the future. It is in keeping with the realistic view now taken of the world as it exists in stark reality that the animals are in this new creation given to man for his food. The glorious times of which the prophets spoke were far removed. Forgiven man had been, would be, but sinful he was yet, and would be so increasingly.

Only "flesh with its life—that is, its blood—you shall not eat." To the ancients blood was sacred, because it was considered the seat of the life given by God. This is the origin of the prohibition of blood in the Jewish dietary or *kosher* laws. In the Law of Moses (Leviticus 17:11) blood served the ritual purpose of expiating sin. The author of Genesis could not know that in turn this was the dim foreshadowing of the bloody sacrifice of Christ whereby the world would be redeemed.

The sacredness of human life, created in the image and likeness of God, is also stressed. The law of God is put in words that correspond to this world of sin and disorder in which God now permits man to live. "Whoever sheds the blood of man, by man shall his blood be shed." This is the law of blood-vengeance. The Bedawin Arabs, who to this day possess this law, know that in an unordered society that acknowledges no moral or judicial sanction against murder, it is the only protection of human life. A man may walk without fear, knowing that the surety of reprisal from his family or tribe is the guarantee of his safety. Moses, who mediated for his people a law and a covenant, was to give them something far better than this.

In a very imperfect way, therefore, this new creation scene can be viewed as the foreshadowing of the covenant made with Israel, as the covenant made with Israel in turn was to be the foreshadowing of the new covenant of the Cross. In a sense, God's relation to Adam had been a covenant, which Adam had violated and thereby forfeited. In Noe the process begins afresh, under the limited terms which God has expressed. The flood in a true sense has marked the end of one age and the beginning of another. God has reached a new understanding with man, and that man may be heedful of the lessons of history, he is bidden to accept as the sign of God's covenant the rainbow in the clouds. When men thereafter would see the rainbow appearing after the rain, they should think of the story of the flood and what it signified; they should remember that they are sinful creatures, and that if sin rages in the world it is not because God is not just, but because in His mercy He has resolved not to destroy.

The end is not yet. Man will abuse God's tolerance, as the following chapters will eloquently prove. We have now reached the final stage of the author's introduction to Why God Chose Israel. Into this last age before the call of Abraham enter Sem, Ham, and Japheth, the remote ancestors of Israel and of the world Israel knew. Mankind is still one, but God will divide mankind for a while by taking a part to Himself, that in time He may gain all.

9: 20 Now Noe was a husbandman, the first to plant a vineyard.
21 When he drank of the wine, he became drunk and lay
22 naked in his tent./ Ham [the father of Chanaan] saw his
23 father's nakedness and told his two brothers outside./ But
Sem and Japheth took a robe, and laying it upon their
shoulders, went backward and covered their father's
nakedness; as their faces were turned away, they did not
24 see their father's nakedness./ When Noe awoke from his
drunkenness and learned what his youngest son had done
25 to him,/ he said:

> "Cursed be Chanaan;
> meanest of slaves shall he be
> to his brethren."

26 Then he said:

> "Blessed be the LORD, the God of Sem;
> let Chanaan be his slave.

27   May God expand Japheth;
> let him dwell in the tents of Sem;
> let Chanaan be his slave."

28 Noe lived three hundred and fifty years after the flood.
29 The whole lifetime of Noe was nine hundred and fifty
years; then he died.

This story reflects some of the fundamental persuasions of the
Hebrew mind, among them that nothing occurs that is not intended by God, and that a father's curse or blessing is sacred and
irrevocable and represents God's will. In view of what later be-

came the lot of the descendants of Noe's sons, this tradition of their father's blessings and curse would have been treasured as the explanation.

Here Ham is represented as an undutiful son, which was and is a capital crime in Semitic eyes. "Cursed be he who dishonors his father or his mother," decreed the Law of Moses (Deut. 27:16). Therefore, while Japheth and Sem are blessed for their reverence to their father, Ham is condemned. Since the author understood this condemnation to have been fulfilled in Ham's descendant Chanaan, however, Chanaan's name is substituted for Ham's in vv. 25, 26, and 27. Who Chanaan was, and why he was deemed accursed, and why Sem and Japheth were blessed, we learn from the following chapter.

10: 1 These are the descendants of the sons of Noe, Sem, Ham and Japheth; sons were born to them after the flood.
  2 The descendants of Japheth are Gomer, Magog, Madai,
  3 Javan, Thubal, Mosoch and Thiras./ The descendants of
  4 Gomer are Aschenez, Riphath and Thogorma./ The descendants of Javan are Elisa, Tharsis, Chetthim and Ro-
  5 danim./ From these sprang the island-peoples. These are the descendants of Japheth in their countries, according to their languages and their families, and by their nations.

We have by now had it amply proved that the Hebrews employed family trees in ways greatly different from our own. Chapter 5 contains religious teaching in the form of a genealogy, and the same is true of chapter 10.

The purpose of this chapter is to show the relation of the nations of the world into which Abraham was born, according to the mentality of the Old Testament Jew. By "world" I mean, of course, the world that the Hebrews knew, which they called *tebel* and the later Romans *orbis terrarum*, the circle of countries about the Mediterranean Sea. I must also stress "the mentality of the Old Testament Jew." He did not classify peoples according to the racial and national distinctions and affinities that we know, but according to facts rooted in Hebrew history and religion.

Among "the descendants of Japheth" we have grouped together the more remote Gentile peoples: the names in the list are not of individuals, but of nations. Most of these names can be localized, either from other parts of the Bible or from the discoveries of archaeology. Gomer, Magog, Thubal, Mosoch, Thogorma, Aschenez, and Riphath are the ancient names of regions we know as Turkey and, farther north, the Caucasus, around the Black Sea. Javan is the Hebrew name for Greece. Tharsis is probably Tartessus, in the southern part of Spain. Rodanim is the island, or rather, the island people of Rhodes, and Elisa is probably the island of Cyprus. Chetthim may be the name of the Cypriotes or some other island people. Madai is further east, the land of the Medes, in modern Iran.

These were the "good" Gentiles, whose relations with the people of God were harmonious. Now we see why in 9:27 Japheth was blessed—he would "dwell in the tents of Sem," that is, share in the blessings of the chosen people.

10:6   The descendants of Ham are Chus, Mesraim, Phut and
  7   Chanaan./ The descendants of Chus are Saba, Hevila, Sabatha, Regma and Sabathacha. The descendants of Regma
  8   are Saba and Dedan./ Chus was the father of Nemrod; he
  9   was the first to be a conqueror on the earth./ He was a mighty hunter before the LORD. Hence the saying, "Like Nemrod, a mighty hunter before the LORD."
  10 The beginning of his kingdom was Babylon, Arach and
  11 Acchad, all of them in the land of Sennaar./ From that region Assur went forth and built Nineve and Rohoboth-Ir
  12 and Chale and Resen/ between Nineve and Chale; that is the great city.
  13 Mesraim became the father of Ludim, Anamim, Laabim,
  14 Nepthuhim,/ Phethrusim, Chasluhim and Caphthorim—
  15 from whom the Philistines sprang./ Chanaan became the
  16 father of Sidon his first-born, and Heth,/ and the Jebusite,
  17 the Amorrite, the Gergesite,/ the Hevite, the Aracite, the
  18 Sinite,/ the Aradite, the Samarite and the Hamathite. Afterward, the families of the Chanaanites spread abroad.
  19 And the border of the Chanaanite extended from Sidon, in the direction of Gerara, as far as Gaza; in the direction of

Sodom, Gomorra, Adama and Seboim as far as Lesa.
20 These are the descendants of Ham according to their families and their languages, in their countries, by their nations.

Most of the places and peoples named in chapter *10* can be
found on the map illustrating Hebrew Geography on page 55,
or on the map of the Ancient Near East, page 57.

From Ham the Hebrews derived those Gentiles who were their
enemies: Chus, Mesraim, Phut, and Chanaan—that is to say, Ethiopia, Egypt, Libya, and the Chanaanite peoples. The "descendants"
of Chus in v. 7 are various localities in the Arabian peninsula.

Also derived from Chus is Nemrod, a hero of the past whose
name has been preserved by other peoples of the Near East; he
and his family are here associated with the founding of great cities
in Sennaar (Babylonia) and Assur (Assyria), the two Mesopotamian countries most cordially detested by the Hebrews. Some of
these cities we know, the rest have never been identified. Babylon,
of course, is the most famous, and Arach, today known as Warka,
was in olden times an equally powerful city-state in southern Mesopotamia. In northern Mesopotamia Acchad, better known as Ak-
kad, was only a memory before the Hebrews began. Nineve became the famous, and in Hebrew eyes infamous, capital of the
Assyrian Empire.

Divers peoples making up the Egyptian Empire, or bordering
on it, are named as "children" of Mesraim (Egypt) in v. 13 f. The
Egyptians enslaved and persecuted the Israelites for four hundred
years; it was after Moses liberated them from this slavery that the
covenant of Sinai was enacted between God and Israel. With the
Egyptians are associated the Caphthorim and Philistines. Caph-
thor was probably Crete. The Philistines who were, in all likelihood, from somewhere in the Mediterranean islands, became the
rivals of the Israelites for control of Chanaan. Ironically enough,
they eventually gave their name to the land: Palestine (*Phelishtim*,
"the Philistines," in Hebrew).

The Jebusites, Amorrites, Gergesites, etc., of v. 16 ff., were the
Chanaanite peoples who resisted the Israelite conquest of the
Promised Land and became their most persistent and hated ene-
mies. We can see now why Chanaan, the "son" of Ham, was cursed

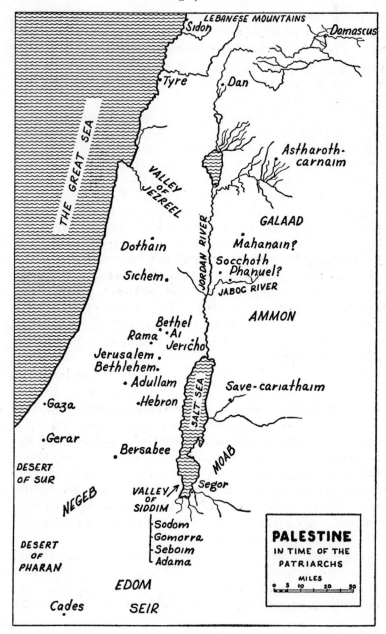

THE GREAT SEA

LEBANESE MOUNTAINS

Sidon

Damascus

Tyre

Dan

Astharoth-carnaim

VALLEY OF JEZREEL

JORDAN RIVER

GALAAD

Dothain

Mahanain?

Socchoth

Sichem

Phanuel?

JABOC RIVER

AMMON

Bethel

Rama ·Ai

Jericho

Jerusalem

Bethlehem

·Adullam

SALT SEA

Save-cariathaim

·Gaza

·Hebron

·Gerar

·Bersabee

MOAB

DESERT OF SUR

NEGEB

VALLEY OF SIDDIM

Segor

DESERT OF PHARAN

Sodom

Gomorra

Seboim

Adama

EDOM

Cades

SEIR

PALESTINE
IN TIME OF THE
PATRIARCHS

MILES
0 5 10   20   30

by Noe in 9:25. The author speaks of Sidon as the "first-born" of Chanaan in v. 15, but in v. 19 f. he makes clear what Sidon was, one of the chief cities of Chanaan, as can be seen on the map of Palestine on page 102. Some of these cities we shall encounter further on in Genesis. With the Chanaanites the author names Heth (v. 15), the putative ancestor of the Hethites, more familiarly known as the Hittites. The Hittites treated in our history books possessed a great empire in what is now Turkey, to the west of the mountains of Ararat (Armenia), where Noe's ark came to rest. The author was probably thinking of a related people in Palestine, however, whom he called Hethites and simply equated with the Chanaanites.

We can pause for a moment to note again that while some of these peoples actually are related racially or nationally, the author has not made this fact the basis of his distinctions. To the extent that there is a science in the study of race, considering affinities in color, features, language, and the like, we scientifically class with the Jews as Semites various peoples such as the Arabs and Ethiopians, and just as certainly exclude the Hittites, Greeks, Persians, etc., who are Indo-Europeans or Aryans. In point of fact, the Chanaanite peoples were mostly Semitic in the scientific sense, and not related to the Egyptians racially. Neither of them were related to the Philistines. There was no science of race or linguistics in the time of Genesis. The author's divisions are partly geographical, but chiefly historical in motivation.

10: 21 To Sem also, the father of all the descendants of Eber, the
22 elder brother of Japheth, children were born./ The descendants of Sem were Elam, Assur, Arphachsad, Lud
23 and Aram./ The descendants of Aram were Us, Hul,
24 Gether and Mes./ Arphachsad became the father of Sale;
25 and Sale became the father of Eber./ Two sons were born to Eber; the one was Phaleg—for in his time the
26 world was divided—and his brother was Jectan./ Jectan became the father of Elmodad, Saleph, Hasarmoth, Jare,
27-29 Adoram, Uzal, Decla,/ Ebal, Abimael, Saba,/ Ophir, Hevila and Jobab; all these were the sons of Jectan.
30 Their settlements extended from Messa in the direction
31 of Sephar, to the mountains of the East./ These are the

descendants of Sem according to their families and their languages, in their countries, by their nations.

32 These are the families of the sons of Noe according to their descent in their nations. From these the nations branched out over the earth after the flood.

From Sem the Hebrews derived themselves and all those peoples with whom they were willing to acknowledge relationship. These, especially the Hebrews of course, had received Noe's particular blessing in 9:26. Since the Jews were indeed God's chosen, this is not idle boasting but a true historical fact.

In this final section there is a mingling of the names of peoples and of individuals. Some of them, Abraham's traditional ancestors, we shall meet again in the genealogy of *11*:10 ff. used to span the period from the flood to historical times. These are Arphachsad, Sale, Eber, and Phaleg. From Eber (or Heber) the name "Hebrew" was thought to originate. The notice of Phaleg in v. 25 may contain an historical allusion: "in his time the world was divided." His name means in Hebrew "canal," and some think that the text refers to the division of Mesopotamia by the vast system of irrigation canals which had existed there from time immemorial and which were periodically renewed and enlarged.

The ancestors of the Hebrews were Mesopotamians; consequently they counted among their relations the neighboring people of Elam (part of modern Iran) and Aram, northwestern Mesopotamia later to be known as Syria. The Arameans were actually racially akin to the Hebrews. Along with Aram went Us, of the same general region, and probably for the same reason Hul, Gether, and Mes, though the identification of these is doubtful. Some of the other names we do not know at all.

The mingling of individuals and peoples in this section has also been accompanied by a mingling of traditions. Because historical considerations played so large a part in fixing these relationships, it is not surprising that at different times the arrangements might be varied. Thus Assur in v. 11 was a Hamite, but in v. 22 he is made a Semite. The same thing has taken place with regard to Saba and Hevila, who were Japhethites in v. 7, but Semites in v. 28 f. All the names in v. 26 ff. are of Arab tribes and sites. The Arabs and Assyrians were, it is true, Semites in the racial sense of the word.

Though we may find such a catalogue of names somewhat tiresome, we should try to sympathize with the author's purpose in bringing it together. That he was frankly hostile to some of the peoples whom he has listed, need not disturb us. His was a primitive age, without the benefit of a Christian law which holds up to us the obligation of loving our enemies, a law which we often find it easy to forget. According to his lights, he has maintained a high religious tone throughout this chapter. The enemies of God's people were, in a strict sense, the enemies of God Himself; and the enemies of God were indeed accursed.

Primitive though the author's thinking may have been, it was more genuinely moral than that of many of our contemporaries. He was no victim of the modern heresy of racism, which achieved its ultimate horror in Nazism. He knew that all men were united in blood in the one human race. He began his teaching with the flood story, which supposed the nations of the world to have a common ancestor. The sources of his animosities were honorable, conclusions from the religion and history of his people. He would have regarded as the irreligious superstition it is a frame of mind that can despise a man for the color of his skin or the shape of his nose.

11:1 The whole earth used the same language and the same
2 speech./ While men were migrating eastward, they discovered a valley in the land of Sennaar and settled there.
3 They said to one another, "Come, let us make bricks and bake them." They used bricks for stone and bitumen for
4 mortar./ Then they said, "Let us build ourselves a city and a tower with its top in the heavens; let us make a name for
5 ourselves lest we be scattered all over the earth."/ The LORD came down to see the city and the tower which
6 men had built./ And the LORD said, "Truly, they are one people and they all have the same language. This is the beginning of what they will do. Hereafter they will not be re-
7 strained from anything which they determine to do./ Let us go down, and there confuse their language so that they
8 will not understand one another's speech."/ So the LORD

scattered them from that place all over the earth; and they
9 stopped building the city./ For this reason it was called
Babel, because there the LORD confused the speech of
all the earth. From there the LORD scattered them all
over the earth.

In the long introduction to Genesis which is now drawing to its
close, we have seen that the author had a complete, very elevated
religious doctrine to set before his people. We have seen what he
taught about God, who is one, almighty, Creator of all things. We
have seen that he taught the unity of the human race, and that man
is the chief of God's visible creation. We have seen how man was
raised to a state above his nature, how he forfeited this state, and
how his sin infected the whole human race, increased, and grew.
We have seen the promise of redemption. We have seen, above all,
that the author was especially conscious of man's sinfulness—and
rightly so, that he might impress upon his readers, in the times
before the promised Redeemer, their need of salvation and the
purpose God had in choosing a people unto Himself to become
the bearers of this hope to the world.

It is on this theme of human sinfulness, and of the inadequacy of
man without God, that the introduction is concluded. These lessons the author has drawn from this ancient story of the tower of
Babel.

The story arose in the East, in Mesopotamia, and must have been
brought into Palestine by Abraham and the other early ancestors
of the Hebrews. Babel is the Hebrew name of the city of Babylon,
and Sennaar, as we have seen, was their word for Babylonia or
southern Mesopotamia. The building mentioned, the "tower," was
a peculiarly Mesopotamian structure known as a *ziggurat*, a
stepped temple that towered high above the other buildings in
each city. A sketch of one of these temples as reconstructed by
archaeologists may be seen on page 107. The construction material described in the story, mud bricks joined with bitumen, is
also proper to Mesopotamia, where there was no stone to speak of.
We notice that the author is at some pains to explain this unusual
type of fabric to his readers.

There was probably a genuinely historical event behind this

story, but all efforts thus far to pin it down have been fruitless. Babylon had a *ziggurat*, of course, but there is no record of its ever having been destroyed or arrested in construction. Quite likely the city in the story has been called Babel because in the Hebrew mind Babylon was just about the oldest city in the world.

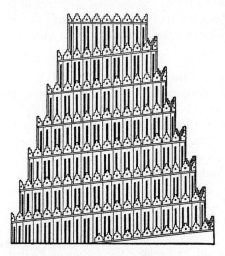

A Mesopotamian Ziggurat

It is easy to see that in the folk tradition by which the story was passed down to the author of Genesis it had been adapted to provide a fanciful explanation of the difference in the world's languages. Originally, it was told, the whole earth had used the same language and the same speech, but the LORD frustrated the plans of these people by dividing their languages and scattering them about the earth. This application of the story was doubtless suggested by the word *balal*, "confuse," which sounds enough like Babel to become a folk etymology.

But the author of Genesis has not used the story to teach us the origin of languages, a matter in which he had little or no interest. In his preceding chapter he has already presupposed the existence of the different languages and nations of the world (cf. *10*:5,20,31). Rather, he has used it as an example of human pride vaunting itself in the presence of the Almighty, a pride which is as dangerous as

it is pathetic. "Let us build ourselves a city and a tower with its top
in the heavens," say the builders of Babel. "Let us make a name for
ourselves lest we be scattered all over the earth." This disposition,
to decide their own destinies independently of God, the author
condemned. It was the sin of Adam all over again.

Man without God was self-doomed. Yet man had learned nothing from the frustration of his own devices. If the world was to be
saved, it must be in some new way, for in man as a whole there
could be no hope.

11:10 These are the descendants of Sem. When Sem was one
hundred years old he became the father of Arphachsad,
11 two years after the flood./ Sem lived five hundred years
after the birth of Arphachsad, and had other sons and
12 daughters./ When Arphachsad was thirty-five years old
13 he became the father of Sale./ Arphachsad lived four
hundred and three years after the birth of Sale, and had
14 other sons and daughters./ When Sale was thirty years
15 old he became the father of Eber./ Sale lived four hundred and three years after the birth of Eber, and had
16 other sons and daughters./ When Eber was thirty-four
17 years old he became the father of Phaleg./ Eber lived
four hundred and thirty years after the birth of Phaleg,
18 and had other sons and daughters./ When Phaleg was
19 thirty years old he became the father of Reu./ Phaleg
lived two hundred and nine years after the birth of Reu,
20 and had other sons and daughters./ When Reu was
21 thirty-two years old he became the father of Sarug./ Reu
lived two hundred and seven years after the birth of
22 Sarug, and had other sons and daughters./ When Sarug
was thirty years old he became the father of Nahor.
23 Sarug lived two hundred years after the birth of Nahor,
24 and had other sons and daughters./ When Nahor was
twenty-nine years old he became the father of Thare.
25 Nahor lived one hundred and nineteen years after the
26 birth of Thare, and had other sons and daughters./ When
Thare was seventy years old he became the father of
Abram, Nahor and Aran.

Once again the author races across time to tie together the story of the flood and the coming of Abraham. If we compare the ages of these patriarchs with those in chapter 5, we see that they are on an average less than half. Following the symbolism established before, the author tells us that as mankind grew older it became less wise, less righteous before the LORD. The lesson of the tower of Babel is being repeated.

The numbers in this chapter are even more obviously symbolic than they were in chapter 5. The author allows only two hundred and ninety years from the time of the flood to the birth of Abraham, yet he gives a total age of six hundred years to Sem. This would mean, if we were to take the figures as representing historical ages, that when Abraham died one hundred and seventy-five years old, "at a good old age, an old man, after a full life" (25:8), Sem would have just been entering upon the full vigor of his manhood. But obviously the author means nothing of the kind. Sem and Arphachsad and Sale and the rest were the shadowy remains of half-remembered traditions in the time of Abraham, let alone the time of the writing of Genesis.

It is likewise a bit easier to unravel the symbolism of these numbers. As before, there are wide discrepancies in the figures as given by our Hebrew text, by the LXX, and the SP. It is not necessary to spell them out; suffice it to say that the differences are of the same sort, but wider in extent. The LXX seems to have missed the point of the chapter rather thoroughly: it has levelled off the figures as much as possible by adding hundreds here and there, and it has even produced another generation, borrowing the name of Cainan from chapter 5 and inserting him between Arphachsad and Sale (giving him exactly the same number of years as Sale). The LXX thought that there should be ten generations after the flood as well as before, but it sold short the subtlety of our author. There *are* ten generations: Abraham is the tenth, whose life is told in chapter 12 ff. It is in this highly artistic way that the author has welded his introduction to the body of his book.

The SP makes the lifespans of the patriarchs decline in unvarying regularity—it is so orderly, in fact, that we suspect some later scribe has made it so. It seems best to take the Hebrew text as having the original numbers. When we add them in each case we get a succession of 600, 438, 433, 464, 239, 239, 230, 148, and 205. This means that there is a diminishing order except for Eber and Thare. It would no doubt have appeared only right to the author that an exception should be made for these two, one of whom had given his name to the Hebrews while the other had ushered in their career as a distinct people by bringing his clan out of Mesopotamia and setting them on the road to Chanaan (v. 30 ff.). With Abraham a new series begins, as will later be shown.

Genesis no more gives a complete genealogical tree of Abraham's forebears in this passage than it did of Noe's in chapter 5. There may not be as many names in these lists as there were thousands of years between one time and the other. In both instances the names themselves are the residue of traditions that had held to the name and little more. Thare is known to have been a personal name used in the Near East, and it would not be remarkable if tradition had correctly preserved the name of Abraham's father. Sarug and Nahor have been discovered in Babylonian records as names of cities, and such may well be their significance in the primitive genealogy of Genesis. About the rest we cannot be sure.

"Thare became the father of Abram." With Abraham will once more come the promise of salvation, repeated for the first time since God predicted Satan's defeat after the fall of man. It will be repeated now not vaguely but as a practical programme that can cheer the pragmatic heart of a Jew. In Abraham, whom the Bible styles God's friend, this programme of the divine mercy will begin to unfold.

PART TWO:
HEBREW BEGINNINGS

11:27 These are the descendants of Thare. Thare was the father
28 of Abram, Nahor and Aran./ Aran became the father of
Lot. Aran died before his father Thare in the land of his
29 birth, in Ur of the Chaldees./ Abram and Nahor married.
Abram's wife was Sarai and Nahor's wife was Melcha, the
30 daughter of Aran, father of Melcha and Jescha./ Now
31 Sarai was barren; she had no children./ Thare took his
son Abram and his grandson Lot, the son of Aran, and his
daughter-in-law Sarai, the wife of his son Abram, and led
them from Ur of the Chaldees toward the land of Chanaan; but when they reached Haran, they settled there.
32 The lifetime of Thare was two hundred and five years;
and he died in Haran.

As closely as we can figure it, Abraham, who was at first called
Abram, entered Palestine and history sometime after about 1850
B.C.

From the findings of archaeology and ancient historical texts, we
have reason to believe that a rather large migration of people took
place around this time or a little earlier from the city of Ur in
southern Mesopotamia to the city of Haran in the north, exactly as
is supposed in v. 31. Presumably Thare and his family were part of
this migration.

Haran, one of the few really old cities of the world, still exists
with its name unchanged. Situated in the centre of the so-called
Fertile Crescent of land encircling the Arabian desert from the
Persian Gulf in the east to Egypt in the west, it was a strategic
crossroads of the trade routes which passed from Ur northward

into Asia Minor and westward from Assur to Carchemish. (The reader will find it helpful from now on, without being told each time, to take an occasional glance at the maps of the Near East and Palestine.) It is thought that Haran was a daughter-city of Ur, if not founded by citizens of Ur at least dominated by them later. The two cities worshipped the same gods, especially the moon-god Sin, which is a strong argument for their political unity.

The reason for the migration from Ur of a sizeable population was the loss of power which Ur had to endure in the second half of the twentieth century B.C., about the time that Babylon was founded. A half-millennium before Ur had dominated practically all of Mesopotamia. Even when it had had to take second place politically in subsequent generations, it had always retained a primacy of honor, and just before its final catastrophe it had been at the height of its prestige in every aspect. But about the time that Abraham's father would have been born, Ur was undergoing the novel and bitter experience of having become insignificant. A flood of invading peoples, some from the East and some from out of the vast desert, began to pour into the Fertile Crescent, toppling thrones and setting up new orders and new values. Ur was invaded, conquered, deprived of its subject lands, and not for another century or more was it to regain a token of its former esteem.

It is well that we underline the history of Ur and its age-old civilization, for this is the city that had moulded Abraham's ancestry. The Hebrews did not begin as barbarians from the steppes. Recorded history in Mesopotamia begins about 5000 B.C., and Ur had inherited and distilled the finest of its traditions. From this civilization had come writing, the numeral system which we still use, and principles of law which we yet observe. It was a civilization that first produced the state, a government based on treaties and defined rights, agreements between city and city to further a commonweal of civilized men. It converted the unpromising arid land between the two great rivers into a fertile plain that supported a population several times that of the present day. Whoever flies over the land that we now know as Iraq can observe the traces of the dykes and the network of canals by which this was effected, which have disappeared through centuries of neglect in which the desert has inevitably returned. In the sands of the desert still stand the mud brick walls of the great cities that flowered from this land when Europe was an uninhabited waste. Not the least of these cities was Ur, whose splendors have been unveiled by the excavations of Sir Leonard Woolley and others.

Ur in Abraham's time had a mixed populace strongly Semitic in culture. The first inhabitants of Ur about whom we know very much were the Sumerians, a non-Semitic people whose origins are obscure, but who set the tone of the durable civilization that was to last through thousands of years and outlast its conquerors. These had been succeeded by the Akkadians who built up the world's first empire, extending as far as Asia Minor, Eastern Semites related to Western Semites like the Jews much as the Scandinavians are related to the Germans. Last of all came the Western Semites, it is thought from the Arabian desert: before that, their origins are lost in prehistory.

The precise relation of Abraham and his family to Ur is uncertain. We may presume, however, that they lived there as they later lived in Chanaan, as semi-nomads, dwelling rather on the edge of the city than in it, preferring the freedom of the pastoral life to that of commerce or trade, yet forming an essential to the city's economy and sharing in all that is implied in the word urbanity. It is possible that from this fact they acquired the name "Hebrew," a term which originally seems to have been a social rather than a racial distinctive, applied to the non-sedentary elements of the population which moved from city to city, sometimes hiring out as mercenary soldiers in time of war. "Abram the Hebrew" appears as such a figure in chapter 14. By the time Genesis was written the source of this name had been forgotten, and the Jews rarely used it of themselves. They derived it, as we have seen, by folk etymology from a man named Eber who had lived beyond the Euphrates.

Genesis quite unintentionally affords evidence to link Thare's family to the migration to Haran that took place after Ur had gone down in defeat. Abraham's ancestors were pagans, as the Hebrews never forgot: "In times past your fathers, down to Thare, father of Abraham and Nahor, dwelt beyond the River and served other gods" (Josue 24:2). Their names show them to have been worshippers of the moon-god Sin whose cult was transplanted to Haran when Ur's identity as a city had been lost. Sarai, "queen," and Melcha, "princess," were common Mesopotamian names for women, titles honoring Nin-gal, the moon-god's consort. Nahor's grandson Laban, whom we meet in chapter 24 still living in the neighborhood of Haran, likewise had a name (meaning "white") that proclaimed him a devotee of Sin.

These and other witnesses come forward to confirm the history of Genesis that places the beginnings of the Hebrews in Mesopotamia. As we saw, there are countless links with Mesopotamia in the old traditions which eventually became the first eleven chapters of Genesis. We shall later find that the laws and customs observed by Abraham and his immediate descendants betray the same origin.

The text of Genesis states that Thare was minded to go down into Chanaan but settled in Haran instead; Abraham was to complete the journey. Between about 1900 and 1700 B.C. a general movement of peoples took place throughout the entire Fertile Crescent, and one aspect of this movement was the invasion of Chanaan by those who were called Amorrites, "westerners," by the Mesopotamians, seemingly as a generic name for Western Semites. An earlier phase of the same movement had resulted in the humbling of Ur and the establishment of Western Semitic kingdoms throughout Mesopotamia. It is in connection with this movement that we must doubtless identify Abraham's descent into Palestine.

In such a fashion we are able to fit Abraham into the larger picture of the history of his time. Genesis makes little or no attempt to do so. The traditions enshrined in the Bible are family history, dealing with people who went unnoticed in the annals of empires and kings, who were thought to be of no significance save to their own descendants. The evident unconcern of the biblical author with the broader history of mankind is what makes all the more exciting the rediscovery of ancient times that has come about in our generation. The wealth of knowledge which we now possess through the laborious piecing together of the million shreds of evidence has corroborated detail after detail in the Genesis story and given us a confirmation of their historicity which the author himself did not have.

Not so long ago the story of Abraham was widely dismissed as legend, but today such a viewpoint would be unthinkable and utterly unscientific. In Professor Albright's words, "Abraham, Isaac, and Jacob no longer seem isolated figures, much less reflections of later Israelite history; they now appear as true children of their age, bearing the same names, moving over the same territory, visiting the same towns, practising the same customs as their contemporaries."[1]

Cuneiform Tablet

Cities have been excavated, inscriptions deciphered, whole literatures and long-dead languages newly discovered and read. Especially, two great cities of ancient Mesopotamia which are never mentioned in the Bible, Mari and Nuzu, roughly contemporary with the period covered by Genesis, within the past quarter cen-

[1] *Archaeology of Palestine,* p. 236.

tury have helped to verify beyond our fondest hopes the basic history contained in this book. In each of these places something in the neighborhood of 20,000 texts of all kinds were unearthed by the archaeologists. Inscribed on virtually imperishable baked clay tablets very similar to the one illustrated on page 117, they have told us in detail of the laws and customs of the world of Abraham and Isaac and Jacob. I shall try to highlight the findings of this new knowledge and its bearing on Genesis as we read the text.

Genesis, of course, is still preeminently *religious* history. The traditions have been chosen and arranged so as to demonstrate the author's religious convictions. It is *popular* history. Some think that it was at one time almost entirely epic poetry. Be that as it may, it is certainly filled with poetic qualities, including daring figures of speech, exaggerations, word-plays, and anthropomorphisms. It is *family* history, taking no account of the movers and shakers of the world, but consisting in homely, familiar accounts of family heroes, of their births, deaths, and doings with one another.

But it is also true history. On this score, its agreement with the other records of antiquity leaves no possible doubt.

CHAPTER VII: ABRAHAM THE PATRIARCH

12: 1 The LORD said to Abram:
"Leave your country, your kinsfolk and your
father's house,
for the land which I will show you;
2 I will make a great nation of you.
I will bless you, and make your name great,
so that you shall be a blessing.
3 I will bless them that bless you,
and curse them that curse you.
In you shall all the nations of the earth
be blessed."

Throughout Israel's long history its deepest thinkers forever asked themselves in wonder and in awe why it was that God had chosen this people to be His own. The answer they gave was the only one that could be given: "It was not because you are the largest of all nations that the LORD set his heart on you and chose you . . . *It was because the LORD loved you.*" And the wise of Israel added: "It was because of his fidelity to the oath he had sworn to your fathers" (Deut. 7:7 f.).

In the call of Abraham which we have just read we see the first oath that God swore to the fathers of the Jews. We see, too, why God swore this oath. The promise of the LORD, though delivered specially to the people of Israel, was to embrace all mankind.

Through God's mercy Abraham is removed from the idolatry and pagan error in which he had been reared and directed towards the land of Palestine which would become the inheritance of his descendants. From Abraham would spring the nation of God's

119

choice, and from that nation would come forth Christ the Savior. The purpose of God's blessing of Abraham is thus the measure of its greatness: "In you shall all the nations of the earth be blessed."

This is the beginning of the fulfilment of God's promise in 3:15, that the seed of Eve should crush the head of the serpent. It is to be a fulfilment of which the Old Testament is not to know the end. Abraham is only the first of many whose hearts will be opened to God's saving grace, leading up to that great day when a descendant of Adam shall once for all end Satan's reign over the world and open to all races of man without distinction the doors of salvation. The end of the promise in v. 3 is to be sought in the redemptive suffering, death, and resurrection of Jesus Christ.

The author would not have possessed these traditions about Abraham had not the origins of Israel's religion been truly founded in the life of the great patriarch. Neither would Israel's history be comprehensible if this were not so. The Bible attributes to Moses the establishment and organization of Israelite religion as it was known to its inspired writers. But no man however magnetic and persuasive has been able to change overnight a whole people's thinking and sacred beliefs. Moses could only build on a foundation already laid. Somehow, under circumstances we do not know, through what influences we cannot even guess, Abraham came to a recognition of the one God whose providence was ever after to guide his footsteps.

We realize that we are reading a familiar account, of course, in which direct discourse may summarize a revelation that came only slowly and by degrees. How the LORD revealed Himself to Abraham we are not told. Of the fact itself, however, in all the implications the author has ascribed to it, we can be sure.

The Bible has committed no anachronism, therefore, in picturing Abraham as a monotheist. Scholars today are readier to admit this than they were a generation ago, for the study of Israel's religion has been consistently bringing them to a conviction that its most fundamental principles must be dated very early in history. Some will use the term "practical monotheism," meaning that while Abraham personally served and worshipped one God as he is shown to do in Genesis, there is no evidence that he denied the existence of the gods served by other peoples. This distinction is, however, a reflection of our thinking which would in all probability have been meaningless to an Old Testament Jew. To the Hebrews all knowledge was practical: knowledge and experience were the same thing, and they did not know what it was to accept or reject anything in pure theory. When the Psalmist wrote that "the fool has said in his heart, 'There is no God,'" he did not accuse the fool of denying the rational proofs for God's existence. There was no atheism of this sort in the ancient world when men lived close to the realities of life. He meant that the fool acted as though there were no God to bring down his folly upon his head. In our terminology this is "practical atheism," but it was the only atheism the Psalmist knew anything about. The existence of other gods does not enter upon the patriarchal scene at all. If Abraham covenanted with the God of Israel, He was the only God that Abraham knew.

12: 4 Abram went away as the LORD had commanded him, and Lot went with him. Abram was seventy-five years old
   5 when he left Haran./ Abram took Sarai his wife, Lot his brother's son, all the property they had acquired and the persons they had got in Haran; and they departed for the land of Chanaan. When they came to the land of Chanaan,
   6 Abram passed through the land to the sacred place at Sichem, near the terebinth of More. At that time the Chanaanite was in the land.
   7 The LORD appeared to Abram, and said, "To your descendants I will give this land." So Abram built an altar
   8 there to the LORD, who had appeared to him./ He moved from there to the mountain region east of Bethel, and pitched his tent, having Bethel to the west and Ai to the east. He built an altar there to the LORD and called on the
   9 name of the LORD./ Then Abram journeyed on toward the Negeb.

The regions where Abraham is said to have stayed in Palestine—Sichem, then a Chanaanite shrine, Bethel, Ai, later on Hebron—are all in the hill country in the central part of the land. A writer ignorant of the past who had simply wanted to imagine what the life of his ancestor was like would undoubtedly have located Abraham on the fertile coastal plain, where anyone would surely go if he had the choice. Archaeology, however, has proved the soundness of the Genesis tradition, for during these times it was the hill country that was inhabited, and the coast deserted. Abraham, we notice, did not actually live in the towns, but near them. The terebinth of More must have been a grove nearby Sichem. His movements to the south are doubtless to be accounted for as the seasonal migrations of people mostly concerned with shepherding. He is presented as a wealthy tribal leader or sheikh, with considerable property and household slaves.

The southern Negeb is also mentioned. This is today wasteland, and it was wasteland when the Israelites possessed Palestine and when Genesis was written: the author sometimes refers to it as a desert. The American archaeologist Nelson Glueck, however, through surface surveys and excavations in recent years has shown that during the period from about 2000 until 1600 B.C. the Negeb was a densely inhabited area. Again the biblical tradition knew whereof it was speaking when it placed Abraham in these parts.

12: 10 Now there was a famine in the land and Abram went down to Egypt where he lived as a stranger; for the fa-
11 mine in the land was severe./ When he was about to enter Egypt, he said to Sarai his wife, "I know that you are a
12 woman beautiful to behold./ When the Egyptians see you, they will say, 'She is his wife'; then they will kill me,
13 but will spare you./ Therefore, say you are my sister so that I may be treated well on your account, and my life
14 may be spared for your sake."/ When Abram came to Egypt, the Egyptians saw that the woman was very beau-
15 tiful./ Pharao's princes saw her and they praised her to Pharao. And the woman was taken to Pharao's house.
16 He treated Abram well on her account so that he received flocks, herds, he-asses, men-servants, maid-servants, she-asses and camels.
17 But the LORD struck Pharao and his household with
18 great plagues because of Sarai, Abram's wife./ Then Pharao summoned Abram and said, "Why have you done

this to me? Why did you not tell me she was your wife?
19 Why did you say she was your sister and let me marry
20 her? Here now is your wife; take her and go."/ Then
Pharao gave his men orders concerning Abram; and they
sent him away with his wife and all that belonged to him.

This story has been brought in by the author to give an example
of God's protection of Abraham. There is nothing implausible in
the story, which accurately reflects the times. Drought caused
periodic famines in Palestine, and nothing was more natural than
to take one's flocks and belongings into the proverbially wealthy
Egypt. Egypt at this time was living under its great Twelfth Dynasty and was at the peak of its power and influence; at least technically it was in control of the city-states of Chanaan. Passage between the two countries was easy, and archaeology has proved
that it was frequent. Many Western Semitic names turn up in
Egypt during this period.

If one would know what Abraham and his caravan looked like,
he can gain an idea from the rather well known illustration reproduced on page 124. This is from an Egyptian wall painting of
the Twelfth Dynasty, representing a delegation of Bedawin "Asi-
atics," as the Egyptians called the Chanaanites, being received in
Egypt. From it we can observe what the amenities of Abraham's
life must have been.

We are apt to consider Abraham's treatment of Sara in this story
somewhat shabby, and to question his sense of truth. The author
has not tried to minimize his faults; at the same time Abraham
should not be judged by the delicate standards that did not exist
in his time. We must also understand the situation presupposed.
Marriages were arranged by the nearest of kin, and the brother of
a prospective bride would be well treated while the extensive,
time-consuming negotiations were taking place. On the other hand,
a woman who already had a husband was not marriageable: the
husband would be to an oriental despot simply a temporary obstacle that could be removed. The author has stressed that Abraham
was a "stranger" in Egypt, that is, an alien without the protection
of law. According to his lights, therefore, Abraham acted pru-
dently.

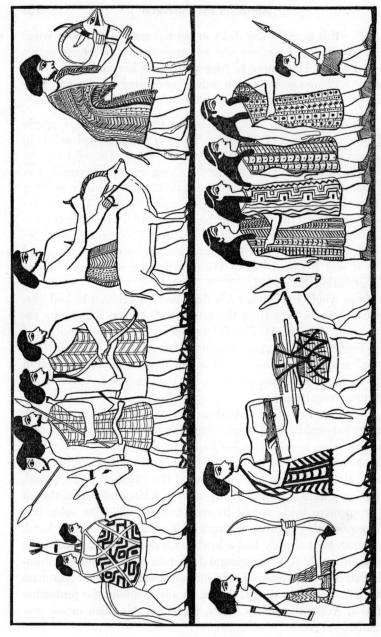

Semitic Bedawin from Beni Hasan in Egypt, 12th Dynasty

God who had promised Abraham the blessing of numerous descendants kept the oath He had sworn. Sara was preserved to her husband, and Abraham, though escorted firmly out of Egypt, was delivered from danger. Thus the story is a token of Abraham's entire life under God's protection.

A question occurs to us in reading this episode that would not have troubled the Hebrew mind. Pharao seems to be punished for something that he had done in perfectly good faith, and this offends our sense of God's justice. We are not told how Pharao discovered the trick that had been played on him, but it is evident that he too recognized the plague that had afflicted his household as the result of some nemesis or divine wrath, the consequence of the act which he had performed in ignorance.

Sin to the Old Testament mentality was a concrete, actual offence to God, even if it had been committed without malice. We know from the flood story that the author of Genesis taught that God does not punish the innocent, and that a man is judged on his individual merits. At the same time an offence to God was an offence to God, which could not be lightly dismissed as though it had never happened. At the same time, too, man is a social creature closely bound up with his fellows. If Pharao had done well and had received God's bounty, the blessing would have been shared by his household. The author thought it only proper that when the converse was true, the household should suffer along with Pharao. The author was no philosopher who would harmonize these divergent conclusions, but he knew that each contained its own truth.

As a matter of fact, we are not capable of an entirely satisfactory reconciliation in our minds of these facts that we know to be true. We believe firmly in individual retribution, yet we know that in some way we cannot wholly fathom the sin of the one man Adam was the sin of us all. We did not actually commit it, but we have suffered its consequences. In the same order, Christ's sacrifice was accepted in atonement for the sins of the whole human race, and it is by our mysterious union with Him that we share in His glorification. We, too, speak of "material" and "formal" sin, evil that has been done unintentionally and evil that was performed of set purpose. We know that a man is not punished for material sin, but we still call it sin.

There is, therefore, not a great deal of difference between our presuppositions and those of the Old Testament. The difference is rather that we are concerned about the resulting problems and the Old Testament was not. Put in our terms, the author of Genesis did not consider Pharao so much punished as simply suffering the inevitable consequences of sin. We do not imprison a criminal lunatic to punish him, but to protect society; yet he may endure the precise deprivation of liberty that would have been his punishment had he been responsible for his deeds. God's laws must also be protected; the moral code must be vindicated against every infraction, whether intended or not. Many a man must suffer for sins he has not personally committed, whether he is the father of a wastrel son, the son of a syphilitic father, or the peace-loving citizen of a war-mongering nation. The whys and wherefores are hidden in a divine will which we know despite all is just and merciful. We can see only the inescapable fact. The Old Testament saw an inescapable connection between sin and human suffering. It was only right that he who had done the sin, however unwittingly, should do the suffering too.

One final observation may not be out of place. The Old Testament writers took a much simpler view than we can afford to take of the relation of cause and effect and the hand of God in human affairs. In the latter part of David's life it is related that God's anger was incited against Israel—we are not told why—and that therefore He inspired David to take a census of the people, that He might punish Israel with its king for this act of pride. This scandalizes us, for it seems to turn God into an arbitrary despot and make a mockery of just retribution. It scandalized some Jews, as far as that goes, for when the story was rewritten at a later date it was revised to read that Satan inspired David to take the census. Yet the earlier writer was right in his convictions though his language from our point of view was unhappily chosen. He started with the agreed fact that Israel had been humbled for a sin of pride. The conception of the project that brought on this punishment, however, could not have come about unless God willed it. And if God willed it, He must have been angry with Israel. To bring in Satan was only to lengthen the story, not change its conclusion, for Satan could do nothing apart from God's power. He would have been impatient with the distinctions we have learned to make, that God's will is only permissive in some respects, imperative in others; and he would note with satisfaction that for all our distinctions we still find the problem of evil quite a mystery, just as he did.

All this is to say that the Old Testament does not hesitate on many occasions to attribute to God's will and even to God's direct command quite a number of disturbing things which our more developed theology will require us to say were only indirectly willed by God, permitted or tolerated by Him. This may at times be misleading: our Lord, for example, had to point out that the Law of Moses had only permitted not commanded divorce. But it arose from the firm conviction of undeniable truths, that God's power is almighty and that His presence is all-pervading in human affairs.

13:1 Abram went up from Egypt to the Negeb, he and his wife
2 and all that belonged to him, and Lot with him./ Now
3 Abram was very rich in cattle, silver and gold./ He journeyed by stages from the Negeb to Bethel to the place
where his tent had been before, between Bethel and Ai.
4 At the place where the altar was which he had previously
built there, Abram called on the name of the LORD.
5 Lot, who went with Abram, also had flocks, herds and
6 tents,/ so that the land would not support them dwelling
together; for their possessions were so great that they
7 could not dwell together./ And there was strife between
the herdsmen of Abram's cattle and the herdsmen of Lot's
cattle. At that time the Chanaanite and the Pherezite
8 dwelt in the land./ Then Abram said to Lot, "Let there be
no strife between you and me, nor between my herdsmen
9 and your herdsmen; for we are kinsmen./ Does not the
whole land lie before you? Withdraw from me. If you go
to the left, I will go to the right; or if you take the right,
10 then I will go to the left."/ Then Lot looked about and saw
that the whole region of the Jordan toward Segor was well-
watered—this was before the LORD destroyed Sodom and
11 Gomorra—like the LORD's garden or like Egypt./ So Lot
chose for himself the whole region of the Jordan and jour-

neyed eastward. Thus they separated from each other.
12 Abram dwelt in the land of Chanaan, while Lot dwelt in
the cities of the Jordan region, pitching his tent near
13 Sodom./ Now the men of Sodom were wicked, and sinned
exceedingly against the LORD.
14 The LORD said to Abram, after Lot had parted from him,
"Raise your eyes, and from where you are now look to
15 the north and the south and the east and the west./ All the
land which you see I will give to you and your posterity
16 forever./ I will make your posterity as the dust of the
earth: if anyone can count the grains of dust, your pos-
17 terity can also be counted./ Arise, walk the length and
18 breadth of the land, for to you I will give it."/ Abram
moved his tent and came to dwell by the terebinths of
Mamre which are at Hebron; and he built an altar there
to the LORD.

Abraham and Lot his nephew possessed the land not as owners
but as users, for the pasturage of their flocks. As they passed from
one watering place to another it was almost inevitable that conflicts would break out between the two households that had to employ the same facilities.

Abraham and Lot acted as civilized men and as brothers in
reaching their agreement to divide the land between them. Lot
chose the region south of the Dead Sea. In those days, says the
biblical tradition, it was well-watered like the LORD's garden or
like Egypt. Archaeological findings reveal that the tradition has
memorialized a fact. The Dead Sea area, today one of the bleakest
and least attractive conceivable, was in olden times a land of fertility and plenty. Natural causes and man's neglect have converted
this garden into a desert.

Abraham retained as his pasturage the territory north of the
Dead Sea, which was later called Juda. The site of Mamre is well
established today by a local tradition that extends back well into
Hebrew times. The Arabs call the place *Ramet el Khalil*, "the
heights of the friend [of God]."

14:1 In the time of Amraphel king of Sennaar, Arioch king of
Ellasar, Chodorlahomor king of Elam, and Thadal king of

2 Goyyim,/ these kings waged war against Bara king of
Sodom, Bersa king of Gomorra, Sennaab king of Adama,
Semeber king of Seboim, and the king of Bala—that is,
3 Segor./ These other kings formed an alliance in the valley
4 of Siddim—that is, the Salt Sea./ Twelve years they had
been subject to Chodorlahomor, but in the thirteenth year
5 they rebelled./ In the fourteenth year came Chodorlahomor and the kings with him. They defeated the Raphaim
in Astharoth-carnaim, the Zuzim in Ham, the Emin in
6 Save-cariathaim,/ the Horrites in the mountains of Seir, as
7 far as El-Pharan, close by the desert./ Then they turned
back and came to En-mesphat—that is, Cades—and sub-
dued all the country of the Amalecites, and also the
8 Amorrites, who dwelt in Hasasonthamar./ Then the king
of Sodom and the king of Gomorra, the king of Adama, the
king of Seboim and the king of Bala—that is, Segor—went
out, and they drew up in battle against them in the valley
9 of Siddim:/ against Chodorlahomor king of Elam, Thadal
king of Goyyim, Amraphel king of Sennaar, and Arioch
10 king of Ellasar, four kings against five./ Now the valley of
Siddim was full of bitumen pits; and as the kings of Sodom
and Gomorra fled, some fell there, but the rest fled to the
11 mountain./ The victors took all the goods of Sodom and
Gomorra and all their provisions, and went their way;
12 they also took Lot, Abram's nephew, and his goods, for he
13 had been living in Sodom./ Then came a fugitive and reported to Abram the Hebrew, who was living near the
terebinths of Mamre the Amorrite, a kinsman of Eschol
and Aner; these were the allies of Abram.

The whole account of chapter *14*, once dismissed as late Israelite
romancing about Abraham's reputation, is now known to be of a
piece with the history of these times.

Four Mesopotamian kings invade Chanaan from the north, having traversed the arc of the Fertile Crescent, and join battle with
five southern kings who had rebelled against them. The leader of
the expedition is an Elamite, a certain Chodorlahomor. We know
now that during Abraham's time the rulers of Elam often de-

manded tribute of the city-states of Chanaan. While we have no records of this precise king, the name is authentically Elamite. Amraphel is not otherwise known, but his name is Semitic as we would expect of a king of Babylon. There were several Mesopotamian kings whose name was Arioch (Ariwuk), though we do not know the identity of Ellasar; it may have been Larsa. The fourth king is not identified by place: *goyyim* means "nations"; probably the tradition had retained nothing more definite than this. The name Thadal (Tidhal), however, was possessed by several Hittite kings, as we know from their recently recovered records. Thus the story in Genesis rings true as an historical account.

The route of march followed by these kings takes them first through the country east of the Jordan river. The sites of Astharoth-carnaim, Ham, and Save-cariathaim are known by almost the same names today. Nelson Glueck has explored this country inch by inch, and from his investigations it is clear that in Abraham's time there were in it large cities and a settled population, but beginning about 1700 B.C. it became uninhabited for some four hundred years. Again the tradition utilized by Genesis is true to history.

From Transjordan they proceeded through the Dead Sea country, gave battle to the coalition of Chanaanite kings, then marched victoriously northward through western Palestine. The valley of Siddim where the battle occurred is identified by Genesis with the Salt Sea, and is said to have been filled with bitumen pits. It is a fact that the Dead Sea has been increasing its area through the centuries, and that much of what is now under its salty, asphalt-filled waters, was once marshy and even dry land.

14: 14 When Abram heard that his kinsman had been taken prisoner, he called out three hundred and eighteen of his trained men, born in his house, and went in pursuit as far
15 as Dan./ He and his servants formed parties against them by night, defeated them and pursued them as far as
16 Hoba, north of Damascus./ He recovered all the goods; and his kinsman Lot and his goods he also recovered, be-
17 sides the women and the people./ When Abram returned from the defeat of Chodorlahomor and the kings with him, the king of Sodom went out to meet Abram in the

21 valley of Save—that is, in the king's valley./ The king of
Sodom said to Abram, "Give me the people, keep the
22 goods for yourself."/ But Abram answered him, "I raise
my hand to the LORD God Most High, creator of heaven
23 and earth,/ that I will not take thread or sandal-strap or
anything that is yours, lest you should say, 'I have made
24 Abram rich';/ nothing but what the young men have
eaten, and the share of those who accompanied me. Let
Aner, Eschol and Mamre take their share."

Abraham, whose extensive household we have already seen,
counted a large number of trained soldiers in his service. This is not
at all extraordinary. Tribal chieftains or sheikhs of the semi-no-
madic population often were used as the professional soldiers hired
by the kings of the cities of Chanaan. By now we should have no
difficulty in recognizing that the "kings" of our story were simply
the heads of communities, some of them probably quite small by
our standards.

Abraham overtook the raiders at the extreme north of Palestine,
and then harassed them by repeated attacks and retreats until he
had escorted them out of the country. These tactics are still used
against superior forces to great advantage by the modern Arab
Bedawin. By these means he recovered Lot and the goods stolen
from Chanaan.

The chief point and lesson of the story, or at least one of them,
probably is to be found in Abraham's declaration when he made
his report to the king of Sodom, the Chanaanites' leader, in the
valley of Save, which was probably near Jerusalem. Abraham had
already shown himself a dutiful uncle in rescuing Lot, and now he
appears as the generous, disinterested benefactor whom the Israelites knew their ancestor to have been. This is the man who was
worthy of God's friendship.

14: 18 Then Melchisedec, the king of Salem, brought out bread
and wine; for he was a priest of the Most High God. He
blessed Abram and said,
19 "Blessed be Abram by the Most High God,
creator of heaven and earth.

20   Blessed be the Most High God,
        who has delivered your enemies into your hand."
    Then Abram gave him a tenth of everything.

I omitted these verses from the story we have seen above for two
reasons; because they deserve special mention, and because they
are not missed when the main story is read as a unit. It is generally
admitted that the incident of Melchisedec was originally a separate
tradition and has been inserted into the story of chapter *14* by the
author or by someone before him. It was a very precious tradition
which contained associations dear to the writers of Hebrew history: here was an early story that connected Abraham their father
with the city of Jerusalem, which not in Abraham's time but
centuries later under King David was to become and to remain
forever the religious capital of the Jews.

Jerusalem was probably never actually known as Salem. In
Eastern Semitic documents it is called Urusalim, which in Western
Semitic Hebrew became Jerusalem. Urusalim meant "Salem [the
name of a god] founded [this city]." It is likely that the text of
Genesis deliberately shortened the name to remove the pagan con-
notations. Such is the opinion of Father Hughes Vincent,[1] the
Nestor of Palestinian archaeologists, and it deserves respect.

Melchisedec was both king and priest. This is in accord with
what we know Chanaanite custom to have been, for the civil leader
of a city was likewise its religious chief. The same practice was
current among the Hebrews before the establishment of a regular,
separated priesthood. Abraham (according to *12*:8, for example)
performed the priestly work of sacrifice as head of his tribe.

This priest-king blessed Abraham. On what occasion we cannot
be sure, if the story did not originally belong to the context of the
expedition of the kings. Abraham, in gratitude, "gave him a tenth
of everything." This may have been the enactment of a covenant
such as Abraham had made with others in this region (Eschol and
Aner "were allies of Abram," v. 13). Gifts were commonly exchanged at such times. As a common meal together seems to have
been the custom in making a covenant, this may be the meaning of
v. 18, that Melchisedec brought out bread and wine. The text does

[1] L. H. Vincent, O. P., "Abraham à Jérusalem," *Revue biblique* 58 (1951)
360–371.

not say that there was a sacrifice; our translation adds *"for* he was a priest of the Most High God," but the "for" is not in the Hebrew.

Melchisedec is a mysterious character who appears momentarily in Genesis only to disappear forever. His precise relationship to the patriarch Abraham we do not know. Because he has been taken as a type of Christ and of the Christian priesthood some have thought that he must have been a priest of the one true God. This would be extraordinary if it were true. It is not impossible, of course, but it is highly unlikely. Chanaan was a land of pagans, and it is not to be presumed that the king of one of its cities would be anything else. Abraham's own monotheism is described in the Bible as the result of special divine revelation.

When we say that a person or thing is a "type" of Christ, we mean that it has some likeness or similitude by which it can be compared to Him under a particular aspect. The Passover lamb whose blood sprinkled on the doorposts saved the Israelites from the destroying angel is a type of Christ, whose blood has saved us from eternal destruction. But that does not mean that the Passover lamb was a rational creature, as Christ was and is, or that its sacrifice was voluntary or an atonement for sin. St. Thomas has wisely remarked in this connection that "we must not look for a similitude under every respect, for if we had this there would no longer be a similitude but the reality itself."

Therefore, while Father Sutcliffe,[2] for instance, still maintains that Melchisedec must have adored the same God as Abraham, I think that Father Chaine more fairly represents the interpretation of present-day Catholic authors when he says: "It is possible that through a miracle of God's mercy and power the Chanaanite leader of Salem would have been a monotheist; but we have no reason to think so. The Bible speaks of no miracle, and the sacred writer who uses his sources to praise Abraham says nothing of such a thing."[3]

Melchisedec has become a type or symbol quite apart from his historical character. In later years when a Hebrew prophet wrote of the coming Messias he said of him, "You are a priest forever, after the manner of Melchisedec" (Psalm *109*:4). By this he meant that just as Melchisedec had been both priest and king (and a

2 *Catholic Commentary,* p. 194.
3 *Genèse,* p. 207.

priest-king of the holy city Jerusalem), so would be the Redeemer Messias, joining in himself these two supreme offices which were carefully distinguished by the Israelites under the Law of Moses.

In the New Testament the symbolism has been carried to much greater lengths. In the Epistle to the Hebrews (chapters 5–7) the author exploits the popular etymology of Melchisedec's name ("king of justice"), the fact that he was king of Salem (which sounds very much like the Hebrew word for "peace"), and other coincidences, to show how aptly he was a typical foreshadowing of Christ. Even his abrupt appearance and disappearance in Genesis *14* is fitted into the symbolism: "Without father, without mother, without genealogy, having neither beginning of days nor end of life . . . he continues a priest forever" (Heb. 7:3). In this the author saw a figure of Christ's eternal priesthood which was not inherited like the Jewish priesthood but came through God's special dispensation.

Later Christian writers went even beyond the New Testament. Clement of Alexandria and St. Cyprian in the third century built on the analogy now firmly set up between Melchisedec and Christ, seeing in the bread and wine of v. 18, which the author of Hebrews had ignored, a prefigurement of the Eucharistic sacrifice. It is this beautiful allegory that is now enshrined in the canon of the Mass, where the priest-king has received a dignity he never knew in life.

Melchisedec had a pagan name, very similar to that of another king of Jerusalem named in Josue *10*:1, Adonisedec—signifying, respectively, "Sedec [the name of a god] is my king," "Sedec is my lord." It has been concluded from this that the deity Sedec, who is known from other sources, Eusebius for one, must have received a special veneration in pre-Israelite Jerusalem.

"The Most High God" whom Melchisedec invoked in blessing Abraham was another pagan deity worshipped in Chanaan: in Hebrew, El Elyon. As Abraham in v. 22 swears to the king of Sodom in the name of the LORD God Most High (Jahweh El Elyon), it might be as well that we pause a moment to notice the names used of God in Genesis.

Just as we do, the Hebrews used a common word, *el* and its longer form *elohim*, "god," both for the true God whom they worshipped and for the gods of the Gentiles. To distinguish their God from all others they had the proper name Jahweh, which however they rarely pronounced, through a sense of reverence (even as we so often unconsciously avoid the name "Jesus" and substitute "Christ" or "our Lord" in its stead). They ended by never using it at all, to the result that its very pronunciation was forgotten (in pre-Christian times the vowel sounds were not written in Hebrew), which gave rise to the false reconstruction "Jehovah." In place of Jahweh they said LORD; hence the traditional translation. Though Jahweh is habitually put on the lips of the patriarchs throughout Genesis, Exodus 6:2 f. tells us this is an anachronism, that Jahweh was a name revealed to Moses and that the patriarchs knew God by another. "I am Jahweh," said God. "As El Shaddai [translated "God the Almighty"] I appeared to Abraham, Isaac and Jacob, but my name, Jahweh, I did not make known to them." God identifies himself to Abraham in Genesis 17:1 as El Shaddai.

The Israelites freely appropriated the names and titles of pagan deities and applied them to Jahweh. The author of Genesis has given a splendid example of this in 14:22. Here the title and name of Melchisedec's El Elyon, creator (the pagan sense of this word was "ruler") of heaven and earth, have been given to the God of the Jews. There are numerous other instances. In 21:33, for example, Abraham is said to have "called on the name of the LORD, the everlasting God," that is, "Jahweh El Olam." El Olam, we have good reason to think, was another Chanaanite deity. The Jews reasoned that Jahweh, not the pagan gods, had the real right to be called Most High and Everlasting. Far from cheapening their theology, this process testifies to their uncompromising monotheism. Quite analogous to this was the Christian policy of baptizing pagan festivals and usages—the rogation days, for instance, or Easter, the goddess of spring, or the title Pontifex Maximus. This sort of thing, it is true, got out of hand during the Renaissance, but by then it was no longer natural, only pedantic. Happily we do not have to refer to Christ as "Apollo" or to nuns as "vestals." But we can extol Divus Thomas with as right a monotheistic heart as when we go to Mass on the day dedicated to the sun-god.

CHAPTER VIII: ABRAHAM THE FRIEND OF GOD

15:1 After these things the word of the LORD came to Abram
     in a vision,
          "Fear not, Abram, I am your shield;
               your reward shall be very great."
   2 And Abram said, "O Lord GOD, what will you give me? I
     am childless, and the steward of my house, Eliezer, is my
   3 heir."/ Abram also said, "To me you have given no de-
     scendants; the slave born in my house will be my heir."
   4 But the word of the LORD came to him. "He shall not be
   5 your heir; your heir shall be one of your own flesh."/ Then
     the LORD led him outside and said, "Look at the heavens
     and, if you can, count the stars." And he said to him, "So
   6 shall your posterity be."/ Abram believed the LORD, who
   7 credited the act to him as justice./ He said to him, "I am
     the LORD, who brought you from Ur in Chaldea, to give
   8 you this land to possess."/ But he said, "O LORD God,
     how am I to know that I shall possess it?"

The author of Genesis had several traditions relating the promises which God made to Abraham. The present one is particularly
valuable for its theology.

Abraham had despaired of having an heir through natural generation. Accordingly he had chosen the steward of his household, a
trusted slave, to be his heir. From the documents of Nuzu we have
learned that this was a custom of the time. Childless people would
adopt a son to serve them during their lifetime and to bury and
mourn for them when they died. He would be their heir. If, however, a natural son should be born after this adoption, the adopted

son would have to yield to him the rights of chief heir. This happened with Eliezer.

"Abram believed the LORD, who credited the act to him as justice." By his faith in God, says St. Paul, Abraham became in truth the father of all nations who are the children of God. "Know therefore that the men of faith are the real sons of Abraham. And the Scripture, foreseeing that God would justify the Gentiles by faith, announced to Abraham beforehand, 'In thee shall all the nations be blessed.' Therefore the men of faith shall be blessed with faithful Abraham" (Gal. 3:7 ff.).

Abraham believed God's promise that he would be the father of a posterity more numerous than the stars of heaven, through which he would be a blessing to all the nations of the earth. The righteousness which he gained in God's sight through his faith is the righteousness which we also receive through Christ's grace. It is the same grace from the same Redeemer, Christ our Lord. Abraham and the men of faith of the old order before Christ's coming could only believe in what was to be. We believe in what has come to be. But as the object of our faith is one, we are the sons of Abraham who first believed.

Abraham was to prove his faith in many ways, even as our faith must occasionally be proved. His supreme test, surely an heroic act of faith, we shall see in chapter 22. But for the present, the author has another beautiful truth to communicate. Here he has described God's promise as a sign given to Abraham in the form of a solemn covenant.

15:9 He answered him, "Bring me a heifer three years old, a she-goat three years old, a ram three years old, a turtledove
10 and a young pigeon." He brought him all these and cut them in two, and laid each half opposite the other; but the
11 birds he did not cut in two./ Birds of prey swooped down
12 on the carcasses, but Abram drove them off./ As the sun was setting, Abram fell into a deep sleep; and terror came
13 upon him, a great darkness./ The LORD said to Abram, "Know for certain that your posterity will be strangers in a land not their own; they shall be subjected to slavery and
14 shall be oppressed four hundred years./ But I will judge

that nation which they shall serve, and afterward they shall
15 go free with great possessions./ And you shall go to your
16 fathers in peace, and be buried at a good old age./ In the
fourth generation they shall return here; for the wickedness of the Amorrites is not yet complete."
17 Now when the sun had set and it was dark, a smoking oven
18 and a fiery torch passed between the pieces. On that day
the LORD made a covenant with Abram, saying, "To your
posterity I will give this land, from the river of Egypt to
19 the Great River [the Euphrates],/ the land of the Cinites,
20 Cenezites, Cedmonites,/ Hethites, Pherezites, Raphaim,
Amorrites, Chanaanites, Gergesites and Jebusites."

Covenants were the equivalent of the treaties and contracts of
our day, the forms of agreement which made civilized life possible
among people who knew little of organized social life. The covenant was essentially a solemn oath undertaken by two parties
with an appropriate ritual, by which they guaranteed to fulfil mu-
tual promises. In view of the prevalence of covenants in Israelite
society, it was inevitable that God's election of this people and the
obligations they acknowledged from this election should have been
conceived in the manner of a covenant. God in His condescension
reveals Himself to men in terms that men can understand, if only
imperfectly: if He did not, a theology would be impossible. It was
inevitable, too, that the Israelites would conceive of the promise
made to Abraham which had prepared for the covenant as itself
being a kind of covenant.

The Bible (see Jeremias 34:18) and other historical sources tell
us that sometimes a covenant was solemnized between parts of
animals that had been split in two and laid with the halves facing
each other. The contracting parties walked between these pieces
as they pronounced their oaths. This rite was supposed to symbolize their readiness to be treated as the animals had been if they
failed to keep their word.

That is the background of the rite which Abraham carried out
at God's direction. The halves of the animals are disposed according to custom; the turtledove and young pigeon, too small to be
divided, each serves as a half of an animal. Then, after the LORD

has repeated His solemn oath, He passes between the carcasses in the form of fire, a symbol of divinity that figures again and again in the Bible, that accompanies the covenant of Sinai and the new covenant of the Church on the first Christian Pentecost. Only God, not Abraham as well, passes between the pieces, for the promise He has made to Abraham is due wholly to His free will. If God is now obligated to Abraham, it is because He has voluntarily obliged Himself. Abraham had done nothing himself that he should have a claim on God.

The Israelites did not forget that what God had done for them He had done of His goodness. The first act of His goodness was that extended to their father Abraham.

The Egyptian captivity from which the Israelites were delivered by Moses is described in v. 13 ff., and an explanation is given why Chanaan was delivered to the Jews: because of the wickedness of the Gentile inhabitants. A list of the names by which the Israelites knew these Chanaanite peoples is found in v. 19 f. Of the significance of some of the distinctions we cannot be sure.

16: 1 Sarai, Abram's wife, had borne him no children. She had an
    2 Egyptian maid named Agar. Sarai said to Abram, "The LORD has kept me from bearing; go in to my maid; perhaps I shall get children through her." Abram listened to
    3 Sarai./ After Abram had lived ten years in the land of Chanaan, Sarai his wife took Agar, her Egyptian maid, and gave her to Abram, her husband, to be his wife.

The reader who is unprepared for it is apt to find Sara's action disconcerting and strange, if not scandalous. We must not imagine, however, that she was doing anything extraordinary or that was thought in any sense immoral. Rather, it was a custom sanctioned by all the force of law.

Legal contracts unearthed at Nuzu make it evident that a childless wife was actually obliged to do what Sara did, unless she preferred to see her husband choose another wife for himself. She was unlikely to prefer this—it was a far less evil if the supplementary wife would be someone over whom she had some control, that she might keep her superior position in the household.

In Israelite times the Jews had adopted the institution of monogamy at least as an ideal, though polygamy was occasionally practised. The teaching of Genesis, we have seen, is all in favor of monogamy. Still the writers of the Bible knew that their ancestors had practised polygamy without a second thought, and they made no effort to hide it in telling their history. It was a sign that they had not perfectly grasped the idea of the sanctity of marriage, but such was the undeniable fact. It would be centuries yet before a developing moral sense would finally forbid it entirely, as it is, of course, forbidden under Christian law.

Islam, the other great religion that sprang from the Near East, never entirely eradicated polygamy, though it imposed limitations on it. Even in Moslem countries today, however, monogamy is almost always the rule, though for practical reasons. The ordinary man simply cannot afford to support more than one wife.

16: 4 And he went in to Agar, and she conceived. When she was aware that she had conceived, she looked with disdain on
5 her mistress. Then Sarai said to Abram, "The injury done me is your fault! I gave my maid to your embrace and when she was aware that she had conceived she looked on me with disdain. The LORD judge between you and me!"
6 Abram answered Sarai, "Your maid is in your power; do to her what seems good to you." Then Sarai humiliated her,
7 and she fled from her./ Afterward an angel of the LORD found her beside a spring of water in the desert, the spring
8 on the road to Sur./ He said, "Agar, maid of Sarai, where have you come from and where are you going?" She an-
9 swered, "I am fleeing from my mistress Sarai."/ The angel of the LORD said to her, "Return to your mistress and sub-
10 mit to her authority."/ The angel of the Lord added, "I will so multiply your posterity that it shall be too many to
11 count."/ The angel of the LORD also said to her:

> "You are with child,
>   and shall bear a son;
> You shall call him Ismael,
>   because the LORD has heard of your humiliation.
12   "He shall be a wild ass of a man,
>   his hand against everyone,

And everyone's hand against him;
    he shall dwell apart, opposing all his kinsmen."
13 She named the LORD, who spoke to her: "You are the
    God of vision"; for she said, "Have I really seen God and
14 remained alive after my vision?"/ Therefore the well was
    called Beer-lahai-roi. It is between Cades and Barad.
15 So Agar bore Abram a son; and Abram called his son
16 whom Agar bore, Ismael./ Abram was eighty-six years old
    when Agar bore him Ismael.

Situations of the kind that arose in Abraham's household were inevitable in a polygamous society. The law had anticipated the case, however, and had provided for it.

"When a man has married a woman who has given a female slave to her husband"—so ran the law as it was formulated in Babylonia—"and this slave has borne children and has later claimed equality with her mistress because she bore children, her mistress may not sell her, but she may mark her with the slave-mark and count her among the slaves."

This is what Sara did when she "humiliated Agar." Having with feminine logic blamed Abraham for the unpleasantness that had come about, and receiving from her husband nothing but lofty disdain for the foibles of women, Sara did what the law allowed her to do to Agar. She could not sell her, for Agar's child would be Abraham's heir. But she could and did deprive her of her privileged place as the master's wife and sent her back to her slave status. Henceforth there would be no question who was mistress of Abraham's house.

Agar felt her humiliation deeply, so much so that she fled the patriarchal home, doubtless intending to return to Egypt. This furnished the occasion for God's blessing of Agar and her unborn son, part of the fulfilment of His promise to protect Abraham's descendants. The Hebrews recognized as sons of Abraham along with themselves various of the Arab peoples. Thus the ancient poem cited in v. 11 f. describes Ismael as a nomad, leading the life of wild freedom that still characterizes the Arabs of the desert. A popular explanation is given of Ismael's name, "God has heard."

It may be remarked that the "angel of the LORD" who appeared to Agar speaks simply as the LORD Himself in v. 10, and is named the LORD by Agar in v. 13. These primitive stories undoubtedly originally pictured the LORD speaking directly with His servants just as in the very anthropomorphic accounts of chapter *18*. Later generations, however, adopted a greater reserve thought to be more in keeping with God's transcendence and represented Him as revealing Himself through an intermediary (the Hebrew "angel" means "messenger"). The same tendency is found in the New Testament. While the Pentateuch shows God revealing the Law directly to Moses, St. Paul refers to "the Law delivered by angels" (Gal. *3*:19).

The real meaning of Beer-lahai-roi is unknown, and Agar's speech in v. 13 is quite obscure. The three Hebrew words signify something like "well-living-vision." The tenacity of place names in Palestine, however, from Chanaanite to Hebrew and now into Arabic, can be seen in the fact that there is today a Bir-mayin between Ain Qedes and Umm el-Bared even as in Agar's time Beer-lahai-roi was between Cades and Barad.

17:1 When Abram was ninety-nine years old, the LORD appeared to him and said, "I am God the Almighty. Walk in
2 my presence and be perfect./ I will make my covenant between you and me, and will multiply you exceedingly."
3.4 Abram fell prostrate, and God spoke to him thus,/ "This is my covenant with you: You shall be the father of a mul-
5 titude of nations:/ you shall no longer be called Abram, but your name shall be Abraham; for I will make you the
6 father of a multitude of nations./ I will make you exceedingly fruitful; I will make nations of you, and kings shall
7 descend from you./ I will establish my covenant between you and me and your descendants after you throughout their generations, as a perpetual covenant, that I may be a
8 God to you and to your descendants after you./ I will give you and your descendants after you this land in which you are immigrants, all the land of Chanaan as a perpetual possession; and I will be their God."

This begins another impression of the covenant made between God and Abraham, from a different source than that of chapter *15*.

This present story shows the spirit of Old Testament history at its very best, which has seen the facts known about Abraham as the pieces of a religious mosaic.

Previously the utter gratuity of God's covenant had been stressed. Here the obligations of the covenant on the part of Abraham and his descendants are brought out more clearly, the obligation of a moral law (v. 1), for example, and the obligation of monotheism, the exclusive worship of the one God (v. 7).

Human covenants had some tangible sign by which the obligation of the covenant would become a matter of public record. In chapter *31* we shall see that in one instance a heap of stones served as the sign of the contract that had taken place. In the change of Abram's name to Abraham the author of Genesis saw a sign of God's covenant with him. The two names were actually the same: one was the form used in Abraham's ancestral Mesopotamia, while the other was used in Chanaan, just as Sara was the Chanaanite spelling of Sarai (cf. v. 15). Because Abraham's coming to Chanaan was the result of divine inspiration, a part of the covenant which God made with him, the sacred writer was certainly not mistaken in giving this religious interpretation to what a modern historian would set down as dialectical variation. "What interested him was not the etymology of a name, but the greatness of the promise," says Father Chaine.[1] Similarly he found a happy coincidence in the new spelling of Abra*h*am with his title *ab hamon*, "father of a multitude (of nations)." He has attributed no special meaning to Sara's name, for Abraham, not Sara, was the principal party in the covenant.

17:9 God also said to Abraham, "You shall keep my covenant, you and your descendants after you throughout their gen-
10 erations./ This is my covenant which you shall keep, between you and me and your descendants after you: Every
11 male among you shall be circumcised./ You shall circumcise the flesh of your foreskin; it shall be a token of the
12 covenant between you and me./ He that is eight days old among you shall be circumcised, every male throughout your generations, including the slave born in your house,

[1] *Genèse*, p. 229.

or bought with money from any foreigner, not of your own
13 race./ Both he that is born in your house and he that is
bought with your money must be circumcised. My cove-
14 nant shall be in your flesh as a perpetual covenant./ If any
male have not the flesh of his foreskin circumcised, that
person shall be cut off from his people; he has broken my
covenant."

The divine promise was a perpetual covenant; therefore it had
to have a sign that would endure after Abraham. This sign was
found in the rite of circumcision.

Circumcision had been practised from time immemorial. In
general, it is a Semitic custom, but it was also found in Egypt as
early as 4000 B.C. Its purpose was usually hygienic, or a part of
tribal puberty rites. Only the Jews ever gave it the religious meaning which we find in this passage.

Its practice among the Hebrews dates from Abraham's coming
into Chanaan, for it was not used in Mesopotamia. In the truest
possible way, then, it was a sign of the covenant made with Him
who had plotted Abraham's course and would continue to protect
his heirs according to His promise. Circumcision became the sign
of the true Jew and of those who had been brought into the house
of Israel to share its privileges.

If the covenant of circumcision has passed away, it is because
the promise which it symbolized has been realized in Christ. It
is this fulfilment that has made the spirit of the covenant truly
perpetual. We are heirs of Abraham not through the fleshy rite of
circumcision, but with the spiritual faith which we share with
Abraham, his in the Christ who was to come, ours in the Christ
who has both come and redeemed us.

Without this true spirit of the promise, circumcision was of no
avail to constitute one an heir of Abraham. The following passage,
the end of this episode, teaches this. The promise was to descend
through Isaac, the son whom God had predicted for Abraham,
not through Ismael, Abraham's son by Agar. Fleshy descent from
Abraham counts for nothing apart from this promise of God. Thus
St. Paul said of us, the spiritual sons of Abraham, "It is written
that Abraham had two sons, the one by a slave-girl and the other

by a free woman. And the son of the slave-girl was born according
to the flesh, but the son of the free woman in virtue of the promise
. . . Now we, brethren, are the children of promise, as Isaac was"
(Gal. 4:22 f., 28).

17: 15 God said to Abraham, "Sarai your wife you shall not call
    16 Sarai but Sara./ I will bless her, and will also give you
        a son by her; yes, I will bless her, and she shall be the
        mother of nations; kings of peoples shall descend from
    17 her."/ And as Abraham fell prostrate, he laughed and
        said to himself, "Shall a son be born to one who is a hun-
        dred years old? Shall Sara who is ninety bear a child?"
    18 Then Abraham said to God, "Oh, that Ismael may live in
    19 your favor!"/ God answered, "No, but Sara your wife
        shall bear you a son, and you shall call him Isaac. I will
        establish my covenant with him as a perpetual covenant
        for his descendants after him.
    20 "As for Ismael, I have heard you. I will bless him and
        make him fruitful and multiply him exceedingly. He shall
        become the father of twelve princes, and I will make
    21 him a great nation./ But my covenant I will establish with
        Isaac, whom Sara shall bear to you at this time next year."
    22 And when he had finished talking with him, God left
        Abraham.
    23 Then Abraham took his son Ismael, and all who were
        born in his house, and all who had been bought with his
        money, every male in his household, and he circumcised
        the flesh of their foreskins on that very day, as God had
    24 commanded him./ Abraham was ninety-nine years old
    25 when he was circumcised in the flesh of his foreskin./ Is-
        mael his son was thirteen years old when he was circum-
    26 cised in the flesh of his foreskin./ That very day Abraham
    27 and his son Ismael were circumcised./ All the male mem-
        bers of his household, including the slaves born in his
        house or bought with money from a foreigner, were cir-
        cumcised with him.

"But my covenant I will establish with Isaac. . . ." God's ways
are not ours, and it is not always easy to see the path that He

has traced in His providence. Late Jewish interpreters of Genesis, who were perhaps a bit too serious for their own good, were convinced that Abraham could have laughed only for joy at the annunciation of Isaac's birth. But Abraham was a human being, with the little demon of unbelief that resides in every human heart. Very much like us, he found it easier to believe in the tangible, solid, positive actualities than in an unknown, faceless future. If Abraham was a man of faith, he was still a man, and therefore his faith was not perfect.

Abraham could not believe he would again become the father of a son, therefore he laughed. Herein is a perennial truth that shows how Abraham's story is the story of all men. Abraham believed the substance of God's promise but doubted the details. Here was Ismael, an undeniable existing fact, with whom the covenant could be established. Why exchange what can be seen for what cannot and may never be? There is the temptation that has plagued the men of faith throughout the centuries. Faith generally meets its test in small things rather than in great. The man who can cheerfully face death in the arena where the issues are clear and drawn may thread his way only with difficulty through a world which is not all black and white but considerably grey. He may renounce all his goods with never a backward glance yet become so attached to a book or a chair or a lampshade that he cannot conceive doing without it. He may believe that faith is an assent of the mind yet try to relieve his mind of any part in it by ignoring rather than facing the challenges to faith, so that faith, as Newman insisted, becomes no longer faith but only prejudice.

There is a lesson for us in Abraham's laughter. In the other story of the annunciation of Isaac's birth which follows, we shall see that Sara laughed. The author, as a matter of fact, has had a bit of gentle humor of his own. Isaac, whose name had not yet been mentioned, has a sound in Hebrew very much like the word "laugh."

18:1 Now the LORD appeared to him by the terebinths of
    Mamre as he sat at the entrance of his tent in the heat of
2 the day./ And when he raised his eyes he saw three men

standing at a distance from him. As soon as he saw them,
he ran from the entrance of the tent door to meet them, and
3 bowed down to the earth,/ and said, "My Lord, if I find
4 favor with you, do not pass by your servant./ Let a little
water be brought that you may wash your feet; and then
5 rest yourselves under the tree./ Since you have come to
your servant, I will bring you a little food that you may
refresh yourselves; then you may go on." They replied, "Do
as you have said."
6 Then Abraham hastened into the tent to Sara and said,
"Quick, three measures of fine flour! Knead it, and make
7 loaves."/ And he ran to the herd, picked out a good tender
bullock, and gave it to the servant who hastened to pre-
8 pare it./ Then he took curds and milk and the bullock
which had been prepared, and set it before them; and he
9 stood by them under the tree while they ate./ They said to
him, "Where is Sara your wife?" He answered, "She is in
10 the tent."/ "I will surely return to you at this time next
year," he said, "and Sara your wife shall have a son."
11 Sara was listening inside the entrance of the tent./ Now
Abraham and Sara were old, advanced in years; and Sara
12 no longer had periods as is customary with women./ So
Sara laughed to herself and said, "Now that I am grown
13 old and my husband is old, shall I have pleasure?"/ The
LORD said to Abraham, "Why did Sara laugh, saying,
14 'Shall I indeed bear a child, though I am old?'/ Is anything too wonderful for the LORD? At this time next year
15 I will return to you, and Sara shall have a son."/ But Sara
denied it, saying, "I did not laugh"; for she was afraid. But
he said, "You did laugh."

One of the most charming scenes in the whole Bible is this of
Abraham the generous host, who discovers that he is entertaining
not men but angels, and even God Himself. It is charming because
it reflects the virtues of simple people. The author of this story
reverently depicted the great patriarch as the man he knew he
must have been, a man gifted with that quality which orientals
prize almost to excess, hospitality. The discreet request for hos-

pitality in the East is that of the three men in the story, standing before Abraham's tent. If we think of Abraham's dwelling as something like the Bedawin tent illustrated on this page, we shall not be far wrong. The generous man, like Abraham, extends to the wayfarer making this silent request the best that he has in his house, water to wash with, and food and drink. Anyone who has traveled in Abraham's homeland will recognize how this picture has been taken from life. I was once entertained in precisely this way, a hot afternoon in the desert of Iraq, by a kindly Arab who was surely one of Abraham's descendants through Ismael.

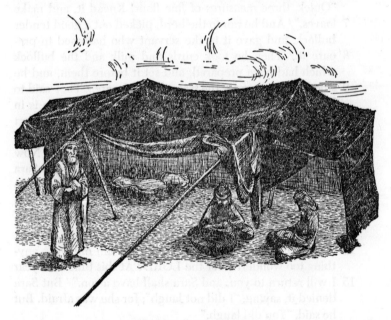

Modern Bedawin Tent

In its touching simplicity this story does not hesitate to apply to God traits which we know cannot be literally true. God does not, of course, sit down under the shade of a tree and eat with men, not even with such a man as Abraham. The author of Genesis knew this as well as we, just as he knew that God did not walk in the garden of Eden in the cool of an evening. But he did not alter the story that had come down to him. It was the work of a mind to whom God was very personal, taking a real and sincere interest in the affairs of His creatures, a God who cares. If he gave utterance to these beliefs in a story that knew nothing of the distinctions of theology, the underlying truths are no less certain for all that. Only one of a deep and childlike faith could tell such a story, only one who knew a great deal about God which some theologians may not know.

This story has been made the vehicle of the foretelling of Isaac's birth, which is found in the preceding chapter from another tradition. There is agreement on the essentials. Isaac was the child of promise, and his birth was due to a special divine favor when his parents were beyond the normal age for having children.

Sara, in keeping with the custom still observed in the East, was excluded from the meal taken by the master of the house and his guests, but in keeping with a custom by no means confined to the East she was curious enough to overhear their conversation. Here it is Sara rather than Abraham who was skeptical when she heard the promise.

18:16 Then the men set out from there and looked toward Sodom; and Abraham walked with them to escort them
17 on their way./ The LORD said, "Can I keep from Abra-
18 ham what I am about to do?/ For Abraham will surely become a great and powerful nation, and all the nations
19 of the earth shall be blessed in him./ Indeed, I have chosen him, that he may charge his sons and his household after him to observe the way of the LORD, doing what is good and right, so that the LORD may fulfill for
20 Abraham what he has promised him."/ Then the LORD said, "Because the outcry against Sodom and Gomorra is
21 great, and their sin is very grave,/ I will go down to see whether they have done all that the outcry which has
22 come to me indicates; if not, I will know."/ So they turned from there, and went toward Sodom, while Abraham remained standing in the presence of the LORD.

The story of chapter 18 had a higher purpose than only to show Abraham's generosity and kindliness. There has been a gradual awareness on his and Sara's part of the supernatural character of their guests. Sara had taken the statement that she was to have a son as one of those polite aspirations which a man will make to his host, unmindful that the host's wife is past childbearing. When she perceived, however, that her secret mirth had been known, and that the statement had been made with a full realization of her condition, she feared. Abraham had greeted his visitors with the deferential "My Lord" which a man used with his superiors and which any well-bred Easterner would address to one he had invited under his roof. Now, as he walks with them a part of the way on their continued journey, fulfilling another of the amenities demanded by hospitality, he knows that he is in the presence of the very LORD Himself.

This episode, therefore, shows Abraham as the true friend of God. "Can I keep from Abraham what I am about to do?" asks the LORD. God is very near to those whom He loves, and to them He manifests Himself. With Abraham God has made His covenant. If Abraham has grave obligations that follow from this fact, so the LORD has obliged Himself to be near to Abraham and to make known to him His ways.

The revelation of God's intentions with regard to Sodom and Gomorra is the occasion of the appealing interchange that follows. It is another scene taken from life, repeated a thousand times daily in the East, in the bazaars and wherever men congregate who dearly love to bargain and match wits. Abraham bargains with God, but for the lives of men. If Abraham is God's friend, he can speak with Him familiarly as a friend.

18: 23 Abraham drew near and said, "Will you destroy the good
24 with the wicked?/ If there be fifty just men in the city, will you then destroy the place and not spare it for the
25 sake of the fifty just men within it?/ Far be it from you to do such a thing as kill the just with the wicked, treating just and wicked alike! Far be it from you! Shall not the
26 judge of all the earth act justly?"/ And the LORD said, "If I find that there are fifty just men in the city, I will
27 spare the whole place for their sake."/ Abraham answered, "I have ventured to speak to the LORD though I

28 am but dust and ashes./ What if there be five less than
    fifty just men? Will you destroy the whole city on account
    of five?" He said, "I will not destroy it if I find forty-five
29 there."/ And Abraham spoke to him again, "What if forty
    be found there?" He said, "I will not do it for the sake of
30 the forty."/ Then he said, "O LORD, be not angry if I
    speak; what if thirty be found there?" He answered, "I
31 will not do it if I find thirty there."/ Abraham said, "I have
    ventured to speak to the LORD, what if twenty be found
    there?" And he said, "I will not destroy it for the sake of
32 the twenty."/ Abraham said again, "O LORD, be not
    angry if I speak once more; what if ten be found there?"
    He said, "I will not destroy it for the sake of the ten."
33 The LORD departed after he had finished speaking to
    Abraham, and Abraham returned to his place.

Abraham is a shrewd bargainer, naming a good round number
on his first attempt, lessening it by only five on his second, then
having gained confidence dropping quickly by tens until he realizes he has reached the irreducible minimum. If we are tempted
to smile at the primitive notion of God engaged in friendly argument with His creature, we must not allow it to obscure for us
the tremendously elevated idea of God's real nature which it contains.

It was a childlike, but surely no childish faith that could say of
God what is quoted of Abraham in v. 25. God, the judge of all
the earth, is both just and merciful. His mercy in our regard out-
strips His justice, for He would have spared Sodom and Gomorra for the sake of only ten just men. Not from philosophers
and the wise of the world, but from inspired narrators of plain
and unaffected speech, did the world first learn that there is a
God who truly cares for the mankind He has made.

19: 1 Now the two angels came to Sodom in the evening, while
    Lot was sitting at the gate of Sodom. When Lot saw them,
  2 he rose to meet them, and falling prostrate to the earth,/ he
    said, "Come aside, my lords, into the house of your servant,
    stay overnight and bathe your feet; then you may arise
    early and go on your way." They said, "No, we shall pass

3 the night in the public square."/ But he urged them so strongly that they turned aside and entered his house; and he prepared a meal for them, and baked unleavened bread,

4 and they ate./ They had not yet retired when the townsmen, the men of Sodom, all the people from every quarter,

5 both young and old, surrounded the house,/ and called Lot, and said to him, "Where are the men who came to your house tonight? Bring them out that we may abuse

6 them."/ Lot went out to the men, and shut the door behind

7 him,/ and said, "I entreat you, brethren, do not act wick-

8 edly./ I have two daughters who have not known man. Let me bring them out to you; do as you please with them. Only do nothing to these men, for they have come under

9 the shelter of my roof."/ But they said, "Stand back! This fellow came in as a stranger, and he would play the judge! Why, we will treat you worse than we will them!" Then they pressed hard against Lot, and drew near to break in

10 the door./ But the visitors reached out their hands, and drew Lot back into the house with them, and closed the

11 door./ Those who were at the door of the house they struck with blindness, from the least to the greatest, so that they could not find the door.

Over a thousand feet below sea level lies the malignant smear of water called the Dead Sea, deep in the cleft of the Jordan valley. Hundreds of thousands of years before man appeared on the earth the violence of nature split the Mediterranean shore from the mountains of Syria all the way through Palestine down to the Gulf of Aqaba on the Red Sea, to form this vast depression. Thus imprisoned, the Jordan has no outlet and can only flow endlessly into a landlocked sea. Dead Sea water supports no life, and masses of bituminous asphalt are from time to time disgorged from underwater deposits to float heavily to the surface. The region is oppressive and unhealthy, though when the Israelites first espied it from the heights of the mountains of Moab to the east, the sea's deceptively blue surface shimmering in the sun must have impressed them as it so easily does the modern traveler.

Great cities once graced the Dead Sea's shores, for when the surrounding land was cared for it was fertile. But this was long before the Israelites entered Palestine after the death of Moses. Tradition told them of five great cities that had stood to the south of the Dead Sea in the days of Abraham—Sodom, Gomorra, Adama, Seboim, and Bala or Segor—in a region called the Valley of Siddim now sunk beneath the surface of this Salt Sea (cf. *14*:2 f.). Of these cities, said the tradition, all but Segor had perished violently (see Deut. *29*:22).

There is evidence to support the tradition. Even today part of the southern shoreline of the Dead Sea is called by the Arabs *Usdum* or *Sdum*. It is a fact that the land in this area has been gradually retreating before the encroachment of the sea. The biblical Sodom is in all likelihood to be located beneath the oily surface of these saddest of all waters.

What happened to these cities, long ago? Possibly there was an earthquake, as occurs not infrequently in these parts. Possibly there was a fire ignited from the bituminous gases; something of this sort is said to have taken place in Roman times. Precisely how the thing happened is not so important as why. Genesis says that the destruction of the cities was divine punishment for their evil ways, and Genesis is our only source of information on this point.

The story in chapter *19* is to give an example of the evil that caused the LORD to blot out Sodom and Gomorra. It takes up from *18*:22; the two angels who come to Sodom are those who left Abraham standing in the presence of the LORD. In violent contrast to the hospitality shown them by Abraham, the wicked men of Sodom leave these strangers standing in the public square. Only Lot, Abraham's kinsman, is aware of the duties towards strangers.

The sin of the men of Sodom, which ever after has been called by its name, was common among the pagans of antiquity, was defended and even praised by the authors of pagan ethics. The superior religion of the Hebrews rejected it as a foul iniquity, as Genesis makes quite clear; under the Mosaic Law it was punishable by death. At the same time, there is primitive as well as enlightened morality in this story. We shall be inclined to think

that Lot showed himself a better host than father in the proposal
he made to the Sodomites. Female virtue, however, was not prized
in that age as it has become through Christian teaching. A Hebrew
of Lot's day would have found little to praise in his proposal, but
neither a great deal to blame. He was bound, it was thought, by
a superior obligation, for to betray a guest who had entered one's
house was an inexcusable crime.

19: 12 Then they said to Lot, "Have you anyone else here? Sons-
in-law, sons, daughters, or anyone you have in the city,
13 take them out of the place; / for we are about to destroy
this place, because the outcry against them has become so
14 great before the LORD that he sent us to destroy it." Lot
went out therefore to speak to his intended sons-in-law,
and said, "Come, leave this place; for the LORD shall
destroy the city." But they thought he was jesting.
15 When morning came, the angels urged Lot on, saying,
"Come, take your wife and your two daughters here, lest
16 you perish in the punishment of the city."/ And as he
lingered the visitors took him, his wife and his two
daughters by the hand, through the mercy of the LORD
toward him, and led him forth, and set him outside the
17 city./ When they had brought them forth, they said, "Flee
for your life; do not look behind you nor stop anywhere in
18 the valley; flee to the hills, lest you perish."/ But Lot said
19 to them, "No, my lords;/ surely, your servant has found
favor with you, and great is the mercy which you have
shown me in saving my life. I cannot flee to the hills, lest
20 the disaster overtake me and I die./ But there is a city
nearby to which I can flee; it is a little one.[2] Let me save
myself there; it is a little one, is it not? So let me live."
21 He said to him, "I grant you this favor also; I will not de-
22 stroy the city of which you speak./ Make haste, seek
safety there; for I can do nothing till you arrive there."
Therefore the city was called Segor.
23 The sun had risen on the earth when Lot entered Segor.
24 The LORD poured down on Sodom and Gomorra sul-

[2] "Segor" means "small"; cf. v. 22.

25 phur and fire from the LORD out of heaven./ He overthrew those cities and the whole region, all the inhabitants of the cities and the plants of the soil.

26 But his wife who was behind him looked back, and became a pillar of salt.

27 Early in the morning Abraham came to the place where
28 he had stood before the LORD./ He looked toward
   Sodom and Gomorra and toward the whole region and
   saw smoke rising from the earth as though from a furnace.

God is again the just punisher of evil, but merciful to the just
man. Lot, the good man, is saved together with his family, as Noe
was saved, "through the mercy of the LORD to him." Segor is
saved for Lot's sake. If God is terrible in His anger, He is lavish in
His salvation.

"Only his wife who was behind him looked back, and became
a pillar of salt." Lot's wife has thereafter remained a monument
of hesitation between good and evil, salvation and destruction.
The salt formations resembling stalagmites that line the Dead Sea
shore doubtless suggested the poetical description "a pillar of
salt" of this one who tradition said had perished in the ruin of
Sodom. (See the illustration below.) There is, as a matter of fact,
one such formation that is still called by the Arabs *bint Lut,* now
"the daughter" rather than "the wife of Lot."

Salt Pillar by the Dead Sea

This verse at one time worried commentators exceedingly. Before much attention had been given the literary forms of Genesis, it was fashionable to interpret the text as meaning that Lot's wife had been engulfed by the salt water and so covered with salt that she took on the appearance of a pillar of salt. But as Father Lagrange wryly remarked. "This is rationalist interpretation in the pure sense of the word. It is precisely the way Paulus, in the beginning of the last century, went about denying the miracles of the gospel—natural facts which had been poorly observed and enlarged."[3] The text says that Lot's wife became a pillar of salt, not that her body took on what could appeal to a daring imagination as the likeness of a pillar of salt. Either the author of Genesis must be taken as recording factual history, as the gospels did, in which case we must conclude that God worked a spectacular and rather strange miracle; or we must recall that the author has accepted this as merely one detail in probably the most primitive story that has been used as a source of Genesis. If we do the latter, we shall have no trouble agreeing with Father Lagrange, that "popular imagination, finding a human resemblance in a certain block of salt, mingled it with the remembrance of a woman who had perished in a great catastrophe."[4]

There is an impressive conclusion to the story of Sodom in v. 27 f. Ever after Sodom and Gomorra were to remain for the Jews a byword for the potentialities of human sin and the power of the divine wrath.

The source used by the author of Genesis, however, extends to the end of chapter 19 and includes the following story.

> 19: 29 While God destroyed the cities of the region, he remembered Abraham, and led Lot away from the catastrophe, when the cities where Lot lived were overthrown.
> 30 Lot went up from Segor, and lived in the hills with his two daughters; for he was afraid to live in Segor. He and his
> 31 daughters lived in a cave. Then the elder said to the younger, "Our father is old, and there is no man in the
> 32 land to marry us as is the custom everywhere./ Let us

---

[3] *La méthode historique,* p. 202 f.
[4] Loc. cit.

give our father wine to drink, then lie with him, that we
33 may have offspring by our father."/ So they gave their
father wine to drink that night, and the elder went in, and
lay with her father; but he did not know of it when she
34 lay down, or when she arose. The next day the elder said
to the younger, "Last night I lay with my father. Let us
give him wine to drink tonight also; then you go in, lie
35 with him that we may have offspring by our father."/ So
they gave their father wine to drink that night also, and
the younger went and lay with him; but he did not know
36 of it when she lay down, or when she arose./ Thus both
37 daughters of Lot were with child by their father./ The
elder bore a son, and called him Moab. He is the father of
38 the Moabites of the present day./ The younger also bore a
son and called him Ben-ammi. He is the father of the Ammonites of the present day.

It matters very little, of course, whether Lot's wife was actually
turned into a pillar of salt or not. No one who believes in the in-
finite power of God would question the possibility of such a thing.
If we conclude that it is, however, a legendary element in a story
that the author has used and passed on without comment, it is
on principle, as a piece of sound interpretation that also follows
the papal injunction of *Divino afflante Spiritu,* that we must
determine at all costs the biblical author's literary forms if we are
to know his meaning. It is gratifying for other reasons besides
these, on the other hand, to be able to say that by applying the
same principles we can be sure that the thoroughly unedifying
story we have just read never really took place.

This is a savage Hebrew tale told at the expense of their hated
enemies, the Moabites and Ammonites, peoples with whom they
were forbidden by law to have friendly dealings or intermarriage
(so Deut. 23:4 ff.), degraded pagans whom the Israelite prophets
continually denounced as enemies of God and of His people (see
Ezechiel 25:1-11, for example). The author has included this story
as he found it in his sources, for he fully shared the aversion to
these peoples.

The Moabites and Ammonites, too, claimed descent from the

Hebrew patriarchs, for by race and language they were akin to the Jews. This story, consequently, is the cruel and contemptuous retort which the Hebrews made to their claim. Descendants of the patriarchs? Very well—but such as Ammon and Moab could have descended only by some unclean connection such as the incest narrated in this tale. Incest the Hebrews abominated above every other sin (see Deut. 27:20, 23).

This is, indeed, a cruel satire, and "satire is not history," Father Lagrange insists.[5] St. Jerome has recorded apparently with approval that the Jewish interpreters of his day did not believe the story to be historical. It is, in fact, an elaborate play on words. A folk etymology for the Ammonites (*bene-Ammon* in Hebrew) has been manufactured in the name Ben-ammi ("the son of my parent") ascribed to the child of Lot's younger daughter, while the Moabites (*Moabi* in Hebrew) have been taken as though derived from the "[offspring] by my father" (*me-abi*) spoken throughout by the elder daughter and given as a name to her son. She hath a way, Anne Hathaway. This device has been used, for ridicule or for praise, through all of man's varied history.

[5] *La méthode historique*, p. 207.

20:1 Abraham journeyed from there toward the land of the
Negeb, and dwelt between Cades and Sur. While he lived
2 in Gerara,/ Abraham said of Sara his wife, "She is my
sister." So Abimelech, king of Gerara, sent and took Sara.
3 But God came to Abimelech in a dream by night and said
to him, "You shall die because of the woman you have
4 taken; for she is married."/ Now Abimelech had not approached her; so he said, "Lord, will you slay the innocent?
5 Did not he himself say to me, 'She is my sister'? and did
not she herself say, 'He is my brother'? With a sincere
6 heart and with clean hands I have done this."/ Then God
said to him in the dream, "I know that you have done this
with a sincere heart. It was I who kept you from sinning
against me; therefore I did not allow you to touch her.
7 Therefore, restore the man's wife; since he is a prophet he
will pray for you that you may live. But if you do not restore her, know that you will surely die, you and all that
8 are yours."/ So Abimelech rose early in the morning, and
calling his servants, told them all these things. And the
men were very much afraid.
9 Abimelech called Abraham, and said to him, "What have
you done to us? And how have I offended you that you
should bring down on me and my kingdom a great sin? No
10 one should be treated as you have treated me."/ Abimelech
also said to Abraham, "What had you in mind in doing this
11 thing?"/ Abraham answered, "I thought, 'Surely there is no
fear of God in this place; and they will kill me on account

12 of my wife!'/ Besides, she is indeed my sister, my father's
daughter but not my mother's; and she became my wife.

13 When God brought me out of my father's house, I said to
her, 'This favor you must do for me; in every place to which
we shall go, say of me that I am your brother.' "

14 Then Abimelech took flocks and herds and cattle, men
and women servants, and gave them to Abraham, and re-

15 stored Sara his wife to him,/ and said, "My land is before

16 you; settle wherever it pleases you."/ To Sara he said, "I
am giving your brother a thousand pieces of silver; it is
your compensation in the eyes of all who are with you; and

17 before all men you are vindicated."/ Then Abraham
prayed to God; and God cured Abimelech and his wife

18 and maid-servants, and they bore children./ For the
LORD had closed the wombs of Abimelech's household
because of Sara, the wife of Abraham.

The "there" from which Abraham journeyed to Gerara would
presumably be the terebinths of Mamre, near Hebron (cf. *18*:1);
however, this story is only loosely connected with the surrounding material. We have seen the essence of the story before in
12:10-20.

Did such a thing happen again with so many of the same details? It is not impossible, of course. What is more likely, however,
is that a single historical fact has been handed down by different
traditions that varied the details in the telling. The story in chapter *12* and the present one do, in fact, exhibit the separate characteristics of language and viewpoint that relate them to one or
another of the series of traditions which can be perceived in the
composition of Genesis. When the author of Genesis gathered
the material for his work he included all the forms of this story,
because all taught the same important lesson: how God had continually safeguarded the promise He had made to Abraham. It
has been put in the present context as an object lesson of this
truth to introduce the story of Isaac's birth which follows. We shall
see it again, almost exactly as it is here, told of Isaac in chapter *26*.

Evidently it has been inserted with no regard to the chronology
of Abraham and Sara's life. It obviously supposes Sara to be a

young wife whom Abimelech found desirable, yet in chapter *18* Sara was an old woman, past the age of childbearing.

It is interesting to see how the traditions had varied the story, apart from the trivial detail that one had set the scene in Egypt and the other in Gerara. In this version there is greater stress on God's vigilance, and Abraham's deception is partially justified on the plea that Sara was indeed his sister as well as his wife. Marriages between children of the same father but not the same mother were forbidden under the Mosaic Law, but were common enough in more primitive times.

More important is this story's taking into account Abimelech's point of view. While sin is still taken as an objective thing, it is acknowledged that Abimelech was acting in perfectly good faith. The story had been handed down among Israelites, of course, who told it from the standpoint of their conviction of the one God who holds men to the moral law. Abimelech was a pagan. The pagans too, however, acknowledged the injustice of adultery and punished it in their laws quite as severely as the Jews. While the story glorifies Abraham it likewise praises Abimelech, and this from the viewpoint of Israelite exclusivism was a generous concession.

21:1 The LORD looked after Sara as he had said; the LORD
2 did to Sara as he had promised./ Sara conceived and bore Abraham a son in his old age at the time which God had
3 promised./ And Abraham called the son whom Sara bore
4 him, Isaac./ When his son Isaac was eight days old, Abra-
5 ham circumcised him as God had commanded him./ Abraham was one hundred years old when his son Isaac was
6 born to him./ Sara said, "God has given me cause for laughter, and whoever hears of it will laugh with me."
7 Again she said, "Who would have said to Abraham that Sara would nurse children? Yet I bore him a son in his old
8 age."/ The child grew and was weaned; and Abraham gave a great feast on the day of his weaning.

At last we see the long awaited and promised birth of Isaac. Again the author draws our attention to the resemblance of his name to "laughter."

Here seems as good a place as any to take up once for all the ages attributed to Abraham and his descendants in Genesis. There are certain chronological data in these stories which are doubtless historical: Genesis' sources agreed, for example, that Isaac was born to Abraham and Sara in their old age. The precise years, however, that are strewn throughout the book here and there are not historical. We do not know how long Abraham lived, nor how old he was when he entered Chanaan, nor what was his age when Ismael or Isaac was born.

Commentators have long realized that to take these ages as historical is to commit Genesis to a series of absurdities. The story of Abraham and Sara in chapter 12 could not have happened in Abraham's lifetime before he came to Chanaan; yet if Abraham was seventy-five years old when he left Haran (12:4) and Sara ten years younger than he (17:17), she would already have been sixty-five years old or more when Pharao desired her for a wife and Abraham described her as "a woman beautiful to behold," and, if the similar story in chapter 20 were in its proper order, she would have been ninety when Abraham was fearing that men would kill him for her sake. If Abraham was eighty-six years old when Agar bore him Ismael (16:16) and a hundred when Isaac was born, then one of the two children playing together in 21:9 was approximately sixteen years old, the same "child" whom Agar carried about with her in the desert in the story that follows. At sixteen in the Semitic way of life a lad would be married and beginning a family of his own. Much later on we shall see Isaac's wife Rebecca worrying about a wife for her son Jacob who, if the chronology of Genesis were historical, would just about have reached the tender age of one hundred and twenty years.

These ages are all from one series of traditions, the same series that furnished the ages of the patriarchs before and after the flood in chapters 5 and 11. The author of Genesis has included them not for any historical purpose, but for their symbolic value.

The ages of the patriarchs in Chanaan have been worked out to allow the Hebrews half the time in Chanaan that they spent as Israelites in Egypt. By tradition their stay in Egypt was 430 years (Ex. 12:40). Therefore they have been given 215 years in Chanaan: twenty-five years from Abraham's entry until the birth

of Isaac (*12*:4, *21*:5), another sixty years until the birth of Jacob
25:26), and a final 130 years until the entry into Egypt (*47*:9).
Within this framework the lives of the patriarchs have been disposed, with some striking coincidences. Abraham is one hundred
years old at Isaac's birth, the same age at which his ancestor Sem
begot the first generation after the flood. Abraham lives seventy-
five years before he enters Chanaan and seventy-five years after
he begot Isaac. Abraham is in Chanaan one hundred years all
together, passing up and down the length of the land, as it were
sanctifying it for his descendants, and as Father Schildenberger
reminds us, a hundred years in the viewpoint of Genesis is a
"generation" (cf. *15*:13, 16).[1] Isaac is one hundred years old at
the marriage of his son Esau (*25*:26, *26*:34), and both Isaac and
Esau are forty years old when they marry (*25*:20, *26*:34), a highly
unlikely thing of itself among a people historically noted for early
marriages. All these numbers again are multiples of five. Joseph,
as we shall see, has a symbolism all his own in the number of his
years.

The system goes on and on through the Pentateuch. The great
Moses has his life divided into three periods of forty years: forty
years in Egypt learning the wisdom of the Egyptians (see Acts
7:22), forty years in Madian preparing to liberate his people, and
forty years in the wilderness with the Israelites. It was fitting that
he have a longer life than Joseph, who attained one hundred and
ten years, because Moses led the Israelites out of Egypt and Joseph brought them down. Yet he should not have a longer life
than Jacob, who gave the Israelites his name, and who lived a
hundred and forty-seven years (Gen. *47*:28); nor should his elders, his father and the ancestor of his tribe, Levi, who are accordingly given one hundred and thirty-seven years, ten less
(Ex. 6:16, 20).

And so on and so on. We cannot pretend to work out all the
complicated relations between these numbers and point out what
in each case was the intended significance. What we have shown
has been enough to convince us that there is no real history intended in these numbers, unless it is of the very vaguest kind.
Their primary purpose is to serve religious or historical ends en-

[1] *Vom Geheimnis des Gotteswortes*, p. 270.

tirely separate from their chronological accuracy. Genesis was composed of traditions that had taken no account, and indeed could not have taken account, of a genuine historical chronology. The Semitic mind made capital out of this by supplying symbolisms instead. It is not the way we would write history, but it is part of our author's literary forms and we must interpret his text accordingly.

21: 9 Sara saw the son of Agar the Egyptian, whom she bore to
10 Abraham, playing with her son Isaac. She said to Abraham, "Cast out this slave-girl with her son; for the son of this
11 slave-girl shall not be heir with my son Isaac."/ The matter was very distressing to Abraham on account of his son.
12 But God said to Abraham, "Be not distressed on account of the boy and your slave-girl; heed all that Sara says to you; for through Isaac shall your descendants be called.
13 But I will also make the son of the slave-girl a great nation because he is your offspring."
14 Abraham rose early in the morning, took bread and a bottle of water, and gave them to Agar, placing them on her shoulder. Then he dismissed her with the child. She departed, and wandered about in the desert of Bersabee.
15 When the water in the bottle was gone, she left the child
16 under a bush./ Then she went and sat opposite the place at about the distance of a bowshot; for she said, "Let me not see the child die." As she sat opposite the spot, the
17 child cried aloud./ God heard the child's cry, and the angel of God called to Agar from heaven, and said to her, "What is the matter, Agar? Fear not; for God has heard the boy's
18 cry in this plight of his./ Rise up, take the boy, be assured in his regard; for I will make him a great nation."
19 Then God opened her eyes, and she saw a well. She went and filled the bottle with water and gave the boy a drink.
20 God was with the boy, and he grew up. He lived in the
21 desert and became an expert bowman./ He lived in the desert of Pharan; and his mother chose a wife for him from the land of Egypt.

This story evidently supposes Ismael to have been still a child, as we have noted before. Even apart from the difficulty of chronology, which is not really an important one to Genesis, some commentators believe that the story is another version of the tradition preserved in chapter *16*, and it is true that the general purpose of the stories is the same and that they are alike in a number of details. Whether or not they were originally the same story, and one of the traditions put the incident before and the other after the birth of Isaac, they both agree on the historical background and are true to their age.

Agar's son Ismael was by legal right Abraham's heir along with Isaac. Mothers who see their children's future imperilled are not always great sticklers for established custom, however. In demanding that Abraham cast out the slave-girl, Sara was asking him to violate the law. God had to give Abraham permission to countermand the law and to heed Sara's request. It was according to divine providence that Isaac should be the sole heir.

The scene of this story of Agar is the same as that of chapter *16*, and there is the same teaching that the Arab peoples of the desert of Pharan, Ismael's descendants, would be blessed because of Abraham.

21: 22 At that time Abimelech and Phichol, the commander of his army, said to Abraham, "God is with you in every-
23 thing you do./ Therefore, swear to me by God that you will not deal falsely with me nor with my children nor with my descendants. As I have treated you with kindness, so must you treat me and the land in which you live
24.25 as a stranger."/ Abraham said, "I will swear."/ But he chided Abimelech about a well which Abimelech's men
26 had seized by force./ Abimelech said, "I do not know who did this; you did not tell me, nor did I hear of it till today."

27 Then Abraham took sheep and cattle and gave them to
28 Abimelech; and the two men made a covenant./ Abraham
29 set apart seven ewe lambs of the flock./ But Abimelech said to Abraham, "What do these seven ewe lambs mean
30 which you have set apart?"/ He said, "Take these seven

ewe lambs from me, to be proof for me that I dug this
31 well."/ Therefore that place was called Bersabee, because
32 both of them took an oath there./ So they made a covenant at Bersabee. Then Abimelech and Phichol, the commander of his army, returned to the land of the Philis-
33 tines./ Abraham planted a tamarisk tree at Bersabee
where he called on the name of the LORD, the everlast-
34 ing God./ Abraham lived a long time in the land of the
Philistines.

This narrative affords us a typical example of the all-importance
of covenants in the lives of the Hebrews and why their relation
to God would have inevitably received the form of a covenant.
Agreements such as this between Abraham and Abimelech, whom
we have met before, took place every day between men during
these primitive times. A difference of opinion would necessitate a
modus vivendi if peace were to be preserved. Or simply two
households living side by side would require a prior arrangement
for the sharing of common facilities such as a well. A covenant
was the solution. Men have been living under covenants, on a
great or small scale, since civilization began.

This present story, because it is brief, also gives us the opportunity to see demonstrated the method which the author of Genesis followed in gathering together and editing the ancient traditions which he had inherited concerning his ancestors. We have
seen that in some instances when the parallel traditions had become rather widely separated in details he included them as
separate stories. When he could, he joined them together, and
this he did in the present instance. Actually, he had three traditions all told, but the third had associated this covenant with Isaac
instead of Abraham; he has given it in chapter 26. The two traditions about Abraham and Abimelech he made into one.

The first story went like this:

22 At that time Abimelech and Phichol, the commander of
his army, said to Abraham, "God is with you in everything
23 you do./ Therefore, swear to me by God that you will not
deal falsely with me nor with my children nor with my descendants. As I have treated you with kindness, so must

you treat me and the land in which you live as a stranger."
24.27 Abraham said, "I will swear."/ Then Abraham took sheep
and cattle and gave them to Abimelech; and the two men
31 made a covenant./ Therefore that place was called Bersabee, because both of them took an oath there.

This story simply recorded a covenant of friendship and nonaggression entered between Abraham, a powerful chieftain, and
the ruler of the land who permitted him to dwell in his territory.
It uses the common word for God, *Elohim,* as was fitting in the
circumstances, since Abimelech was not a worshipper of the true
God of the Hebrews. The tradition had derived the name of Bersabee (in Hebrew *Beer-sheba*) by folk etymology from the oath
of the covenant made there—*beer shaba* is "well of the oath."
The second tradition was longer, and recorded a dispute between Abraham's men and Abimelech's over this well. It consisted
of the rest of the verses:

25 Abraham[2] chided Abimelech about a well which Abimelech's
26 men had seized by force./ Abimelech said, "I do not know
who did this; you did not tell me, nor did I hear of it till to-
28 day."/ Abraham set apart seven ewe lambs of the flock.
29 But Abimelech said to Abraham, "What do these seven ewe
30 lambs mean which you have set apart?"/ He said, "Take
these seven ewe lambs from me, to be proof for me that I dug
32 this well."/ So they made a covenant at Bersabee. Then Abimelech and Phichol, the commander of his army, returned
33 to the land of the Philistines./ Abraham planted a tamarisk
tree at Bersabee where he called on the name of the LORD,
34 the everlasting God./ Abraham lived a long time in the land
of the Philistines.

Here the particular occasion which necessitated a covenant is
brought out. By accepting this covenant, Abimelech admitted
Abraham's title to the well in question. There are minor differences in the vocabulary of the two stories, and in this one we
find the proper name of the true God, the LORD. Possibly this

---

[2] The Hebrew has the subject "Abraham," not simply "he" as in the translation above.

reference in v. 33 is a recollection of Abraham's having taken over a Chanaanite shrine at Bersabee which he rededicated to Jahweh El Olam, appropriating the Chanaanite title, "the everlasting God." Finally, this tradition derives the name Bersabee evidently from the *seven* ewe lambs which Abraham offered as the sign of the covenant—*beer sheba* is "well of the seven."

Both stories were worth keeping, and both were kept. The sense of neither has been betrayed in the resulting combination. What the author has done here he has done time and again throughout his work.

The tradition calls Abimelech's territory "the land of the Philistines" by anticipation. There were no Philistines in Palestine for centuries yet, but when they did come they settled this region. Abimelech was a Chanaanite ruler with a good Semitic name; the Philistines were not Semites.

22: 1 After these events God put Abraham to a test. He said to
2 him, "Abraham." He answered, "Here I am."/ God said, "Take your only son Isaac whom you love and go into the district of Moria, and there offer him as a holocaust on
3 the hill which I shall point out to you." Early in the morning Abraham harnessed his ass, took with him two of his servants and his son Isaac, and cut wood for the holocaust. Then he set out on his journey to the place which
4 God had indicated to him. On the third day he looked up
5 and saw the place at a distance. He said to his servants, "Stay here with the ass while the boy and I go there to
6 worship; then we shall come back to you." Abraham took the wood for the holocaust and put it upon his son Isaac while he himself carried the fire and the knife. As they
7 walked together,/ Isaac said to his father Abraham, "Father." He answered, "Yes, son!" He said, "You have the fire and the wood, but where is the sheep for the holo-
8 caust?" Abraham replied, "God himself will provide the sheep for the holocaust, my son." And they went on together.

Rarely was man ever called upon to offer a more convincing evidence of faith and obedience than Abraham in the story that is before us. This is, in fact, the climax in the life of Abraham told by Genesis.

Abraham's heroic example has been held up to us by St. Paul. "Abraham hoping against hope believed, so that he became the father of many nations, according to what was said, 'So shall thy offspring be' . . . In view of the promise of God, he did not waver through unbelief but was strengthened in faith, giving glory to God, being fully aware that whatever God has promised he is able also to perform. Therefore it was credited to him as justice" (Rom. 4:18, 20 ff.). And the Apostle has added, "Not for his sake only was it written that 'It was credited to him,' but for the sake of us also, to whom it will be credited if we believe in him who raised Jesus our Lord from the dead, who was delivered up for our sins, and rose again for our justification" (v. 23 ff.).

The faith that Abraham manifested was in the promise of God, which we have seen fulfilled in a manner beyond anything Abraham could have dreamed in the coming of Jesus Christ. The faith that saved Abraham saves us also in Christ.

The story of chapter 22 is thus a touching demonstration of faith, touchingly told both in the example of Abraham's unswerving obedience and Isaac's unsuspecting trust. When God's will was made known to Abraham it apparently sounded the death-knell of all his hopes. Isaac was the child of promise through whom God's word was to be fulfilled that Abraham might become the father of many nations, yet he was being asked to destroy this life and the promise with it.

The sacrifice of a human being, so repugnant to us and with such difficulty associated with a divine command, would not have appeared too strange to Abraham. There is no evidence that human sacrifice was ever practised by the Hebrews, but it was common among the Chanaanites with whom Abraham lived, and how was he to know that God, the ruler of life, would not require this thing of him?

22: 9 When they arrived at the place of which God had told him, Abraham built an altar there and arranged the wood on it. Then he bound his son Isaac and laid him on the wood
   10 upon the altar./ Abraham stretched out his hand, and took

11 the knife to kill his son./ But an angel of the LORD called
to him from heaven, "Abraham, Abraham!" He answered,
12 "Here I am."/ He said, "Do not lay a hand on the boy; do
nothing to him. I know now that you fear God, since you
13 have not withheld your only son from me."/ Abraham
looked about and saw a ram caught by its horns in the
bush. He went and took it, and offered it as a holocaust in
14 place of his son./ Abraham named the place, "Yahweh-
yireh."[3] Hence even to this day people say, "On the mountain of the LORD provision will be made."

15 Again the angel of the LORD called from heaven to Abra-
16 ham/ and said, "I swear by myself, says the LORD, since
you have done this and have not withheld your only son,
17 I will indeed bless you, and will surely multiply your descendants as the stars of the heavens, as the sands on the
seashore. Your descendants shall possess the gates of their
18 enemies./ In your descendants all the nations of the earth
19 shall be blessed, because you have obeyed me."/ Abraham
returned to his servants, and together they went to Bersabee where Abraham made his home.

God was but trying Abraham. After the great patriarch had
successfully passed this test, hoping against hope, he received
the consolation of once more obtaining the assurance of the divine
promises. He became not only the one who has made our faith
possible, but an example for the faith of us all.

It is small wonder that Abraham has been singled out from all
the other men of the Old Testament as the man of faith and the
father of all who believe, as St. Paul called him. God could have
worked out His promise to save mankind in any number of ways,
but the way He actually chose was through the descendants of
Abraham. If Abraham had failed God's test, the promise would
have been fulfilled otherwise. As it is, we are Abraham's spiritual
sons according to the promise.

[3] This name means "the LORD will provide." The location of the place is
unknown; later Jewish tradition identified it with the temple-site of Mount
Moria in Jerusalem.

22: 20 After these events, Abraham was told, "Melcha too has
21 borne sons to your brother Nahor:/ Us, the first-born,
22 Buz, his brother, Camuel, the father of Aram,/ Chased,
23 Hazau, Pheldas, Jedlaph, and Bathuel."/ [Bathuel was
the father of Rebecca.] Melcha bore these eight to Nahor,
24 Abraham's brother./ As for his concubine, whose name
was Roma, she brought forth Tabee, Gaham, Thahas and
Maacha.

These final verses of chapter 22 have been taken from an old genealogy which the author of Genesis has inserted as he draws near the conclusion of the patriarch's life history. The genealogy is also a preparation for the story of Isaac's marriage which is to follow. As with the genealogies we have seen before, the names in the list are for the most part of peoples and places rather than of individuals. The purpose was to link these peoples with the Hebrews; many of them turn up later on in the Bible.

Us and Buz, for example, are parts of Arabia or Idumea, named as such in the book of Job (*1*:1, *32*:2). From another tradition in *10*:23 Us was made the son of Aram. Aram and Chased are the names of peoples, the first of the Semites who later came to be called Syrians, the latter of another Semitic people, the Chasdim or Chaldeans, who established the powerful Babylonian dynasty which ruled Mesopotamia. In *11*:28 Ur was called by anticipation "of the Chaldees." Aram in *10*:22 was made the son of Sem. These peoples were truly related to one another and to the Hebrews. Hazau was another region of the Arabian peninsula. Tabee was a city near Damascus later captured by Kind David; Thahas and Maacha were also places in the Lebanon region. The significance of most of the other names is unknown. Rebecca, however, the daughter of Bathuel, we shall see in chapter *24*.

Before the author proceeds to tell us the story of Isaac's marriage which brings to a close the history of Abraham, he has recorded the moving description of Sara's death and her burial near the famous city of Hebron, later to become a holy city of the Hebrews as it is now of the Moslem Arabs. This following chapter has a particular historical interest owing to recent discoveries.

23:1.2 Sara lived one hundred and twenty-seven years./ She
died in Cariath-arbe, that is, Hebron, in the land of
Chanaan. Abraham prepared to mourn for Sara and
3 weep over her./ He left the side of his dead wife and
4 said to the Hethites,/ "I am a stranger resident among
you; give me burial ground among you that I may bury
5.6 my dead."/ The Hethites answered Abraham,/ "Hear us,
my Lord, you are a mighty prince among us. Choose
any of our tombs to bury your dead. None of us will re-
7 fuse you a tomb for your dead."/ Abraham rose and
bowed low before the Hethites, the natives of the land.
8 He said to them, "If it is acceptable to you that I bury my
dead, then hear me: ask Ephron, the son of Sohar, in my
9 behalf/ to give me the cave of Machpela which he has
at the end of his field. Let him sell it to me in your pres-
10 ence for its full value, as a burial ground."/ Now the Hethite Ephron, sitting among the Hethites, answered
11 Abraham in the hearing of all his fellow citizens,/ "No,
my lord! Hear me: I give you the field and the cave that
is in it. In the presence of my people do I give it; bury
12 your dead."/ Abraham bowed low before the natives of
13 the land,/ and in their hearing said to Ephron, "If you
are really willing, hear me. I will give you money for the
field; accept it from me that I may bury my dead there."
14.15 Ephron answered Abraham,/ "Hear me, my lord! A piece
of land worth four hundred shekels of silver,[4] what is that
16 between you and me? Bury your dead in it."/Abraham
came to terms with Ephron and weighed out for him the
sum he had mentioned in the hearing of the Hethites,
four hundred shekels of silver of commercial standard.
17 Thus Ephron's field in Machpela, facing Mamre, that is,
the field, the cave and all the trees in the entire field, be-
18 came/ the property of Abraham in the presence of all the
19 Hethites, his fellow citizens./ After this Abraham buried
his wife Sara in the cave of the field at Machpela, facing

[4] The shekel, later a coin, was originally a weight, the exact quantity of
which is unknown.

20 Mamre, that is Hebron, in the land of Chanaan./ Thus
the field with its cave passed from the Hethites to Abraham for use as a burial ground.

Until very lately it was thought that this chapter contained a
mixture of authentic history and some anachronisms. History,
surely, is in the description of Abraham's purchase. The story rings
authentically enough in its picture of a typical bargain struck in
the manner still honored in the Near East. The seller professes
himself willing to give away his goods out of pure friendship,
knowing the while that he will get a good price if the purchaser
really needs what he has to sell. This good price, when pressed
to sell, he mentions carelessly as though it were of no importance:
"Four hundred shekels, what is that between you and me?" Agreements of this kind, witnessed by the whole community in lieu of a
written record, are precisely those that would be the best remembered and historically trustworthy.

What was thought to be an anachronism was the reference to
the inhabitants of Hebron, which the author first calls by its old
Chanaanite name, Cariath-arbe, "the city of the four [quarters]":
to this day Hebron is divided into four parts. These are named
Hethites, that is, Hittites. The Hittites, who later ruled a powerful
non-Semitic empire centred in Asia Minor, are not known to have
lived in Palestine, and certainly not as early as this in history. Centuries after the Hittite Empire was dead and buried, however,
the mixed population that inherited its former territories came
to be called Hittites, much as the Arab population in Egypt are
now called Egyptians, though they have no connection with
those who gave Egypt its name. It was thought that the writer
of Genesis, living at a time when these pseudo-Hittites had thoroughly penetrated Palestine, and ignorant of their origins, had
wrongly ascribed them to the period of Abraham.

Anachronisms are common in popular history, and we expect
them in the Bible. We noted that Abimelech's kingdom in chapter
21 was called "the land of the Philistines," which it was in the
author's day but certainly not in Abraham's. The author used the
term with which he and his readers were familiar. There is nothing extraordinary in this, and we do it every day when we say

that Caesar invaded England, or Clovis was the King of France, or that La Salle explored Texas.

But it now begins to appear that chapter 23 contains more authentic history than was previously imagined. The law codes of the Hittite Empire, which passed into oblivion about 1200 B.C., have lately been unearthed by archaeologists, and it seems that a peculiarly Hittite custom was practised by the people called Hethites in this chapter.

Abraham came before these people as a resident stranger, that is, a person who possessed no land of his own. He asked that he might bury Sara in their territory, and when this proved agreeable he requested Ephron to "give," that is to sell him the cave that lay in his field. Caves were the ready-made tombs of the time. Ephron, however, offered to "give" Abraham the field *and* the cave, and this was the arrangement that was finally made. Abraham wanted only the cave, he concluded by acquiring a field for four hundred shekels. Ephron would not relinquish the cave without the field.

This action can be explained by Hittite law. The full owner of a field owed the Hittite overlord certain specified duties; just what they were, we are not sure. The owner of only a minor part of a holding, however, was not obliged to these duties, which always pertained to the principal owner. Seemingly Abraham wanted to avoid these duties, which may have had some religious connection distasteful to him; he tried, therefore, to acquire only a small part of Ephron's field. Ephron was just as anxious to be rid of them himself, and so insisted that Abraham become full owner.

If this is the correct understanding of this episode, Genesis has become once more a source of knowledge of what has otherwise been passed over in history. If the Hethites of this story shared the same laws with the people who built the Hittite Empire, there must have been a relation between them.

Sir Leonard Woolley has recently theorized (in his Penguin book, *A Forgotten Kingdom*) that these Palestinian Hittites were part of a migration from the Caucasus which split up in Anatolia, part of which came south into Palestine while the rest proceeded into Asia Minor, eventually to establish the Hittite Empire.

24: 1 Abraham was now an old man well advanced in years. The
2 LORD had blessed him in every way./ Abraham said to
the oldest servant of his household, who had charge of all
3 his possessions, "Put your hand under my thigh / that I
may adjure you by the LORD, the God of heaven and the
God of earth, not to obtain a wife for my son from the
4 women of the Chanaanites among whom I live,/ but to go
to my land and kindred to obtain a wife for my son Isaac."
5 The servant answered, "Perhaps the woman will not wish
to follow me to this land; shall I then take your son back to
6 the land from which you came?"/ Abraham said to him,
7 "Never take my son back there./ The LORD, the God of
heaven, who took me from my father's house, from the land
of my kindred, who spoke to me and swore to me, 'I will
give this land to your descendants,' will send his angel
ahead of you and you will obtain a wife for my son there.
8 If the woman does not wish to follow you, you will be released from this oath; but do not take my son back there."
9 So the servant put his hand under the thigh of his master
Abraham and swore an oath to him in this matter.

The author of Genesis did not have a great deal of information
about Isaac, most of whose life story is included in that of his
father Abraham or of his son Jacob. The little we know of Isaac,
however, is found in stories like this one, warm in their familiarity
with the daily facts of human experience as they were lived some
eighteen hundred years before Christ.

Abraham's family formed a religious oasis in a vast desert of
the most degraded paganism. It is easy to understand why Abraham wanted a wife for his son from his own kindred, so as not
to form any alliance by marriage with the neighboring peoples.
At the same time, it is understandable why he did not wish Isaac
to return to the land of origins, for there too paganism reigned.
God's mercy had brought Abraham into a new life, and there
must be no return to the old for any of his family. Thus the oldest
servant of his household, possibly the Eliezer who had been his
intended heir before Isaac's birth (15:2), was sent to obtain a wife
for Isaac.

24: 10 The servant then took ten of his master's camels and a variety of his master's treasures. He set out and journeyed to the city where Nahor lived in Aram Naharaim.[5]

11 In the evening, at the time when the women came out to draw water, he made the camels kneel near the well out-

12 side the city./ Then he said, "LORD, God of my master Abraham, grant me success this day; be gracious to my

13 master Abraham./ I stand here at the spring, and the young women of the city are coming out to draw water.

14 Now if I say to a young woman, "Lower your jar that I may drink,' and she answers, 'Drink, and I will also water your camels,' she it is whom you have chosen for your servant Isaac. Thereby shall I know that you have shown

15 your favor to my master."/ He had not yet finished speaking when Rebecca came out, the daughter of Bathuel, son of Melcha, wife of Abraham's brother, Nahor. She came out with a jar on her shoulder.

16 The young woman was very beautiful, a virgin undefiled. She went down to the spring, filled her jar, and as she

17 came up,/ the servant hastened to meet her and said, "If

18 you please, let me drink a little water from your jar." /She answered, "Drink, sir," and quickly lowered the jar to her

19 hand and gave him a drink./ When she had given him the drink, she said, "I will draw water also for your camels

20 until they have finished drinking."/ She quickly emptied her jar into the trough, hastened again to the well, and

21 drew water for all the camels./ All the while the man was watching her, waiting to learn whether or not the LORD

22 had prospered his journey./ When the camels had finished drinking, the man took out a gold ring, a half shekel in weight, and he put on her wrists two gold bracelets

23 weighing ten shekels./ He said to her, "Tell me whose daughter you are! Is there room in your father's house for

24 us to stay overnight?"/ She answered him, "I am the daughter of Bathuel, a son of Nahor whom Melcha bore to

[5] "Aram of the two rivers," northwest Mesopotamia, the region about Haran. This is the name by which it was known to the author of Genesis. The Greeks called it Syria, as we do after them.

25 him."/ She added, "We have plenty of straw and fodder,
26 and there is room to spend the night."/ Then the man
27 bowed in worship to the LORD,/ saying, "Blessed be the
    LORD, the God of my master Abraham, whose constant
    favor to my master has not ceased. Me also the LORD has
    guided on my way to the house of my master's kinsmen."
28 Meanwhile the maiden hastened to inform her mother's
    household of what had happened.

This charming scene pictures an apparently chance meeting
of Abraham's servant and Rebecca, which the author is convinced
was providential. The canny servant had decided on something
more than an arbitrary sign to know that his journey had been
blessed with success. To refuse a drink of water to a passing
stranger is unheard of in the East. It would be a goodhearted
girl of more than ordinary generosity and diligence, however,
who would offer to water the camels as well. Anyone who has
seen a camel drink will know why this is so.

The gold bracelets and ring (a nose-ring is meant) were Abraham's bridal gift. Rebecca's family could tell from this gift that
they were entertaining someone with an important message. Perhaps the author has intended a dash of irony in the following
scene. We learn from a later chapter that Laban was a man not
wholly immune to the allure of wealth.

24:29.30 Now Rebecca had a brother named Laban. As soon as
        he saw the ring, and the bracelets on his sister's wrists,
        and heard his sister Rebecca say, "Thus the man spoke
        to me," Laban hastened to the man at the spring. When
        he reached the man he found him standing by the
     31 camels near the spring./ He said, "Come in, blessed of
        the LORD! Why should you stay outdoors when I
        have made ready the house, as well as a place for the
     32 camels?"/ So the man went into the house, Laban un-
        loaded the camels, and provided them with straw and
        fodder. Then he brought water for the man himself
        and for those who were with him, to wash their feet.
     33 Food was placed before the men, but he said, "I will

not eat before I have delivered my message." They answered, "Speak."

34.35 So he said, "I am Abraham's servant. / The LORD has blessed my master abundantly so that he has become a rich man. He has given him flocks, herds, silver, gold,

36 men and women servants, camels and asses./ My master's wife Sara bore a son to my master in her old age,

37 and he has given him all his property./ My master adjured me, 'You must not choose a wife for my son from the women of the Chanaanites in whose country I

38 live,/ but you shall go to my family and kindred to

39 choose a wife for my son.'/ I answered my master,

40 'Perhaps the woman will not follow me.'/ He said, 'The LORD in whose sight I have lived will send his angel with you and prosper your journey. You will choose a

41 wife for my son from my kindred and family;/ then will you be released from your oath to me. If you go to my kindred and they refuse you, you will be free from your oath to me.'

42 "Today when I came to the spring I said, 'LORD, God of my master Abraham, may you prosper the journey

43 I am making!/ Here I stand at the spring; if I say to a girl coming out to draw water: Give me a little water

44 from your jar to drink,/ and she answers me: Drink, and I will also draw water for your camels, she is the wife whom the LORD has chosen for my master's son.'

45 "I had not yet finished planning this when Rebecca came with her jar on her shoulder, went down to the spring, and drew water. I said to her, 'Give me a drink,

46 please.'/ She quickly lowered her jar and said, 'Drink; and I will also water your camels,' So I drank and she

47 also watered the camels./ Then I asked her, 'Whose daughter are you?', and she replied, 'I am the daughter of Bathuel, son of Nahor and his wife Melcha.' Then I put the ring in her nose and the bracelets on her wrists.

48 And I bowed and worshiped the LORD, blessing the LORD, the God of my master Abraham, who guided me along the right road to choose the daughter of my

49 master's kinsman for his son./ Now tell me whether my master can depend on your favor; if not, let me know, that I may determine my course."

50 Laban and his family answered, "This comes from the
51 LORD. We can say nothing at all to you./ Here before you is Rebecca; take her and go. Let her be married to
52 your master's son as the LORD has decided."/ When Abraham's servant heard their answer, he bowed to the
53 ground before the LORD./ He brought out silver and gold jewelry, and clothing, and gave them to Rebecca. He also gave costly presents to her brother and mother.
54 Then he and the men with him had food and drink. They stayed overnight, and when they rose the next
55 morning he said, "Let me go to my master."/ Her brother and mother answered, "Let the girl stay with
56 us some days, say ten, and then she may go."/ But he said to them, "Do not detain me, because the LORD has prospered my journey; let me go and return to my
57 master."/ Then they said, "Let us call the girl and ask her in person."

58 They called Rebecca and asked her, "Will you go with
59 this man?" And she answered, "I will."/ So they let their sister Rebecca and her nurse go with Abraham's
60 servant and his men./ They blessed Rebecca and said, "May you, sister, become a thousand times ten thousand,
and may your descendants conquer the gates of their foes."
61 Then Rebecca and her maids mounted camels and followed the man. So the servant took Rebecca and departed.

We can hardly accuse the author of abbreviating his sources. The repetition of such a story, which may at times be irksome to us, is in the best tradition of Semitic narration; constant telling, and a joy in telling, these ancestral tales encouraged this.

Rebecca's family speak throughout as though they were worshippers of the LORD. We already know, and are told explicitly later on, that they were pagans. We can set this down to the Hebrew author's levelling things off to his own viewpoint, though this is hardly necessary. It was in keeping with politeness to praise or attribute blessings to the deity of a friend, even if one knew nothing about him. In the broad bosom of paganism there is always room for another god.

Laban was apparently the head of the household, after the death of his father Bathuel who does not figure in the story at all. This would be in line with the legal custom: although Rebecca's mother still lived, the heir of the father was the eldest son. Thus it is Laban who gives the consent to his sister's marriage, and both he and his mother receive the gifts of Abraham's servant.

The servant refused to remain in Aram Naharaim for the often tediously drawn out celebrations that accompanied betrothals and marriages. He was anxious to return to Chanaan, his mission happily accomplished. As it was, Abraham was probably already dead by this time. He is mentioned no more, and the account of his death in the following chapter is not related chronologically to the present. The mission of his servant to Aram Naharaim sounded very much like a deathbed instruction.

Rebecca's consent was asked before she was sent away. This may mean one of two things, depending on the custom then followed by her kindred. According to one law known from Nuzu, the consent of the girl was necessary when it was her brother rather than her father who was giving her in marriage. According to Assyrian law, on the other hand, while the brother could give his sister to someone of her own country, he could not marry her to a person in a foreign land against her will. In either case, Rebecca had to be consulted.

24:62 Isaac had gone to the desert of Beer-lahai-roi; he was liv-
   63 ing in the district of Negeb./ One day toward evening,
      when he went out in the field for a walk, he looked up and
   64 saw camels approaching./ Rebecca too looked up, and
   65 when she saw Isaac she dismounted from the camel,/ and
      asked the servant, "Who is the man coming through the
      field toward us?" The servant said, "It is my master." Then
      she covered herself with her veil.

66.67 The servant told Isaac all he had done. Isaac led Rebecca into the tent and took her to wife. Because he loved her, Isaac was consoled for the loss of his mother.

Isaac was now living in southern Negeb, in the land about Beer-lahai-roi, where he went after the death of Abraham according to 25:11. Abraham as well as Sara was doubtless no more, which is suggested, too, by the fact that Abraham's servant called Isaac his master.

In obedience to the custom still observed in the land of Isaac's birth, the bride veiled herself before meeting her promised husband. Another custom is indicated in the mention of the marriage tent in v. 67. A vestige of this ancient ritual is preserved in Orthodox Jewish marriages, in the canopy under which the marriage rite is solemnized.

25:1 Abraham married another wife whose name was Cetura.
   2 She bore him Zamran, Jecsan, Madian, Madan, Jesboc and
   3 Sue./ Jecsan became the father of Saba and Dedan. The descendants of Dedan were the Assurim, the Latusim and
   4 the Loommim. The descendants of Madian were Epha, Epher, Henoch, Abida and Eldaa. All these were the descendants of Cetura.

Genesis now ends the story of Abraham with a number of miscellaneous details drawn from different traditional sources. Firstly is this list of his descendants by another wife nowhere else mentioned, Cetura. As usual, the purpose of the genealogy is to show the relation of various peoples, some of whom we have seen before. In fact, there is some conflict in the sources which the author has used here and elsewhere. The Saba and Dedan of v. 3, for example, are in 10:7 named descendants of Chus and Ham, therefore not relatives of the Hebrews at all. The variation in the traditions probably marks an earlier friendship and a later hostility towards these neighboring peoples, for as we saw before, one of the purposes of the genealogies of chapter 10 was to condemn the enemies of God's people.

The names in this list all seem to be those of Arab tribes. This is true of Zamran and Jecsan (the same as the Jectan of 10:25.

where he is again the father of Saba), Madian and Sue. Madan
and Jesboc have not been identified, but they too were most likely
Arab peoples. Sue is named in the book of Job (2:11). The most
important of the tribes is Madian, which is frequently mentioned
in the Bible and later becomes intimately associated with the
Israelites. We shall see some of the Madianites in the story of
Joseph in chapter 37. Saba or Sheba is, however, probably the
best known to the modern reader, because of its famous queen.

Most of the other names are unknown outside this passage.
Epha, however, is found in Isaias 60:6, together with Madian and
Saba, as the name of an Arab country, and Abida turns up in
Assyrian inscriptions as another Arab tribe. Because of the context
the Assurim of v. 3 are unlikely to be the Assyrians of Mesopo-
tamia.

> 25:5.6 Abraham gave Isaac everything he had. Abraham gave
> presents to his children by his concubines, and while yet
> alive sent them away eastward, to the land of the East
> apart from Isaac.

These verses certainly reflect an authentic social practice of
the time of Abraham. Abraham's children by his concubines do
not share the privileges of Agar and Ismael, who because Sara
had given Agar to Abraham were Abraham's legal heirs and could
not legally be sent away.

A Mesopotamian law centuries older than Abraham decreed
that "if a man married a wife [Sara, in this case] who bore
him children who are still living, and if a slave has also borne
him children but he has granted freedom to the slave and her
children, the slave's children shall not divide the estate with their
master's children."

It was in view of this law that "Abraham gave Isaac everything
he had," at the same time giving his slave-wives' children their
freedom and depriving them of any right to be heirs with Isaac.

> 25:7 Abraham's life span was one hundred and seventy-five
> 8 years when he expired./ He died at a good old age, an old
> 9 man after a full life, and was gathered to his kinsmen./ His
> sons Isaac and Ismael buried him in the cave of Mach-

phela, facing Mamre, in the field of Ephron the Hethite,
10 the son of Sohar./ Abraham was buried with his wife Sara
11 in the field which he had bought from the Hethites./ After
the death of Abraham, God blessed his son Isaac, who
made his home near Beer-lahai-roi.

The death and burial of Abraham are briefly told. When they
occurred we do not know. Ismael is supposed present, though
another tradition in chapter 21 separated him permanently from
Abraham at an early age. The statement in v. 9 may be simply a
conventional expression to say "he was buried by his family."

25:12 These are the descendants of Abraham's son Ismael,
whom Agar the Egyptian, Sara's maid, bore to Abraham.
13 These are the names of Ismael's sons, in the order of their
birth: Nabaioth, the first-born of Ismael, Cedar, Adbeel,
14.15 Mabsam,/ Masma, Duma, Massa,/ Hadad, Thema, Jetur,
16 Naphis and Cedma./ These were the sons of Ismael and
these are their names according to their villages and en-
campments: twelve princes according to their tribes.
17 The length of Ismael's life was one hundred and thirty-
seven years when he expired. He died, and was gathered
18 to his kinsmen. The Ismaelites dwelt from Hevila to Sur,
on the border of Egypt on the way to Assur. He died in
conflict with all his kinsmen.

For good measure, the author closes his account with a genealogy of Ismael's descendants. These "twelve princes," the fulfilment of the prediction of 17:20, are known either from the Bible
or other ancient historical sources to have been Arab peoples
dwelling where v. 18 says that they dwelt, "from Hevila to Sur,"
that is, from southern Arabia to the border of Egypt. Somewhere
in this neighborhood was the residence of the Assurim named in
v. 3 above. The most famous of these twelve tribes were the
Nabaioth, who as the Nabateans of later history created a great
kingdom which lasted into Roman times, and whose capital was
the rose-red city of Petra south of the Dead Sea, literally carved
from solid stone, one of the wonders of man's ingenuity.
What are we to say of Abraham as we see the final curtain fall

in his life story? Surely we can do no better than let the Bible account speak for itself. It has shown him a creature of real flesh and blood, not just a glorified symbol, an idealized hero who could do no wrong or whose vices were made virtues. He is one of the first complete men we know from history, with many of the imperfections to which we are all heir and with an uncommon share of the perfections we would like to have.

Perhaps we can best think of him as Father Lagrange thought of the scriptural interpreters of France's past, whose understanding of the Bible was no longer adequate in a scientific age. He lectured the Catholic Institute of Toulouse in 1902, "Gentlemen, do not do Bossuet and Pascal the injury of imagining that they would have obstinately held to their positions if they had been aware of what we now know. If we had lived in their time, we would have thought as they, and we would have expressed it much more poorly."[6]

Abraham lived without the Church, without the sacraments, without the consolation of the fulfilment of prophecy, all of which we have. He had to walk virtually alone, gropingly, with only his strong faith in a future he was not to see in this life. We must candidly confess, if we had lived in the time of our father Abraham, we would only with God's help have done as he, and we would have done it far less well.

[6] *La méthode historique*, p. 219.

CHAPTER X: JACOB THE SUPPLANTER

There is very little, as we have noted, to the story of Isaac, who is almost wholly submerged in the strong characters of his father and son. The emphasis of at least the first part of these following chapters is on the conflict between Jacob and his brother Esau, in which Irving Fineman in his book *Jacob* has seen "that endless struggle for supremacy which has existed since the beginning of mankind on this earth between the two kinds of men who inhabit it—the men of force and action and the men of thought and sensibility, the men of violence and the men of peace, the men for whom life is primarily self-gratification and those for whom it is nothing without aspiration."[1]

The author of Genesis does in fact tell us that, when all is said and done, it is the men of sense and sensibility who triumph, and who leave the world somehow changed for their having been in it. The noisy bluster of an Esau may prevail for the moment, but it is the Jacobs who endure. Esau is the eternal type of the man who wants actions, not words, but Jacob is the quiet man in whose mind alone any lasting and significant action must be planned. This is the scene that is set from the beginning in Genesis.

From Jacob, of course, the Israelites traced their descent, and from Esau the descent of their neighbors the Edomites. The Edomites were a wild, warlike people persistently hostile to Israel; under David they were subjugated and made tributary to the Israelite kingdom. It is to this historical fact that the poetic oracle in the following passage has reference. Through an irony of reversal it was the Edomites' later representatives, the Idumeans, who

[1] New York: Random House, 1941, p. 31.

in the person of the Herods ruled over the Jews in our Lord's time. It almost seemed that the prophecy had been annulled. Yet we have seen the vindication of Genesis' inspired words. Where today is Edom? Where is Idumea? Who acknowledges Esau or the Herods? It is Jacob surnamed Israel that remains, the spiritual Israel which is the Church of Christ.

25:19 This is the family history of Isaac, the son of Abraham.
20 Abraham was the father of Isaac./ Isaac was forty years old when he married Rebecca, daughter of Bathuel, an Aramean of Phaddan-Aram,[2] and sister of Laban the
21 Aramean./ Isaac prayed to the LORD for his wife because she was barren. The LORD answered Isaac and his
22 wife Rebecca conceived./ The children jostled each other within her, and she said, "If this be so, why am I preg-
23 nant?" Then she went to consult the LORD./ He said to her,

"Two nations are in your womb;
  two peoples shall stem from your body.
One people shall be stronger than the other,
  and the elder shall serve the younger."

24 When the time of her delivery came, there were indeed
25 twins in her womb./ The first to come forth was red. His whole body was like a hairy garment, so they named him
26 Esau./ Afterward his brother came forth, with his hand gripping Esau's heel; so he was called Jacob. Isaac was sixty years old when they were born.

The future of these two sons of Isaac is in the story of their birth. They are at odds literally from the womb. This passage is overloaded with popular etymologies. Edom, the land of Esau's descendants, means "the red [land]," and Esau is red at birth. The name Esau itself has never been explained, but presumably it meant something like "hairy." We learn later (33:16) that Edom is also called Seir, which recalls that Esau's body "was like a hairy (*sear*) garment." Jacob comes into the world gripping his brother's heel (*akeb*). In Hebrew *jaakob* is one who follows, who overtakes.

2 "The plain of Aram," another name for Aram Naharaim.

Jacob is the supplanter, the second-born who is to become dominant over his less resourceful brother.

It would be interesting to know how Rebecca consulted the LORD in v. 22. In later times this phrase was used for seeking a divinely revealed oracle from a prophet or priest at one of the sanctuaries dedicated to the LORD. The Law of Moses made specific provisions for this. The priestly or prophetical oracles, like the oracles found in the prophetical books of the Bible, were spoken in the name of the LORD Himself as in v. 23, God speaking through His instrument. Since the Law of Moses ratified much that had been long in practice among the Israelites, some similar means must have been available even in these early days.

25:27 When the boys grew up, Esau became a skillful hunter, a man of the open country, while Jacob was a settled
28 man who stayed among the tents./ Isaac preferred Esau because he was fond of game, but Rebecca preferred
29 Jacob./ Once when Jacob was cooking some food, Esau
30 came in from the field famished./ Esau said to Jacob, "Let me have some of that red food, for I am famished." Hence
31 he was called Edom./ But Jacob replied, "Sell me first
32 your birthright."/ Esau said, "I am dying; of what use to
33 me is the birthright?"/ Jacob said, "Swear to me first." So
34 he swore to Jacob and sold him his birthright./ Then Jacob gave Esau some bread and lentils. He ate and drank and went his way. Thus lightly did Esau value his birthright.

We are not particularly happy at the way Jacob went about supplanting Esau, obtaining a legal title to his brother's first birthright. We cannot admire the mean advantage he took of Esau's hunger. But while the author does not minimize Jacob's fault, he saw the fault of Esau as much greater. "Thus lightly did Esau value his birthright" is a cry of shocked amazement.

From Nuzu documents we know that the sale of a first birthright was perfectly legal. But in Israelite eyes it was altogether incredible that a man would be so base as to make the sale. The first birthright had certain material advantages; when the inheritance was divided the eldest son had the right to a double portion

in the division. Over and above the material advantage was what
was considered far dearer. The firstborn son carried on the family
name; he was the head of the household. It was through the first-
born son that the promise given to Abraham was to descend.

Esau preferred his temporary need, his vulgar appetite of the
moment, to the gifts of God. "He ate and drank and went his way"
is the epitaph of Esau and of all men like him. It was providential
that Jacob, the quiet man, supplanted the feckless Esau.

26: 1 Now another famine occurred in the land, besides the
earlier famine of the days of Abraham. And Isaac went
   2 away to Gerara, to Abimelech, king of the Philistines./ The
LORD appeared to him and said, "Do not go down into
Egypt, but dwell in the land which I shall point out to you.
   3 Reside as a stranger in this land and I will be with you and
bless you; for I will give all these lands to you and your descendants. I will fulfill the oath which I swore to your
   4 father Abraham./ I will make your descendants as numerous as the stars of the heavens. I will give your descendants
all these lands, and in your descendants all the nations of
   5 the earth shall be blessed;/ for Abraham obeyed me and
heeded my charge [my commands, my ordinances and
my laws]."

Not Isaac but his son Jacob was to go down into Egypt. Isaac
was to remain among the "Philistines" a stranger as Abraham had
been, in expectation of the promise to be fulfilled in his descendants. The promise is repeated in almost the same words as it had
been given to Abraham.

26 :6.7 So Isaac dwelt in Gerara. When the men of the place
inquired about his wife, he said, "She is my sister" for
he feared to call her his wife lest the men of the place
should kill him on Rebecca's account, as she was
beautiful.
   8 When he had been there a long time, Abimelech king of
the Philistines happened to look out a window and saw
   9 Isaac fondling his wife Rebecca. Abimelech summoned
Isaac and said, "It is evident that she is your wife; why

did you say, 'She is my sister'?" Isaac replied, "Because I
10 feared that I should die on her account./ Abimelech
said, "Why did you do this to us? How easily someone
could have lain with your wife, and you would have
11 brought guilt upon us!"/ Then Abimelech warned all the
people, saying, "Whoever touches this man or his wife
shall be put to death."

There are some variations between this story and the very similar one in the life of Abraham in chapter 20. This time Abimelech
learns of Isaac's deception not through a divine manifestation but
by the evidence of his eyes, and he had not attempted to take
Rebecca into his harem. Again, therefore, it is not impossible that
we have here a separate fact recorded in tradition. However, the
situation is otherwise so much the same, and there are so many
other coincidences that follow in the two accounts, most commentators today regard the stories as originally one.

Besides the fact that the lesson of the story is, as always, God's
safeguarding of His servants, the author had an additional reason
for preserving this version of the tradition which had been associated with Isaac. This is the only chapter of Genesis in which Isaac
stands alone, not a part of the story of either Abraham or Jacob.

26:12 Isaac sowed a crop in that land, and harvested a hun-
13 dredfold the same year. The LORD blessed him;/ he became rich, and increased in riches until he was very weal-
14 thy./ He had flocks and herds and many beasts for plow-
15 ing. The Philistines became envious of him./ [They had
stopped up and filled with dirt all the wells which his
father's servants had dug in the days of his father Abra-
16 ham.]/ So Abimelech said to Isaac, "Depart from us, for
17 you have become much too strong for us."/ Isaac departed, camped in the valley of Gerara, and settled there.
18 [Isaac reopened the wells dug by the servants of his father Abraham which the Philistines had filled up after the
death of Abraham. He called them by the same names
19 which his father had given them.]/ Isaac's servants dug
20 in the valley and found a well of running water,/ but the

shepherds of Gerara disputed with Isaac's shepherds and said, "The water belongs to us." So he called the well
21 Esec[3] because they had wrangled with him./ They dug another well, but they quarreled over this also, so he
22 named it Sitna.[4]/ He moved from there and dug still another well over which they did not dispute. He called it Rohoboth[5] and said, "For now the LORD has made room for us; we shall prosper in the land."

This is the first explicit notice given to the patriarchs' having led an agricultural as well as a pastoral life. It fits in with what we can surmise from the previous accounts. The patriarchs were semi-nomads, ordinarily devoted to shepherding but occasional farmers depending on the circumstances.

The story introduces the narration that follows of a covenant made between Isaac and Abimelech, which we saw in chapter 21 as a covenant between Abraham and Abimelech. All the traditions in this chapter seem to have had parallels which made them now a part of Abraham's life and now a part of Isaac's. The story of the covenant in chapter 21 was introduced abruptly, without the account of the wells of Esec, Sitna, and Rohoboth. Nevertheless the tradition must have originally included these details, which the author omitted in compiling Genesis. That explains vv. 15, 18 above; they have been bracketed in the text by the translators because they are recognized as the obvious additions of some scribe who was sensitive to the fact that the same events were related of Abraham.

Who was leagued with Abimelech, Abraham or Isaac, is of course unimportant. These stories did not contribute a great deal to the religious purpose of Genesis, but they were all precious souvenirs of the early life of the Hebrew forefathers in the land of promise. The author probably omitted very little of his source material that could possibly be used despite minor inconsistencies.

26: 23.24 From there he went up to Bersabee. The LORD appeared to him that very night and said, "I am the God

[3] "Contention."
[4] "Hostility."
[5] "Wide places." Names similar to the last two are still preserved in the Negeb.

of your father Abraham; fear not, for I am with you. I
will bless you and multiply your descendants for the
25 sake of my servant Abraham."/ He built an altar there,
and invoked the name of the LORD. Isaac pitched his
26 tent there, and his servants dug a well./ Then Abimelech came to him from Gerara with Ochozath, his
27 friend, and Phichol, the general of his army./ Isaac
said to them, "Why do you come to me? You hate me
28 and have driven me away from you."/ They answered,
"We see clearly that the LORD is with you, so we say,
let there be a sworn agreement between you and us.
29 Let us make a covenant with you; you shall do us no
harm as we have not harmed you, but have done only
good to you and sent you away peacefully. You are in-
30 deed the blessed of the LORD."/ Isaac gave a feast
31 for them and they ate and drank./ Early the next morning they exchanged oaths. Isaac sent them away and
32 they departed from him in peace./ That same day the
servants of Isaac came and informed him of the well
they had dug. They said to him, "We have found wa-
33 ter."/ So he named it Siba. Therefore the name of the
city is Bersabee to this day.

After a brief reference to the renewal of the promise to Isaac
which we have seen already in a longer form from another tradition, the covenant with Abimelech is described almost exactly as
in chapter 21, a treaty of nonaggression, one of the two traditions
that had been combined in the Abraham story. Again the name of
Bersabee is attached to the taking of a covenant oath. The form
Siba, however, seems to be a recollection of the "seven" of the
other Abrahamite tradition of the ewe lambs given in token of
ownership of the well. Though there is nothing of that in this present text, the preceding section was all about contentions over
wells between Abimelech's and Isaac's men.

All these traditions and parts of traditions that remain in Genesis testify to the tenacious memory of the Israelites for remote
happenings that appear to us to have been relatively trivial. It
was important to them, however, to remember that the wells and

holy places of Palestine had been hallowed by the presence of their ancestors who had first received the promises which God had fulfilled in giving them the promised land.

> 26: 34 When Esau was forty years old he married Judith, daughter of Beeri the Hethite, and Basemath, daughter of Elon
> 35 the Hethite./ But they were a source of bitterness to Isaac and Rebecca.

These verses begin one of the two traditions which the author had at his disposal to explain why Jacob went back to the land of Abraham's birth. It is continued in parts of the next two chapters. According to this story, when Esau had married Hethite women of the country, contrary to the wishes of his parents, Rebecca expressed her displeasure to Isaac (27:46), whereupon Isaac charged his younger son to go to the land of their ancestors and there get himself a wife from his own relatives (28:1–5). The conclusion of this story was that Esau, now realizing how displeased his parents were at him, tried to make amends by choosing another wife, this time from the daughters of Ismael, Abraham's son (28:6–9).

That was one story. But the author had another, much more exciting. So, as we have seen him do before, he combined the two into one. In any case they did not exclude one another in substance.

The second story begins with 27:1 and presupposes different conditions. According to this version Isaac was near death when Jacob left Chanaan, and Jacob departed at Rebecca's urging in order to avoid the vengeance of Esau (27:41–45).

It is not necessary that we delve into these stories to pin down the bare historical occurrences on which they depended; the author himself was not interested in doing so. It is not likely, for example, that Jacob would have taken no wife before Isaac was dying of old age, not among a people whose tradition it is to marry young. The tradition, therefore, had doubtless simplified matters in joining Jacob's departure with Isaac's deathbed blessings of his sons. In such purely factual data Genesis was not interested. The stories were true in their essentials, they contained valuable memories of the past, and both of them were preserved.

27:1 When Isaac was old and his eyesight had failed, he called
2 his elder son Esau, and said to him, "Son!"/ He replied
"Here I am!" He said, "You see I have grown old; I do not
3 know when I may die./ Take your weapons, quiver and
4 bow; go out into the fields to hunt me some game./ Prepare for me some savory food such as I like; bring it to me
5 to eat, so that I may bless you before I die."/ Rebecca listened while Isaac was talking to his son Esau. When Esau
had gone out into the field to hunt some game for his fa-
6 ther,/ Rebecca said to her son Jacob, "I heard your father
7 tell your brother Esau,/ 'Bring me some game; prepare
some savory food for me to eat, and then I will bless you
8 in the sight of the LORD before I die.'/ Now my son, do
9 what I tell you./ Go to the flock and bring me two choice
kids that I may make of them savory food for your father,
10 such as he likes./ Then bring it to your father to eat, that
11 he may bless you before he dies."/ Jacob said to his mother
Rebecca, "But Esau my brother is a hairy man, while I am
12 smooth./ If my father touches me, it will seem to him that
I am mocking him. Thus I shall bring a curse on myself in-
13 stead of a blessing." His mother replied,/ "Let the curse
fall on me, my son! Do but listen to me; go, get them for
me."
14 He went, selected them, and brought them to his mother,
15 who prepared savory food such as his father liked. Then
Rebecca took the best clothes of her elder son Esau, which
she had in the house, and put them on her younger son Ja-
16 cob. She put the skins of the kids on his hands and over
17 the smooth parts of his neck. Then she gave her son Jacob
18 the savory food and bread she had prepared. He went to
his father and said, "Father!" He answered, "Here I am.
19 Who are you, my son?"/ And Jacob said to his father, "I
am Esau, your first-born. I have done as you told me;
sit up, please! Eat again of my game, that you may bless
20 me."/ Isaac replied, "How did you find it so quickly, my
son?" He answered, "The LORD your God let me come
21 upon it."/ Then Isaac said to Jacob, "Come close that I may
touch you, my son, to know whether you are really my son

22 Esau or not."/ Jacob went close to his father; Isaac touched
　　him and said, "The voice is the voice of Jacob, but the
23 hands are the hands of Esau."/ He did not recognize him
　　because his hands were hairy like those of his brother Esau
　　[so he blessed him].

This story does little credit to either Rebecca or Jacob. Rebecca
is the possessive, unscrupulous mother who will stop at nothing
to advance the future of her beloved son. Jacob might allege that
he had purchased the right of the firstborn, but this could never
excuse his duplicity and deceit. Jacob was as yet far from the
strength of character he would later manifest in keeping with his
dignity as upholder of the promise given to Abraham.

27:24 Isaac said, "Are you really my son Esau?" Jacob an-
　　25 swered, "Yes, I am."/ Isaac continued, "Set your game
　　　near me my son, that I may eat it, and bless you." He set
　　　it before him and he ate of it, and he brought him some
　　26 wine, which he drank./ Then his father Isaac said to him,
　　　"Come close and kiss me, my son." He came close and
　　27 kissed him./ When he smelled the fragrance of his gar-
　　　ments, he blessed him and said:
　　　　"The fragrance of my son
　　　　　is like the fragrance of a field which the
　　　　　LORD has blessed!
　　28 "God give you dew from heaven,
　　　　　and fruitfulness of the earth,
　　　　　abundance of grain and wine.
　　29 "Let nations serve you,
　　　　　peoples bow down to you.
　　　　Be master of your brothers;
　　　　　may your mother's sons bow down to you.
　　　　Cursed be those who curse you,
　　　　　blessed be those who bless you."

This old poetic blessing of Israel extols its destiny to dominate
its neighbor peoples, including Edom. It is interesting to see the
attitude taken by all—by Isaac, Jacob, Esau, and the author of
Genesis—regarding the efficacy and the irrevocable nature of this
blessing. Esau, we note below, did not ask Isaac to take back Ja-

cob's blessing. A blessing once given could not be withdrawn, even if it had been given mistakenly. Esau begged for another blessing for himself.

The primitive mind attached great significance to a father's blessing or curse. Once Jacob had been blessed, he had been blessed for all time. He was now fully recognized as Isaac's heir. For Esau would remain only the sombre words we see in v. 39 f., a description of the wild, semibarbarous Edomites who were his off-spring.

27:30 Isaac had pronounced the blessing and Jacob had just left his father's presence, when his brother Esau re-
31 turned from hunting./ He also prepared savory food and brought it to his father, saying, "Sit up, father, and eat of
32 your son's game, that you may bless me."/ His father Isaac said to him, "Who are you?" He answered, "I am
33 Esau, your first-born son."/ Isaac was greatly disturbed, and asked, "Who was it, then, that hunted game and brought it to me? Before you came I ate heartily and then
34 blessed him; and he shall be blessed."/ On hearing his father's words, Esau uttered a very loud and bitter cry,
35 and said to him, "Father, bless me too."/ But he answered, "Your brother came deceitfully and received your bless-
36 ing."/ Then he said, "Must he, true to his name Jacob, supplant me now a second time? He took my birthright and now he has taken my blessing." He added, "Have you
37 not reserved a blessing for me?"/ Isaac answered Esau, "I have appointed him your lord, and have given him all his brothers as servants. I have enriched him with grain
38 and wine; what then can I do for you, my son?"/ But Esau said to his father, "Have you only one blessing, father? Bless me also, my father." And Esau wept aloud.
39 His Father Isaac answered him:
    "Without the fruitfulness of the earth
shall your dwelling be;
    without the dew of the heavens above.
40 By your sword shall you live;
    you shall serve your brother.

>   But when you become restive,
>   you shall shake his yoke from your neck."

The author appears to be sympathetic to Esau throughout this story. He had only contempt for one who would sell his first birthright, but Esau has been unwillingly deprived of his father's blessing. There is something pathetic in the picture of this crude, somewhat stupid man, forestalled by minds more cunning than his. While we can but rejoice that Jacob did become Isaac's heir, nothing can excuse the means he took.

Esau must look forward to the lot for which nature had endowed him, now confirmed by his father's prayer. Israel's dominance over Edom was at times disputed, at times repudiated; but in the end, it was forever.

27:41 Esau bore Jacob a grudge because of the blessing his father had given him. He said to himself, "The time of mourning for my father is coming; then I will kill my
42 brother Jacob."/ Rebecca was told of these words of her elder son, Esau. She summoned her younger son, Jacob, and said to him, "Your brother Esau intends to revenge
43 himself on you by killing you./ Listen to me therefore,
44 my son; flee to my brother Laban in Haran./ Stay with him awhile until your brother's fury subsides [until your
45 brother's wrath against you relents],/ and he forgets what you have done to him. Then I will send for you and bring you back. Why should I be bereaved of you both on the same day?"
46 Rebecca said to Isaac, "I am disgusted with life because of the Hethite women; if Jacob should marry a Hethite woman like these, a native of the land, what would life mean to me?"
28:1 Isaac therefore called Jacob and having blessed him,
2 charged him, "Do not marry any Chanaanite woman;/ go then to Phaddan-Aram, the home of Bathuel, your mother's father, and there choose your wife from the daughters
3 of your uncle Laban./ May God Almighty bless you, and make you fruitful; may he multiply you so that you may
4 become many nations./ May he bestow on you, and your

descendants also, the blessing of Abraham that you may
inherit this land in which you are immigrants, which God
5 gave to Abraham."/ Isaac sent forth Jacob, who went to
Phaddan-Aram to Laban, the son of the Aramean Bathuel, the brother of Rebecca, mother of Jacob and Esau.
6 Esau learned that Isaac had blessed Jacob and sent him
away to Phaddan-Aram to marry there, and while blessing him had charged him not to marry a Chanaanite wom-
7 an,/ and that Jacob had departed for Phaddan-Aram in
8 obedience to his father and mother./ Since he realized
his father Isaac's displeasure with Chanaanite women,
9 Esau went to Ismael,/ and in addition to the wives he
had, married Maheleth, daughter of Abraham's son Ismael and sister of Nabaioth.

The mingling of the two traditions which we previously pointed
out explains what would otherwise be rather strange anomalies
in this story. Isaac would suddenly and unaccountably have re-
gained his health; he would just as suddenly and unaccountably
have forgotten entirely the deceitful game his son had played
against him: indeed, repeating with good will the blessing that
had been obtained with such guile; and so on.

Whether the tradition that sent Jacob to Phaddan-Aram because of Rebecca's disgust with Esau's Chanaanite wives also included the story of Jacob's theft of the first birthright, and if so,
where it fitted it into the chronology of Jacob's life, we do not
know. Perhaps it had not kept this idea but rather had understood that Isaac had transferred the privilege to Jacob because of
Esau's Chanaanite connections. Both agreed, at any rate, that Jacob had received the promise given to Abraham, and that through
his descendants it would be fulfilled.

28:10 Meanwhile, Jacob left Bersabee and journeyed toward
11 Haran./ He came to a place where he spent the night because the sun had set. He took one of the stones of the
12 place, put it under his head, and went to sleep there./ He
dreamed that a ladder was set up on the ground with its
top reaching to heaven; angels of God were ascending
13 and descending on it./ The LORD stood beside him and

said, "I am the LORD, the God of Abraham your father, and the God of Isaac. I will give you and your descend-
14 ants the land on which you lie./ They shall be as the dust of the earth. You shall spread abroad to the west, to the east, to the north, and to the south; in you and in your descendants, all the nations of the earth shall be blessed.
15 I will be with you and protect you wherever you go. I will bring you back to this land; indeed I will not forsake you till I fulfill my promise."
16 When Jacob woke from his sleep he said, "Truly the
17 LORD is in this place and I did not know it."/ Reverently he continued, "How awesome is this place! This is none other than the house of God; this is the gate of heaven."
18 Jacob arose in the morning, took the stone which he had placed under his head, set it up as a memorial pillar and
19 poured oil over it./ He called the place Bethel; formerly
20 the name of the city was Luza./ Jacob also made a vow: "If the LORD is with me and protects me on my present journey, and gives me food to eat and clothing to wear,
21 and a safe return to my father's house, the LORD shall be
22 my God;/ and this stone which I have set up as a memorial pillar shall be the house of God. I will offer faithfully a tenth part of everything you give me."

For whatever reason, Jacob left Chanaan and journeyed toward the ancestral home in Haran. Before the author takes us with Jacob to Phaddan-Aram, however, he pauses to tell a story about Jacob and Bethel which was important for both.

We have seen time and time again that Genesis is preoccupied with the identification of various sacred places in Palestine with one or another of the patriarchs. Abraham builds an altar to the LORD at Sichem (12:7), and another near Bethel (12:8). Again by the terebinths of Mamre near Hebron (13:18), at Bersabee where he planted a tamarisk tree (21:33), Abraham hallows these places to the worship of the LORD. Isaac builds an altar also at Bersabee to the LORD (26:25). Jacob in the present story erects a memorial pillar at Bethel; later he will build there an altar, and frequently throughout the rest of Genesis we shall see similar stories identifying other sites with the worship of the patriarchs.

All these stories come from one series of traditions, whose purpose was to underline the antiquity of Israelite religion. It is the same series which consistently puts the name of the LORD (Jahweh) on the lips of the patriarchs, though other parts of the Pentateuch make it plain that the God of the Israelites was not known by this name until Moses' time. In a sense, this could be called an anachronism, but only in a sense. What the traditions are insisting on is a fact absolutely true in itself, that by whatever name He was called, the God of Abraham, Isaac, and Jacob was the LORD worshipped by their descendants.

Chanaanite Altars of Undressed and Dressed Stone

Sichem, Bethel, Bersabee were important Israelite shrines in the time when the traditions of Genesis were being developed. The Israelites knew that these had once been Chanaanite sanctuaries, dedicated to one or another of the myriad Chanaanite deities. The very altars on which sacrifice was now offered to the LORD had replaced or had been converted from the simple Chanaanite structures that had once dotted the land. (See above illustration of typical Chanaanite altars.) The same process has taken place everywhere when a change of religion has occurred. The name of Santa Maria sopra Minerva in the Eternal City testifies to the identity of this spot before it became a church dedicated to the Mother of God. Beneath the legendary three hundred odd churches raised by Cortés in Cholula were an equal number of temples laid by the Toltecs in their holy city.

Genesis tells us as much. "Abram passed through the land to the sacred place at Sichem," we were told previously. Here it is written that Jacob "came to *a place*," an emphatic term in Hebrew which makes it clear that the place was no ordinary one. It too was a pagan shrine.

The traditions of Genesis have therefore insisted that, just as the God of the patriarchs was the same LORD of their Israelite descendants, there was likewise a patriarchal origin to the sacred places and sacrificial worship of the Israelites in Chanaan despite the fact that the shrines had lately been wrested from the Chanaanites. The instinct of history here is a true one: there was such a connection, though there was probably no way of showing, after so many hundreds of years, in precisely what places the patriarchs had offered sacrifice. Consequently the traditions were content to find the beginnings of the worship of the LORD at the major shrines of Palestine, the ones with which they were most familiar. All Palestine, for that matter, was a holy land that had been sanctified to the LORD by their ancestors while it was still owned by the Chanaanite deities and their devotees.

Hence the *massebah*, the anointed stone or memorial pillar which existed at Bethel in Israelite times, is attributed to Jacob, together with the offering of tithes at the shrine, which was to be made a part of the Mosaic Law. The name Bethel, "house of God," is associated with Jacob's vision. Originally this name itself seems to have been that of a deity, to whom the shrine was evidently sacred in Chanaanite times. The Luza of v. 19 was actually at one time a separate site nearby (cf. Jos. *16*:2), but when Genesis was written the two had been combined.

The outward forms of the sacrifice of the patriarchs and of the later Israelites, their altars, shrines, and rituals, probably differed very little from those of the Chanaanites, however different may have been their spirit. They were certainly similar enough to make it necessary for the prophets to insist repeatedly that they must not be confused one with the other, that the Israelites could not and must not cheapen the conception of their God by assimilating Him and His worship to those of the Chanaanites. Gradually, chiefly under prophetic influence, the outward forms themselves were altered to make the distinction more apparent. The *masseboth* were later forbidden, and Israelite altars were constructed after a different design. Finally the multiplicity of sanctuaries was done away with, under a tendency that had been present from the first days of the Israelite conquest, and the sacrificial worship of the LORD was confined to the holy city Jerusalem.

This story we have just read is no less important in the life of Jacob. The revelation he received from God, the vision of the ladder to heaven, signified God's nearness to him and the meeting that is possible between God and man. Our Lord applied to Himself the perfect fulfilment of the Old Testament figure in an unquestioned allusion to this passage (see John 1:51). This spiritual awakening of Jacob is connected with the promise given to Abraham and Isaac, which he now received. Henceforth Jacob will have a keener awareness of his relation to God, with whom he is now covenanted as Abraham and Isaac were. Not for some time will he be the ideal of God's humble servant, but there will be in him considerably less of the young man too shrewd for his own good.

What was the "ladder" that Jacob saw? The word so translated appears only in this place in the Bible, and we are not too sure of its exact meaning. Father H. Junker in his commentary on Genesis[6] suggests that the shrine of Bethel was built after the fashion of the Mesopotamian *ziggurat* (see page 107), a stepped structure which actually did symbolize an ascent into heaven (as in the story of the tower of Babel). This would have furnished the occasion of Jacob's dream, after which he recognized God's presence there though he had acknowledged no sanctity to the pagan shrine as such. Others have pointed out that the terrain about Bethel is more or less naturally terraced, and that with a little imagination the countryside itself takes on the appearance of a rocky stairway.

[6] *Genesis* (Würzburg: Echter-Verlag, 1952), p. 85.

CHAPTER XI: RACHEL THE BELOVED

29: 1 Then Jacob continued his journey and came to the land of
2 the people of the East. Looking about he saw a well in
the open country, and three flocks of sheep lying nearby,
for the flocks were watered from this well. But the stone
3 over the mouth of the well was large. After all the shepherds were gathered there, the stone was rolled back from
the mouth of the well and the flocks were watered. Then
the stone was replaced over the mouth of the well.

4 Jacob said to them, "My brothers, where are you from?"
5 And they answered, "We are from Haran."/ Then he in-
6 quired, "Do you know Laban the son of Nahor?"/ And
they said, "We do." He asked further, "Is he well?" They
replied, "He is, and here comes his daughter Rachel with
7 his flock."/ Then he said, "Much of the day is left; it is not
yet time for the stock to be gathered; water the flock and
8 lead them back to pasture."/ But they answered, "We cannot, until all the shepherds have assembled; then they remove the stone from the mouth of the well and we water
the flock."

9 While he was still talking with them, Rachel arrived with
her father's flock; for it was her custom to tend them.
10 When Jacob saw Rachel, the daughter of his uncle Laban,
with the flock, he drew near, rolled the stone from the
11 mouth of the well, and watered his uncle's flock./ Then
Jacob kissed Rachel and wept aloud.

12 Jacob told Rachel that he was her father's relative, a son of
13 Rebecca, and she hastened to tell her father./ When La-

ban heard about Jacob, his nephew, he hastened to meet
him, received him with embraces and kisses, and brought
14 him to his dwelling./ Jacob told Laban all these things,
and Laban said to him, "You are indeed my flesh and
bone." And Jacob stayed with him a whole month.

Jacob meets Rachel under circumstances slightly similar to
those of the meeting of Rebecca and Abraham's servant. The little
glimpse of shepherd life that precedes the story of the meeting
is a token how much at home this tradition was with the ordinary
facts of life. Community arrangements of this kind in the possession of a well in water-conscious Aram Naharaim must have been
rather common. It is remarkable that besides their shrines devoted
to the service of the LORD, the Israelites were most anxious to
remember the patriarchs in connection with wells, as at Bersabee. How cherished these recollections were, and how enduring,
we learn from the conversation of our Lord with the Samaritan
woman in John 4:12. It is possible that our story in Genesis has
been abbreviated, and that originally some point was made of
the fact that the manly Jacob could remove a stone which ordinarily required the concerted efforts of several men.

Thus Jacob entered the house of Laban, and thus begins the
story of Jacob and Rachel, the only love-story in Genesis in the
modern sense of the term.

29: 15 Then Laban said to Jacob, "Should you serve me for nothing because you are a relative of mine? Tell me what
your wages shall be."
16 Laban had two daughters. The elder was called Lia, and
17 the younger Rachel./ Lia's eyes were weak, but Rachel
18 was shapely and beautiful./ Jacob loved Rachel. He said,
therefore, "I will serve you seven years for your younger
19 daughter Rachel."/ Laban answered, "It is better to give
20 her to you than to another man; stay with me."/ So Jacob
served seven years for Rachel, and they seemed to him
but a few days because of his love for her.

Once again our knowledge of ancient Mesopotamian customs
has come to shed light on the biblical account. A Nuzu wedding

contract discovered rather recently has some striking parallels with the story in Genesis. If we were to substitute biblical names for those in the contract, it would come out like this:

Tablet of adoption whereby Laban, the son of Nahor, has adopted Jacob, the son of Isaac. As long as Laban lives Jacob will assure him food and clothing. When Laban dies, Jacob will be his heir. If Laban fathers a son, the latter will divide his inheritance equally with Jacob, but it is the son of Laban who will take Laban's gods. Further, Laban has given his daughter Rachel as the wife of Jacob. If Jacob takes another wife, he loses all right to Laban's goods, land, and buildings.

Apparently Laban "adopted" Jacob according to some such agreement as this. This would explain the episode of the household gods which we shall see in chapter *31*, as it will also explain Laban's subsequent insistence that Jacob is free to marry none other than his daughters. It explains, too, the resentment which Laban's sons will manifest against Jacob, with whom they would have to share their inheritance. These sons are not mentioned at present and in all likelihood were not yet born when Jacob first entered Laban's house. Other aspects of the Jacob-Laban relation become clear against the background of an adoption-marriage contract.

29: 21 Then Jacob said to Laban, / "Give me my wife; for the time has come for me to go in to her."

22 Laban gathered all the men of the place and gave a feast.

23 That night he brought Lia, his daughter, to Jacob, who
24 had relations with her./ Laban gave his servant Zelpha
25 to his daughter Lia to be her maid./ In the morning, to Jacob's amazement, it was Lia. Then he said to Laban, "What have you done to me? Did I not serve you for
26 Rachel? Why then have you cheated me?"/ Laban replied, "It is not the custom in our country to give the
27 younger daughter before the first-born;/ complete the week of this one's nuptials and I will give you the other in return for another seven years of service with me."

28 Jacob did so; he completed her week. Then Laban gave
29 him his daughter Rachel in marriage./ Laban gave his
30 servant Bala to his daughter Rachel to be her maid./ So

Jacob went in to Rachel also; he loved her more than Lia,
and served Laban another seven years.

Laban's deceit in tricking Jacob into marrying Lia as well as
Rachel was, of course, not in the contract. There is an irony in this
story not lost on the author of Genesis, that Jacob who had deluded his father should himself be deluded in almost the same
fashion. That the deception was possible supposes the customs
of the Near East rather than our own. As we saw before (24:65),
a bride was always veiled from her husband's sight until they
had begun to live together.

If we cannot applaud Laban's ethics, we can at least understand that he was being a better father than father-in-law.
Women like Rachel, for whom a man will labor seven years as
though they were a day, can make their own way in life, for the
world is at their feet. Their less favored sisters like Lia sometimes
need circumstances to be bent in their direction. It was not Lia's
fault that she had "weak" eyes, that is, that unlike Rachel she did
not possess the dark eyes which the modern Arab still sets up
as the highest criterion of feminine beauty: "eyes like a gazelle's."

Lia's life, we shall see, probably was not a very happy one.
Laban contrived for her probably her happiest days in the week
when she was Jacob's only wife. And Jacob, after all, though he
was bound over to another period of service, did receive Rachel,
the wife for whom he had labored.

29: 31 When the LORD saw that Lia was disliked, he made her
  32 fruitful, while Rachel remained barren. Lia conceived
   and bore a son, naming him Ruben. "For," she said, "the
   LORD has had regard for my misery;[1] now my husband
  33 will love me."/ Again she conceived and bore a son saying, "The LORD has heard[2] that I am disliked; therefore
   he has given me this one also." She named him Simeon.
  34 She conceived again and bore a son, saying, "This time
   my husband will become attached to me,[3] for I have
   borne him three sons." Therefore she named him Levi.

[1] *Reu ben,* "behold, a son."
[2] *Sema adonai,* "the LORD has heard."
[3] *Yilave,* "he will become attached."

35 Once more she conceived and bore a son, saying, "Now I will praise the LORD."[4] Therefore she named him Juda. Then she ceased bearing.

30: 1 When Rachel saw that she was not bearing children to Jacob, she became jealous of her sister and said to Jacob,

2 "Give me children or I shall die."/ Jacob became impatient with Rachel and answered her, "Can I take the place of

3 God, who has made you barren?"/ She replied, "Here is my slave-girl, Bala; go in to her that she may bear on my knees,

4 and I too may have children by her."/ She gave him Bala, her maid, in marriage, and Jacob had relations with her.

5.6 Bala conceived and bore Jacob a son./ Then Rachel said, "God has pronounced judgment in my favor,[5] for he has heard my prayer and given me a son." Therefore she

7 named him Dan./ Bala, Rachel's maid, conceived again

8 and bore a second son to Jacob. Then Rachel said,/ "I have used a clever device against my sister,[6] and I have indeed prevailed." So she called him Nephthali.

9 When Lia knew that she had ceased bearing, she gave

10 Zelpha her maid to Jacob in marriage./ Zelpha, Lia's maid,

11 bore Jacob a son./ Lia said, "What good fortune!"[7] And

12 she named him Gad./ Lia's maid Zelpha bore Jacob an-

13 other son./ And Lia said, "What happiness![8] Women will call me happy." So she named him Aser.

14 During the wheat harvest, Ruben went into the field, found some mandrakes, and brought them to his mother Lia. Rachel said to Lia, "Give me some of your son's man-

15 drakes."/ She answered her, "Is it a trivial matter to have taken my husband? Will you also take my son's man-drakes?" Rachel said, "Very well! In exchange for your

16 son's mandrakes, Jacob shall lie with you tonight."/ As Jacob was returning from the field in the evening, Lia went to meet him and said, "You are to come to me; for I have bargained for you with my son's mandrakes." So he slept

---

[4] *Odeh,* "I will praise."

[5] *Danani,* "he has pronounced judgment in my favor."

[6] Literally, *naphthule Elohim niphthalti,* "I have used the ruses of God."

[7] *Gad,* "good fortune."

[8] *Aser,* "happiness."

17 with her that night./ God heard Lia's prayer, and she con-
18 ceived and bore Jacob a fifth son./ Then she said, "God has
    rewarded me[9] because I gave my maid to my husband."
19 She called him Issachar. Lia conceived again and bore a
20 sixth son to Jacob. /She said, "God has made me an excel-
    lent gift. Now my husband will honor me;[10] for I have
    borne him six sons." Therefore she named him Zabulon.
21 Afterward she bore a daughter whom she named Dina.
22 But God remembered Rachel; he heard her prayer and
23 made her fruitful./ She conceived and bore a son, and she
24 said, "God has taken away my reproach."/ She named
    him Joseph, saying, "May the LORD give me another
    son."[11]

The author of Genesis, who probably felt rather as we do on
the subject of monogamy, must have viewed with some distaste
the chronicle of the inner-family jealousies and strifes that we find
in this description of a Semitic household where polygamy was the
rule.

Lia, for whom it is not hard to feel sympathy, was the less favored wife, for Rachel was the light of Jacob's life. It was only right,
the author felt, that Lia therefore should have experienced the
joys of motherhood rather than Rachel; this was the LORD's compensation to her. The world in which we live has not entirely
lost its sense of proportion: there are still those among us who look
on children as a divine blessing rather than a burden. Yet it is
hard for us to comprehend what a price was set on parenthood
by the ancient Semites. To be a parent was the entire purpose of
living, and to die without children was indeed a curse. Through
one's children a man's or a woman's memory remained in the world,
among one's people. The Hebrews of this period had precious
little revelation concerning the life after death. They knew that it
existed, but they knew little more than that. It was inevitable that
the sum of their aspirations should be centred in their life in the
world, and parenthood was the fulfilment of this life.

From the sons of Jacob, who was later called Israel, the Isra-

[9] *Sechari,* "my reward."
[10] *Yizebeleni,* "he will honor me."
[11] *Joseph,* "may he add."

elite tribes derived their names and origin. For this reason the author has carefully noted each separate birth in this story, and in each case occurs another of those word-plays by which the tellers of these tales had impressed the details of their stories on the memories of their listeners. Only Dina, Jacob's one daughter, goes almost unnoticed, for no tribe took its name from her.

In *30*:1 ff. we see that Rachel adopted the expedient followed years before by Sara when she was without children by Abraham (*16*:1 ff.). Rachel gives her maid to Jacob, "that she may bear on my knees, and I too may have children by her." This expression originally at least doubtless referred to a literal practice, but it came to be an idiom signifying adoption. As Laban had given this maid to Rachel for this very purpose, and as Bala's children were legally Rachel's, there was no violation of what we have presumed to have been Jacob's agreement not to marry outside Laban's family. The children born to Bala, we note, are named by Rachel: naming the child was the parent's prerogative. Lia also followed the same procedure as Rachel.

The episode of the mandrakes in *30*:14 ff. possibly once introduced an account of Joseph's birth, assisted by this means. If so, the author did not pursue the idea in writing Genesis. Belief in such aids to conception was widespread in ancient times, and in fact still prevails. But Genesis quite properly attributes Joseph's birth to the blessing of God.

30: 25 When Rachel had given birth to Joseph, Jacob said to Laban, "Let me return to my own home and country.
26 Give me my wives for whom I served you, and my children; let me depart. You know well the service I have
27 given you."/ Laban said to him, "If you please, I surmise
28 that God blessed me because of you./ Name your wages
29 and I will pay."/ He answered, "But you know well how I have served you, how your stock fared under my care.
30 Before I came you had little indeed, but now it has greatly increased. The LORD blessed you at my every step. And now, when shall I provide for my own household?"
31 He asked, "What shall I give you?" But Jacob answered, "Give me nothing at all, if you agree to this proposal: I

32 shall again pasture and tend your flock,/ but today go
through your entire flock and separate every speckled and
spotted goat, and all black lambs; then every goat that is
spotted or speckled and every black lamb shall be my

33 wages./ In the future, when the time comes, I will stand
self-condemned before you in the matter of my wages.
Every goat that is not speckled or spotted, and every lamb

34 that is not black, shall be considered stolen."/ Laban said,
"Let it be as you say."

35 That day Laban separated the striped and spotted he-
goats, and all the speckled or spotted she-goats, every
one with white on it, and all the lambs that were black,

36 and he gave them into the care of his sons./ He put a
distance of three days' journey between himself and

37 Jacob, who had charge of the rest of Laban's flock./ Jacob
took green boughs of poplar, almond and plane and by
laying bare the white in the boughs, he peeled white

38 stripes in them./ Then he set the boughs he had peeled in
front of the flock in the watering troughs where they came
to be watered. And they mated when they came to be wa-

39 tered./ Since they mated in front of the boughs, they
brought forth young lambs that were striped, speckled

40 and spotted./ Jacob set these lambs apart, and the young
animals were all speckled or black in a white flock. Thus
he formed droves of his own which he did not join to

41 Laban's flock./ Whenever the hardier sheep were breeding, Jacob placed the boughs in the troughs in front of the

42 sheep so that they might mate in front of the boughs,/ but
not so in the case of the weaker ones. The weaker ones

43 fell to Laban and the stronger to Jacob./ Thus the man
became exceedingly rich and had large flocks, male and
female servants, camels and asses.

Another old belief ingrained in shepherd folk is reflected in
this story. Jacob, as is evident, had by now grown restive in Laban's house and was anxious to terminate the contract by which
he was bound to his shrewd relative. By this time the sons which
Laban had never hoped to have had been born, so that there was

no longer reason for Jacob to remain as provider for Laban's old age. Jacob no longer had the prospect of being Laban's sole heir, by the same token.

Laban was desirous of keeping Jacob's valuable services, but he recognized, or pretended to recognize, Jacob's legitimate desire to build up his own household. Without doing away with the ties that bound Jacob to Phaddan-Aram, therefore, Laban was prepared to agree to a means whereby Jacob could acquire wealth of his own. To the canny Aramean, the strange proposal which Jacob made to him must have seemed heaven-sent and entirely to his advantage. Speckled and spotted kids, and black lambs, were and still are exceptional animals in Syrian flocks. Laban thought that they would be very few.

Just to be sure that they would be few, he removed to a safe distance the males and females that would normally produce such offspring. Laban was nothing if not a practical business man. But he reckoned against someone cannier, who had been tricked once and was not to be tricked again. It is intriguing to watch the counterplay of these two experts in sharp practice; though, to be sure, the story has more of the David Harum about it than anything that would have been counted really dishonest.

The expedient which Jacob is said to have adopted to build up the flock to his advantage contradicts, it is claimed, the Mendelian laws. The author of Genesis, who did not know the Mendelian laws, had no desire to contradict them. He has simply transmitted this traditional account which certainly in his time contained nothing that was deemed implausible. Eminent Greek men of science as well as simple Hebrew shepherds were willing to testify that Jacob's methods were valid, as indeed some breeders of sheep still are, Mendel or no Mendel. Luckily we do not have to decide the science of the matter. The author of Genesis was hardly interested in the principles of genetics or chromosomes. He reported a popular tradition for what it was worth. It is sufficient for us to know that, by whatever cause, Jacob became a wealthy man during his sojourn with Laban. He was to return to Chanaan with wives, a large family, and many possessions. What is more important, as develops later, he was to return spiritually as well as materially enriched.

31:1 Jacob learned that Laban's sons were saying, "Jacob has
    taken all our father had, and he has acquired all these
  2 riches from what belonged to our father." Jacob perceived,
    too, that Laban's attitude toward him was not what it had
  3 previously been. The LORD said to Jacob, "Return to the
    land of your fathers and to your own kin; I will be with
  4 you." Jacob sent for Rachel and Lia, calling them to his
  5 flock in the field, / and said to them, "I see that your fa-
    ther's attitude toward me is not what it was previously;
    but the God of my father has been with me.
  6 "You yourselves know that I have served your father with
  7 all my strength,/ yet your father cheated me and changed
    my pay time after time; but God did not allow him to harm
  8 me./ Whenever he said, 'The spotted animals will be your
    pay,' the entire flock had spotted young; but whenever he
    said, 'The striped ones will be your wages,' then the entire
  9 flock had striped young./ So God took away your fa-
 10 ther's stock and gave it to me./ At breeding time of the
    flock, I saw in a dream that the he-goats mating were
 11 striped, spotted and speckled./ An angel of God said to
    me in the dream, 'Jacob!' and I answered, 'Here I am!'
 12 Then he said, 'Look and take note: all the he-goats mating
    are striped, spotted and speckled; I have seen all that
 13 Laban has been doing to you./ I am the God who ap-
    peared to you at Bethel, where you anointed the memorial
    pillar and made a vow to me. Rise now, leave this land,
    and return to the land of your kin.' "

The relations between Jacob and Laban had now gone from
bad to worse, a situation doubtless aggravated by Laban's sons'
resentment at Jacob's right to share their inheritance. Jacob's res-
olution taken with God's counsel to return to Chanaan was simply
facing the fact that a serene life was no longer possible at Haran.

Jacob offers a rather involved justification of his conduct to his
wives. Like any other man, of course, Jacob wanted to be thought
in the right. But his story differs from the details of his agreement
with Laban which we read in the preceding chapter. Here we
read that the policy of recompensing Jacob from the flock had

been Laban's idea, not Jacob's, and that there had been repeated
arrangements of the kind. There is no mention at all of the way
Jacob had himself taken a hand in the affair. We can see that
the author is now using a different tradition from the former. Both
stories agreed that Jacob had profited at Laban's expense, but
they differed as to how.

> *31:* 14 Rachel and Lia answered him, "Have we any share or
> 15 heritage left in our father's house?/ Are we not regarded
>   as strangers by him? For he has sold us, and entirely used
> 16 up the money he received through us./ Surely all the
>   property God has taken away from our father belongs to
>   us and our children. Do whatever God has told you."

Men rationalize their actions, not wives and mothers. Jacob's
self-justification was somewhat wasted on Rachel and Lia, who
were quite prepared to depart. "He has sold us," they say of their
father. These words were not intended to be as bitter as they
may sound to us. The *mohar* or marriage-price which Jacob had
equivalently paid for his wives by his service to Laban did in
ancient times actually amount to the purchase of a bride. However, while children were expected to conform to the wishes of
their parents, parental love usually guaranteed that a marriage
would be mutually acceptable, as was the case here. Rachel and
Lia's argument is a simple one: What is, is true. Their inheritance
was now with Jacob, no longer with their father. Jacob had been
enriched; that was good. Their destiny and first duty lay with
their husband.

So for the last time Jacob outwits Laban, departing stealthily
with his wives and goods while his father-in-law was away from
home. Once he had crossed the Euphrates he would be outside
Phaddan-Aram and en route to Chanaan through the Transjordan
region of Galaad.

> *31:* 17 Jacob began by mounting his children and wives on
> 18 camels./ Then he took away all his herds, all the property
>   he had acquired [the stock he had obtained] in Phaddan-
>   Aram, to go to his father Isaac in the land of Chanaan.
> 19 When Laban had gone to shear his flock, Rachel stole her

20 father's household idols;/ and Jacob outwitted Laban the
   Aramean by not mentioning to him his intended flight,
21 and fled with all that belonged to him./ Jacob set out,
   crossed the River and made for the highlands of Galaad.
22 On the third day, Laban was informed of Jacob's flight.
23 Taking his kinsmen with him, he pursued Jacob seven
24 days and overtook him in the highlands of Galaad./ But
   God came to Laban the Aramean in a dream at night and
   cautioned him, "Take care not to say anything at all to
   Jacob."

Why was this stealth necessary, and why did Laban feel compelled to pursue Jacob? Why was Jacob not free to do as he chose?

It is possible that Jacob merely feared that Laban would try to keep by force the one whose service he had found profitable. Yet of late the relations between the two men seemed to have become as distasteful to Laban as to Jacob. We have reason to believe that Jacob was technically in the wrong and that Laban followed him with just cause. Laban's profession below that he would have been willing to allow Jacob to depart may have been untrue, yet when he added that Jacob's family and properties really belonged to him, Laban, he was not contradicted by his son-in-law, who was not one to suffer injustice in silence. Apparently, then, the contract between Jacob and Laban was still in effect. Jacob was under law Laban's adopted son, and his wives and possessions did not become his property until Laban's death. This gives point to what Jacob goes on to say, that he was afraid Laban would have taken his daughters back by force. Laban, therefore, quite probably told the truth when he said that it was within his power to do Jacob harm and that he refrained only because he had recognized that this was the divine will.

31:25 Jacob had pitched his tent in the highlands when Laban
      overtook him. Having pitched his tent on Mount Galaad,
   26 Laban said to Jacob, "Why have you acted so, deceiving
      me and carrying off my daughters like prisoners of war?
   27 Why did you flee secretly and steal away from me? You
      did not let me know, so that I could send you off with re-

28 joicing and song, with tambourine and lyre./ You did not
allow me to kiss my sons and daughters; you have acted
29 foolishly./ It is in my power to do you harm; but last night
the God of your father said to me, 'Take care not to say
30 anything at all to Jacob.'/ If you had to leave because you
longed so much for your father's home, why did you steal
31 my gods?"/ Jacob replied to Laban, "I was afraid, for I
thought you would take away your daughters from me
32 by force./ If you find your gods in anyone's possession, he
shall not live. In the presence of our kinsmen, identify
whatever of yours I may have, and take it." But Jacob did
not know Rachel had stolen them.
33 Then Laban went through Jacob's tent, through Lia's and
through those of both the maids without finding them.
34 From Lia's tent he went to Rachel's;/ but Rachel had
taken the household idols, put them in the camel's saddle,
and was sitting on them. When Laban had felt around the
35 whole tent without finding them,/ she said to her father,
"Be not offended, my lord, that I cannot rise in your presence; I am having my periods." Though he searched, he
did not find the household gods.
36 Then Jacob became angry and remonstrated with Laban.
"What is my offense or my crime," he said "that you have
pursued me, and have ransacked all my belongings?
37 What household article of yours have you found? Put it
out here in the presence of your kinsmen and mine that
38 they may decide between us two./ Twenty years now I
have been with you; your ewes and your she-goats have
never miscarried, nor have I eaten the rams of your
39 flock./ I have not brought to you any torn by wild beasts;
I bore the loss myself. You held me responsible for any-
40 thing stolen by day or night./ The heat wasted me by day,
41 the cold by night, sleep fled from my eyes./ This has been
my twenty years with you: I served you fourteen years
for your two daughters, six years for your flocks; you
42 changed my pay time after time./ If the God of my father,
the God of Abraham, and the God whom Isaac fears, had
not favored me, even now you would have sent me away

empty-handed. God saw my affliction and my toil, and last night he pronounced sentence."

43 Laban answered Jacob, "The daughters are mine, the grandchildren are mine, the flocks are mine, indeed all that you see is mine. What can I do today to these daugh-

44 ters of mine and to the children they have borne?/ Come, then, let us make a covenant, you and I; then the LORD shall be a witness between you and me."

Another reason for Laban's pursuit was Rachel's theft of his household gods. These were his *lares* and *penates,* the signs of the family succession. The author of Genesis or his sources have often simplified these ancient stories, even in the present instance, to make it sound as though everyone worshipped the same true God, but in such scenes as this it is evident that Laban and his family were pagans after all. It had been an exceptional grace that he had called Abraham and his descendants from this paganism into the service of the LORD.

From this story we see that it was not for nothing that Rachel was Laban's daughter; slyness was the family trait. Why she had stolen the gods—out of spite, for some legal reason, or because of a personal motive that defies explanation—remains a mystery. Laban's unsuccessful search, however, afforded Jacob the chance once again to make a fine display of righteous indignation; but Laban, as we said before, did not seem highly impressed. His rejoinder is that of a man who, despite all, has the law on his side and knows it.

But Laban was a realist. The encounter ends peaceably with the enactment of another of those covenants by which civilized man showed his yearning for law and order.

31:45 Then Jacob took a stone and set it up as a memorial pillar.

46 Jacob said to his kinsmen, "Gather some stones." And they gathered stones, made a heap, and ate there near the

47 heap./ Laban called it Jegar-sahadutha and Jacob named

48 it Galaad./ Laban said, "This heap is a witness between

49 you and me today." [Therefore he called it Galaad;/ and Maspha, because he said, "May the LORD watch between

50 you and me when we are away from each other.]/ You
shall not mistreat my daughters, or marry others besides
them; even though there be no man near us, remember,
51 God is witness between you and me."/ Laban continued,
"Note this heap and this memorial pillar I have set up
52 between you and me./ This heap is a witness, and the
memorial is a witness that I will not go beyond this heap
toward you, and that you shall not go beyond this heap
53 and memorial toward me to do harm./ The God of Abraham and the gods of Nahor [the gods of their father]
judge between us." Jacob swore by him whom his father
Isaac revered.
54 Jacob offered sacrifice in the highlands and invited his
kinsmen to take food. When they had eaten they spent
the night in the highlands.
32:1 Early in the morning, Laban kissed his grandchildren and
daughters, bade them farewell, and returned to his home.
2 Jacob also resumed his journey and God's angels met him.
3 When he saw them, Jacob said, "This is the encampment
of God"; and he named that place Mahanaim.

Laban permits Jacob to return home, with the proviso that he
is still bound by certain conditions of their previous agreement.
A heap of stones and a memorial pillar witness to the treaty, and
each man swears by his own deity. From the heap of stones a
popular etymology is devised for Galaad (*gal ed*, "heap of witness," translated by Laban into Aramaic in v. 47). The stress on
the two languages, the fact that Laban is called "the Aramean"
throughout this chapter, and the mention of the witness heap *and*
a memorial pillar as the sign of the covenant, suggest that this
story has recalled not only the personal covenant of friendship
between Jacob and Laban, but also an ancient treaty between
the Arameans and Hebrews which had defined the traditional
boundaries of their lands. The covenant is concluded with the
usual sacrificial meal.

Probably v. 49, where Laban rather than Jacob calls the witness
heap Galaad, is a later expansion of the text. The scribe responsible for it also worked in the name Maspha, "watch tower" ("May

the LORD watch . . ."), important in Israelite history, which was indeed in Galaad but probably much farther south.

Thus Laban returned to Phaddan-Aram and Jacob continued his way homeward. In 32:3 another etymology is formed to explain the name Mahanaim (literally, "two camps") given this area. Here it is ascribed to a vision of angels; other explanations are given further on.

32: 4 Then Jacob sent messengers ahead to his brother Esau in
 5 the region of Seir in the country of Edom,/ commanding them, "Thus you shall say to my lord Esau: Your servant Jacob sends you this message: 'I have been dwelling with
 6 Laban and stayed till now./ I have acquired cattle, asses, flocks, men and women servants; so I am sending word to my lord that I may find favor with you.'"
 7 The messengers returned to Jacob and said, "We went to your brother Esau. He is coming to meet you with four
 8 hundred men."/ Filled with fear and anxiety, Jacob divided into two camps the people with him, as well as the
 9 flocks, the cattle, and the camels./ He said, "Should Esau come on one camp and attack it, the other will be saved."
 10 Jacob prayed, "God of my father Abraham and God of my father Isaac, LORD who said to me, 'Return to your land
 11 and to your kin, and I will deal well with you':/ I am not worthy of all the kindnesses and the constant solicitude which you have shown your servant. With only my staff I crossed this Jordan; now I have grown into two camps.
 12 "Save me from my brother Esau; for I fear that he is com-
 13 ing to kill me and all my family./ You have promised, 'I will surely deal well with you. I will make your descendants as the sands of the sea, too numerous to count.'"

Hardly had Jacob settled once for all his difficulties with Laban when this new anxiety beset him. Esau had reason to hate his brother who had supplanted him, and he was now in command of a respectable army of marauders and in a position to harm Jacob if he chose. Resourceful to the end, Jacob planned to forestall his brother once more.

The author of Genesis again had two versions of the account

how Jacob solved his problem. According to the one which appears above, he divided his party into two groups or camps, so that if Esau's intentions should prove hostile at least the second camp would have an opportunity to escape. In this second camp he put the beloved Rachel and her son Joseph (33:2 f.). These two camps are another explanation of the name Mahanaim, which became a very important city in Israelite times. The previous explanation was found in the description of a vision which was begun but never completed, from which the author took only the popular etymology of the place.

Having thus made remote preparations, the caravan settled at Mahanaim for the night (v. 14a). The name "Jordan" in v. 11 must be an error that has occurred in the transmission of the text. Jacob was nowhere near the Jordan. "Jaboc" must have been meant (cf. v. 23), the *wadi* that flows into the Jordan from the east.

32: 14 After sleeping there that night,[12] he chose a present for
   15 his brother Esau from what he had with him:/ two hundred she-goats, twenty he-goats, two hundred ewes,
   16 twenty rams,/ thirty milch camels with their young, forty
   17 cows, ten bullocks, twenty she-asses and ten foals./ He delivered these to his servants, in separate droves, instructing them. "Go ahead of me, but leave a space be-
   18 tween one drove and the next."/ He charged the leaders, "If my brother Esau meets you and asks, 'To whom do you belong? where are you going? and whose animals
   19 are these before you?'/ you shall answer, 'They belong to your servant Jacob; they are a gift sent to my lord Esau,
   20 and Jacob is just behind us.'"/ He also charged the second, the third and all who followed the droves, "Give this
   21 same message to Esau when you meet him,/ and say also, 'Your servant Jacob is just behind us!'" He thought, "I will appease him with the gift that precedes me; then when I see him, perhaps he will be kind to me."
   22 So the gifts went ahead of him while he lodged that night

[12] The Hebrew says literally, "And he slept there that night." This v. 14a is the conclusion of the first version of the preparation; v. 14b begins the second. The action did not extend over two days, but only one.

24 in the camp./ He took them and sent them across the
25a stream, with everything that belonged to him;/ but Jacob
     himself remained behind, all alone.

In this second version of the preparation for Esau there were
not two camps but several. Jacob divided from his possessions such
as would serve as gifts for Esau, distributed into various successive groups, and sent them ahead of himself and his family. Esau
was supposed to become more and more softened as he received
each gift, and thus be prepared to greet Jacob with a forgiving
heart.

According to this story, finally, only Jacob remains behind on
the other side of the Jaboc. His family and possessions have been
sent ahead. This last v. 25a is the introduction to the story of
Phanuel, which we shall omit for the present. On the other hand, v.

23 That same night he arose, took his two wives, the two
   maids and his eleven sons, and forded the Jaboc.

is the conclusion of the first story, the sequel to v. 14a. The first
story did not bring in the episode of Phanuel at this point, and
therefore takes Jacob and his entourage immediately to the inevitable encounter with Esau.

33:1 Jacob looked up and saw Esau approaching with four
     hundred men. So he divided the children among Lia,
   2 Rachel and the two maids,/ putting the maids and their
     children in front, then Lia and her children, with Rachel
   3 and Joseph in the rear./ He himself went ahead of them,
     bowing to the ground seven times, until he reached his
   4 brother./ Esau ran to meet him, embraced him, fell on his
     neck and kissed him. And they wept.
   5 When he looked up and saw the women and the children,
     he said, "What relation are they to you?" Jacob answered,
     "They are the children whom God has graciously given
   6 your servant."/ Then the maids and their children drew
   7 near and bowed down./ Lia and her children also drew
     near, made their bow, and lastly Joseph and Rachel drew
   8 near and bowed./ He said, "What do you mean by all this
     company which I met?" Jacob answered, "To win favor

9 with my lord."/ Esau said, "I have plenty; keep what is
10 yours my brother."/ Jacob replied, "No, I beg you; if only I
find favor with you, accept the gift from my hand, because
I have come before you as before God, and you have re-
11 ceived me kindly./ I beg you, accept the gift I have
brought you, for God has been good to me, and I have all I
need." When he urged him, Esau accepted.

It would seem almost as though Jacob's precautions had been
unneeded, so cordial is the meeting of the two brothers. We can
hardly speak of a reconciliation, since the occasion of their old
enmity is not even mentioned. Still, we may think that Esau
would hardly have required the attendance of a small army to
pay just a social call, and therefore Jacob's flattery and gifts were
probably not misplaced. If Jacob's demeanor strikes us as an
obsequiousness overdone, in an oriental setting the excess would
not be so remarked. There was a point to Jacob's insistence that
Esau accept his gifts; gifts imposed an obligation of friendship
which it would be sacrilegious to ignore.

Even so, Jacob was not yet entirely out of danger. Esau's proposal, rather his taking for granted that Jacob should accompany
him to Seir, was fraught with uncertainty and perhaps worse for
Jacob's future.

33: 12 Then he said, "Let us break camp, and go on; I will march
13 alongside you." But Jacob replied, "My lord can see that
the children are young, and the flocks and herds giving
suck are a care to me; if overdriven for a single day, the
14 whole flock will die. Let my lord go on ahead of his servant and I shall proceed slowly at the pace of the stock
I am driving and the pace of the children, until I come to
15 my lord at Seir." Esau answered, "Allow me to leave
some of my men with you." But he said, "Why all this
trouble for me, my lord?"
16 That same day Esau started back on his way to Seir,
17 while Jacob went to Socchoth, and built a home for himself and made sheds for his stock. For this reason he
named the place Socchoth.[13]

[13] "Sheds," "huts."

Jacob had not lost his prudence, nor did he rate too highly his brother's present good feelings. Why Esau wanted Jacob to go down with him into Edom is not clear, but it is more than conceivable that he intended him for a minor position at his "court"; Esau was evidently in a place of some power. Jacob was well aware that his favor could quickly cool, and he did not intend to be near Esau when this happened.

Hence, while pretending that he will join Esau in Seir, he excuses himself from accompanying his brother's party, nor will he think of Esau's leaving any of his men behind. These men might have been meant for Jacob's protection, but they would also know how to persuade Jacob to follow Esau after all. While Esau journeys south, therefore, Jacob immediately travels west, to Soccoth on the way to Chanaan.

33:18 During his journey from Phaddan-Aram Jacob came
safely to the city of Sichem, in the land of Chanaan, and
19 camped near the city./ For the price of one hundred
pieces of money he bought the plot of ground on which
he had pitched his tent, from the sons of Hemor, the
20 father of Sichem./ There he erected a memorial pillar and
named it "El, God of Israel."

These few verses serve to introduce the story that will be told
in chapter 34 about the sack of Sichem. The sources which the
author had at his disposal to tell of Jacob's subsequent career
seem to have been quite varied. Above it was to Socchoth that
he returned and there he made his home. Here it is near Sichem,
where he is described as settling down rather permanently, buy-
ing land from the inhabitants and erecting a shrine. Further on
another version of the return to Chanaan (35:9 ff.) takes Jacob
to Bethel, whence he eventually comes to Isaac at Mamre. Yet
Isaac had lived in the south, at Beer-lahai-roi (24:62) and Bersabee (26:23 ff.), and it was at Bersabee that Jacob had left him
(28:10); Abraham, not Isaac, had lived at Mamre (13:18). Fur-
thermore, we saw before that Isaac, at least according to one tradition, was near death when Jacob left for Phaddan-Aram over
twenty years before. The order of events throughout this entire
period is consequently far from clear.

Before we go on to these events, however, we must return to a
most important story which the author of Genesis inserted into
the account of Jacob's return to Chanaan. It is surely one of the
oldest traditions which grew up about this patriarch.

32: 25b Someone wrestled with him until the break of dawn.
   26 When he saw that he could not overcome Jacob, he touched the socket of Jacob's thigh so that it was dis-
   27 located while Jacob wrestled with him./ Then he said, "Let me go; it is dawn." But Jacob answered, "I will not
   28 let you go till you bless me."/ Then he asked Jacob,
   29 "What is your name?" and he answered, "Jacob."/ He said, "You shall no longer be called Jacob, but Israel, because you have contended with God and men, and have
   30 triumphed."/ Jacob asked, "What is your name?" He answered, "Why do you ask my name?" But he blessed him
   31 there./ Jacob named the place Phanuel, saying, "I have seen a heavenly being face to face, yet my life has been spared."
   32 The sun rose on him just as he passed Phanuel, limping
   33 because of his thigh./ To this day the Israelites do not eat the hip-muscle on the socket of the thigh, because he touched the socket of Jacob's thigh on the hip-muscle.

The descendants of Jacob spoke of themselves as Israelites, in Hebrew *Bene Israel,* "the sons of Israel." Tradition gave this name Israel to Jacob. Its actual etymology has been lost, but the Israelites knew that it had some relation to the religious life of their great forefather.

The above story is one explanation of the origin of the name. What are we to see behind this narrative about a man who wrestled with God at a place called Phanuel? There is no doubt, indeed, that the "someone" with whom Jacob wrestled was God. In v. 29 the name Israel is explained as "one who strives with God" (*yisreh El*), and in v. 31 Jacob names the place Phanuel ("the face of God") because he saw there "a heavenly being" (literally *Elohim,* "God") face to face.

This story is of the same spirit as those in chapter *18,* where God is pictured sitting and conversing familiarly with Abraham, taking a meal, walking along a road, and in chapter *3,* where He walks in the garden of Eden in the cool of the day and makes garments of skins for Adam and Eve. We know that these descriptions cannot be taken at the letter, but must be taken in the spirit in which they were composed, familiar and primitive impressions of God, not theological definitions.

Therefore we can understand from this present story that a great thing happened in the life of Jacob. Somewhere in his career he underwent a conversion, an experience of God. At some point in his life this ambitious man was truly blessed and touched by God's grace, so that the shrewdness which he had before devoted to pure self-interest in contending with men would in the future have a better service: for he had contended also with God. The mysterious name Israel does, therefore, signify the new person which Jacob became.

The story was told in this form for another reason, as we see from v. 32 f. The dietary law whose origin receives this popular explanation must have been observed by the Hebrews only in very remote times. It had been abandoned before the adoption of the Law of Moses, for it is found nowhere else in the Bible.

We can anticipate the order of the text by a few verses to see another version of the origin of Jacob's new name. In this second tradition the name was connected with Bethel, the venerable shrine which, as we have already seen, the Israelites intimately associated with Jacob's worship of God.

35:1 God said to Jacob, "Rise and go up to Bethel. Build there an altar to the God who appeared to you as you fled from
2 your brother Esau." So Jacob said to his family and to all who were with him, "Do away with the strange gods you have among you, purify yourselves, and change your
3 garments./ Let us be on our way to Bethel, that I may build an altar there to the God who helped me in my dis-
4 tress and was with me on my journey."/ They handed over to Jacob all the strange gods they had, with their earrings;
5 Jacob buried them under the terebinth near Sichem,/ and they departed. But a great fear lay upon the cities in the vicinity, so that they did not pursue the sons of Jacob.

This connected Bethel-episode in vv. 1-15 itself seems to have been composed by the author from more than one tradition. In v. 9 there is an introduction like that of 33:18, which suggests that it was formerly a separate account of Jacob's return to Cha-

naan. However, there is no question that the author intended all
these verses to be read continuously, which can be done without
effort.

As it stands, this story is a sequel to the account of the sack of
Sichem, which we shall see in a moment. Jacob resolves under
divine guidance to return to Bethel to erect an altar in gratitude
just as he had before set up a memorial pillar. This part of the
story is the complement of the preceding narration about Bethel.
Because of these traditions the sacred pillar and altar at Bethel
were held in special esteem by the Israelites. It is again recalled
that Bethel was formerly called Luza (below, v. 6), and once
more its name is attributed to Jacob. Along with this it is noted
that Jacob's family was contaminated with paganism, which is not
surprising since they were all natives of Phaddan-Aram. In ancient
times changing one's garments was symbolic of beginning a new
life: we have kept the symbolism in the investiture ceremonies of
holy orders and the religious life. The earrings worn by these Ja-
cobites were probably those familiar to archaeologists, in the form
of the crescent, which was a sign of the Semitic moongod aeons
before it became the symbol of Islam. Before going to Bethel,
therefore, Jacob purified his people of their idolatrous tendencies
and trappings and consecrated them to the God whom he worshipped.

> 35:6 So Jacob and all who were with him came to Luza [now
> 7 called Bethel] in the land of Chanaan./ He built an altar
>   there and named the place Bethel, because God had ap-
>   peared to him there when he was fleeing from his brother.
> 8 Debora, Rebecca's nurse, died and was buried below
>   Bethel at the foot of an oak tree, so the place was called
>   Allon-Bachuth.

A quite incidental detail such as that in v. 8 shows how eager
the author was to preserve his source material intact. A tree near
Bethel known as "the oak of weeping" had been associated by
tradition with the nurse of Rebecca who was mentioned fleet-
ingly in 24:59.

Thus 28:10-22 and 35:1-8 together explain Bethel's name, its
sacred pillar and altar, and the custom of giving tithes there. Still

another parallel to these stories which is also the other version
of the origin of Israel, is in the following verses.

35:9 As Jacob returned from Phaddan-Aram, God appeared to
   10 him again and blessed him./ God said to him, "Your name
      is Jacob; no longer shall you be called Jacob, but Israel
   11 shall be your name." Thus he named him Israel./ God said
      to him, "I am God Almighty. Be fruitful and multiply; a
      nation and many nations shall spring from you; kings shall
   12 stem from you./ I will give you the land which I gave to
      Abraham and Isaac; this land will I give also to your de-
   13 scendants."/ Then God departed from him at the place
   14 where he had spoken to him./ But Jacob erected a memo-
      rial pillar in the place where God had spoken with him, a
      pillar of stone, and he poured out a libation and oil on it.
   15 The place where God had spoken to him, Jacob named
      Bethel.

This story is far more laconic than that of Phanuel. There is no
"wrestling," for no significance is attached to the meaning of the
name; it is simply ascribed to God's doing. Nevertheless, the
change of name is connected with the renewal of God's promise
first given to Abraham and then to Isaac. The stories also agree
that this event took place after Jacob's withdrawal from Phaddan-
Aram: in a sense, the story of Jacob is that of Abraham once
again. This much is clear, that by whatever chain of circumstances
God had chosen Jacob as he chose Abraham, to be the one through
whom the nations of the earth would be blessed. As the chosen of
God Jacob becomes Israel.

Now it is time to return to the story of Sichem. It is the only account of any length that remains from the life history of Jacob.

34:1 Dina, the daughter whom Lia bore to Jacob, went to pre-
   2 sent herself among the women of the region./ When Sic-
      hem, son of Hemor the Hevite, prince of the region, saw
   3 her, he took her, and lay with her by force./ He became
      attached to Dina, Jacob's daughter, and fell in love with
   4 the girl, speaking tenderly to her./ Sichem said to his fa-
   5 ther Hemor, "Get me this girl as my wife."/ Now Jacob

heard that Sichem had defiled his daughter; but his sons were out in the fields with his stock, so he held his peace until their return.

The narration of the sack of Sichem by Jacob's sons is most interesting, chiefly because we suspect that there is more to the story than appears on the surface.

On the face of it, there seems to be simply a private quarrel between a young man of the land and the bloodthirsty brothers of a girl whom he had wronged. Not so obvious is some other information that the story gives us. The young man's name has been lost in the past, and for want of a better he is called by the name of the city, Sichem. His father's name Hemor is another makeshift. All the Sichemites were called *Bene Hemor*, "sons of Hemor," just as all Jews were later called *Bene Israel*, "sons of Israel." *Hemor* is Hebrew for "ass." We saw before in chapter 15 that sometimes a covenant was made between the parts of an animal that had been split asunder, and Jeremias 34:18 tells us that the animal used was frequently an ass. "Sons of Hemor," therefore, could be the equivalent of "sons of the covenant." This becomes really probable when we learn from Judges 9:4 that the god of Sichem was Baal-Berith, that is, "lord of the covenant."

If the Sichemites were a people who felt themselves related to their god through a covenant, did the Israelites, who also had this notion, borrow it from them? It is quite possible: the books of Josue and Judges indicate that Sichem had considerable influence on the Israelites during the early times of their conquest of Chanaan. Of course, the fact that God had chosen the Israelites as His special people is an historical certainty which stands by itself independent of the terms used for this fact. The way the Israelites thought and spoke of their relation to God, however, after the analogy of a human covenant, they may easily have borrowed from this more advanced people.

The Sichemites were not Semites. As we shall see, they did not practise circumcision, a common trait of the Semites of Chanaan. Our text calls them Hevites, a people who are an unknown quantity. But the LXX used the word "Horrites" instead, and it is therefore probable that that is what the Hebrew originally had (the two words are almost identical in Hebrew spelling). The Horrites, or Hurrians as they are better known in archaeology, we know very well as an important non-Semitic people with an ancient cultural background who had built up a very advanced civilization during this period. The documents of Mari, which contained significant Hurrian elements, employ the idiom "slaughter an ass" to designate the ceremony of covenant-making. Consequently we would like to know much more about the Sichemites than our story tells.

34:6 Hemor, the father of Sichem, came out to Jacob to speak
7 with him./ Now Jacob's sons came in from the field as soon as they head the news. They were aroused and very angry because Sichem had committed a crime against Israel by
8 lying with Jacob's daughter—an intolerable crime./ Hemor said to them, "My son Sichem has set his heart on your
9 daughter; give her to him as wife./ Intermarry with us;
10 give us your daughters in marriage and marry ours./ Live with us, and the land will be yours; dwell and trade and
11 settle here."/ Sichem, too, said to her father and brothers, "Let me find favor with you; I will pay whatever you de-
12 mand of me./ Increase the marriage price and gifts as you will. I will give you whatever you demand of me; only give me the girl as wife."

Again the author has fused two traditions to derive this story. According to one version, Sichem had violated Dina (vv. 2b–3) and Jacob heard of it (v. 5). He told his sons, who were enraged (v. 7), but Sichem was willing to make amends by marrying the girl (vv. 11–12). Then, in the rest of the story which we see below, the Israelites imposed the condition of circumcision (vv. 13–14), to which Sichem agreed (v. 19). Thereupon Simeon and Levi deceitfully killed Sichem and his father, and carried away their sister who was still in Sichem's house (vv. 25a–26); and at the same time they pillaged his house (v. 29b).[1] Jacob rebuked these two sons for the treachery that had brought consequent danger to his family, but they were proudly obdurate (vv. 30–31). Here we have a family drama that was probably common enough in

[1] The Hebrew of v. 29b has, "and they looted everything that was in the house." Our translation has taken "house" to be a collective noun.

those days. In 49:5 ff. we find another reference to this tradition.

In the other version of the story Sichem had seen Dina in the neighborhood and became enamored of her (vv. 1–2a); he asked his father Hemor to obtain her for his wife (v. 4). Hemor approached Jacob for this purpose (v. 6) and at the same time made a proposal of general alliance between the Israelites and Sichemites (vv. 8–10). The sons of Jacob answered deceitfully, laying down the condition of circumcision before they would consider such an alliance (vv. 15–18). (In this story, as v. 17 shows, Dina was with the Israelites, not in Sichem's house.) Sichem and Hemor set out to persuade their townspeople to agree to the Israelite condition, and were successful (vv. 20–24). When this had taken place, the sons of Jacob in general—not merely Simeon and Levi—went forth and sacked the town (vv. 25b, 27–29).

The two stories do not differ enough to matter seriously, but they do presuppose different situations.

34: 13 The sons of Jacob answered Sichem, who had defiled their sister Dina, and his father Hemor; and they spoke

14 deceitfully./ They said to them, "We cannot do this: give our sister to a man who is uncircumcised; for to us that

15 would be a disgrace./ We will agree to you only on condition that you become like us, by having every male

16 among you circumcised./ Then we will give you our daughters and take yours; we will live among you and

17 become one people./ But if you refuse to be circumcised, we will take our daughter and depart."

18 Their proposal pleased Hemor and his son Sichem.

19 The young man carried out the proposal without delay because he was in love with Jacob's daughter; and he

20 was the most distinguished member of his family./ So Hemor and his son Sichem went to the gate of their city

21 and spoke to their fellow citizens./ "These men," they said, "are friendly; let them dwell with us and trade in the land, since there is ample room for them. Let us marry their daughters and give them our daughters to marry.

22 Only on this condition will the men agree to live with us and form one people: all the males among us must be

23 circumcised as they are./ Will not their stock, their property and all their beasts be to our advantage? Let us agree with them, so that they may dwell with us."

24 All their fellow citizens were persuaded by Hemor and
25 his son Sichem, and all the males were circumcised./ On the third day, when they were in pain, the two sons of Jacob, Simeon and Levi, Dina's brothers, took their swords, advanced boldly against the city and slew all the males.
26 They put Hemor and his son Sichem to the sword, and
27 took Dina from Sichem's house./ Then the sons of Jacob went out, attacked the sick men, and sacked the city, be-
28 cause their sister had been defiled./ They took its flocks, herds and asses, whatever was in the city and in the fields.
29 All its wealth, its women and children they carried off; and they looted whatever was in the houses.
30 Jacob said to Simeon and Levi, "You have brought trouble on me, making me loathsome to the inhabitants of the land, the Chanaanites and the Pherezites. I have but few men; if they unite against me and attack me, my
31 family and I will be destroyed."/ They answered, "Should our sister have been treated as a harlot?"

Two separate histories may be imbedded in these two traditions. The first and obvious one is the family history of revenge of the rape of Dina. Not so obvious is the tribal history that is suggested. For just as Sichem and Hemor are the names of peoples, so Simeon, Levi, and the rest are the names of tribes as well as of individuals.

Curiously, in the book of Josue which describes the Israelite conquest of the promised land of Chanaan, no mention is made of any attack on Sichem, one of the strategically important cities of the country. In fact, Sichem is referred to as though it was already in Israelite hands. Archaeology has shown, further, that it was neither besieged nor destroyed during the time of the conquest.

Have we, then, in this present story the recollection of an ancient occupation of Sichem by some of the Israelites long before the general conquest of Palestine under Josue, Moses' successor?

There is some reason to believe that not all the Israelites descended into Egypt under Joseph, but that some remained in Palestine and therefore never went through the Exodus. Perhaps that is what this tradition has dimly remembered, and perhaps it can explain the mystery of Sichem during the later conquest. We cannot, however, on the basis of present knowledge, give a definite answer to this question.

With this story, Genesis has almost concluded the life of Jacob. What remains is a collection of miscellaneous episodes which have been gathered together in the following chapter without any particular chronology or order.

We have already seen that 35:1–8 is the second part of an account beginning with 28:10–22, which explained the origins of the Israelite shrine of Bethel. We saw too that 35:9–15 form another, briefer account of the same fact, and also give an alternate explanation of the change of Jacob's name to Israel, in parallel to the dramatic story of 32:22 ff. which localized this event at Phanuel.

After these passages follows the story of the birth of Jacob's last son by the beloved Rachel. We are left to surmise the pathos concealed in this simple account. When we remember Jacob's devotion to Rachel, we know the loss he must have felt in her death.

35: 16 They journeyed from Bethel, and when they were still a distance from Ephratha, Rachel gave birth to a child amid
17 great pain./ While she was in painful labor the midwife said to her, "Fear not; for this time also you have a son."
18 As her soul was departing her—for she was at the point of death—she named him Benoni, but his father called
19 him Benjamin./ Rachel died and was buried on the way
20 to Ephratha, that is, Bethlehem./ Jacob erected a memorial over her grave; and this memorial marks Rachel's grave to this day.

That Rachel should have called her son Benoni, "son of sorrow," is typical of the oriental mentality that sets great store in symbolic names. But no parent would seriously wish such an unlucky title on his offspring. Hence the child was called Benjamin, interpreted by the Hebrews as "son of the right hand," the right hand being the position of dignity and power.

Rachel was buried near Ephratha: "that is, Bethlehem," our text adds. This is most certainly wrong: we have here a later, incorrect explanation tacked on the original story. Ephratha was originally near Rama, north of Jerusalem, whereas Bethlehem is south. Much later some of the inhabitants of Ephratha moved south and gave the region the name of their homeland, by the same process that so many old-world names are now found in America. Bethlehem and Ephratha were then identified. The text as it now stands has given rise to the local tradition in Palestine of "Rachel's tomb" (an ordinary Moslem mausoleum) which the Arabs point out near Bethlehem. It is not the one mentioned by Genesis.

> 35: 21 Israel moved on and pitched his tent beyond Magdal-
> 22 eder./ While Israel was living in that region, Ruben went
> and lay with Bala, his father's concubine; and Israel heard
> of it. . . .

This brief story is never completed: the text passes over the distasteful episode briefly, though it will be mentioned again in chapter 49, with a reference to the dire consequences it had for Ruben. Ruben's act, apart from the question of adultery, was deemed a heinous crime; that a father and son should have relations with the same woman was thought unnatural.

The site of Magdal-eder, "the tower of the flock," is unknown. There were many such towers of stones erected by shepherds for the better guarding of their flocks.

> 35: 23 The sons of Jacob were twelve: / the sons of Lia: Ruben;
> Jacob's first-born, Simeon, Levi, Juda, Issachar and Zabu-
> 24.25 lon;/ the sons of Rachel: Joseph and Benjamin;/ the
> 26 sons of Bala, Rachel's maid: Dan and Nephthali; / the
> sons of Zelpha, Lia's maid: Gad and Aser. These were
> the sons of Jacob who were born to him in Phaddan-
> Aram.

How generalized is this entire chapter we can see from this summary list of Jacob's son by his various wives. They are all said to have been born in Phaddan-Aram, though immediately before occurred the story of Benjamin's birth at Ephratha.

35: 27 Jacob went to his father Isaac at Mamre in Cariath-arbe,
that is, Hebron, where Abraham and Isaac had sojourned.
28 The lifetime of Isaac was one hundred and eighty years.
29 Isaac breathed his last and died, and was gathered to
his kin, an old man who had lived a full life. His sons
Esau and Jacob buried him.

We need not imagine that Esau returned after he went to dwell
in Seir. The conventional description of Isaac's death is very similar to that of Abraham's in 25:8 f., and what was said at that time
applies in this case as well. Where Isaac's death should be fitted
into the chronology of Jacob's life it is impossible to say.

In concluding this section of his book, the author has ap-
pended some miscellaneous material relating to Esau. The whole
of chapter 36 is thus a collection of genealogies, probably drawn
chiefly from Edomite sources. The lists contain details which differ sharply from others previously given, and even among themselves they differ. While the reader may think these lists rather
unimportant to the *Heilsgeschichte* of Genesis, they do have
historical value, and they show again quite clearly how the author
went about making up his book.

36: 1.2 These are the descendants of Esau, that is, Edom./ Esau
married the Chanaanite women, Ada, daughter of Elon
the Hethite, and Oholibama, daughter of Ana, son of
3 Sebeon the Hevite;/ also Basemath, daughter of Ismael
4 and sister of Nabaioth./ Ada bore Eliphaz to Esau, Base-
5 math bore Raguel,/ Oholibama bore Jehus, Jelom and
Core. These are the sons of Esau who were born to him
in the land of Chanaan.

There is evident disagreement among the traditions that have
handed down the names of Esau's wives. Before (in 26:34 and
28: 9) we read of Judith, daughter of Beeri the Hethite; Basemath, daughter of Elon the Hethite; and Maheleth, daughter of
Ismael the son of Abraham. Here only one of the wives' names
is the same, and she is given a different father; two of the fathers'
names are the same, but they have different daughters.

The names of Esau's sons are rather common in the Semitic world, and some of them occur again in the Bible.

36: 6 Esau took his wives, sons, daughters, and all the members of his household, his stock, all his beasts, and all he had acquired in the land of Chanaan, and went to the land of
7 Seir, out of the way of his brother Jacob;/ for their possessions were too great for them to live together, and the land where they sojourned could not support them because of their stock.
8 Esau settled in the highlands of Seir, that is, Edom.

Here a new note is struck. Either this tradition knew nothing of Jacob and Esau's quarrel over the first birthright, or it had confused it with a difficulty about the practical affairs of the two brothers' households, similar to the difference between Abraham and Lot (*13*:1 ff.).

36: 9 These are the descendants of Esau, father of the Edomites in the highlands of Seir.
10 These are the names of Esau's sons: Eliphaz, son of Ada, Esau's wife, and Raguel, son of Basemath, the wife of Esau.
11 The sons of Eliphaz were Theman, Omar, Sepho, Gatham
12 and Cenez/ [Thamna was a concubine of Esau's son Eliphaz and bore Amalec to Eliphaz]; these are the descendants of Ada, Esau's wife.
13 The sons of Raguel were Nahath, Zara, Samma and Meza. These are the descendants of Basemath, Esau's wife.
14 The following are the sons of Esau's wife Oholibama, daughter of Ana, son of Sebeon: she bore Jehus, Jelom and Core to Esau.

Here the text has set out again to do what it did in v. 1 ff. It retraces the same ground, but also adds the names of Esau's grandsons through two of his wives. Some of these names, Theman for example, and Cenez and Amalec, are, as before, those of related Semitic peoples of Palestine or its environs.

36: 15 These are the chiefs of the descendants of Esau, the sons of Eliphaz, the first-born of Esau: the chiefs Theman,

16 Omar, Sepho, Cenez,/ [Core,] Gatham, Amalec. These
were the chiefs of Eliphaz in the land of Edom; they are
the descendants of Ada.

17 The following are the sons of Raguel, son of Esau: chiefs
Nahath, Zara, Samma, Meza. They were the chiefs of
Raguel in the land of Edom; they were the descendants
of Basemath, Esau's wife.

18 The following are the sons of Esau's wife Oholibama:
chiefs Jehus, Jelom and Core; these are the chiefs of Oho-

19 libama, daughter of Ana, wife of Esau./ These are the descendants of Esau, and these are their chiefs. Esau is
Edom.

This text goes through the whole process once more, and has
precisely what the preceding list contained. Between the various
lists there are occasional differences in spelling some of these
names. These differences have been smoothed out in the translation where it is obvious that a reference to the same person was
intended. The bracketed words are those which commentators
agree are corruptions, additions to the primitive text. There may
be others besides.

36: 20 The following are the descendants of Seir the Horrite, the

21 aborigines of the land: Lotan, Sobal, Sebeon, Ana,/ Dison, Eser and Disan. These are the chiefs of the Horrites,

22 the descendants of Seir in the land of Edom./ The sons
of Lotan were Hori and Heman; Thamna was the sister of

23 Lotan./ The following are the sons of Sobal: Alvan,

24 Manahath, Ebal, Sepho and Onam./ The following are
the sons of Sebeon: Aia and Ana. He is the Ana who discovered the hot springs in the desert when he was pastur-

25 ing the asses of his father Sebeon./ The following are the
children of Ana: Dison, the son of Ana, and Oholibama,

26 his daughter./ The following are the sons of Dison: Ham-

27 dan, Esban, Jethran and Charan./ The following are the

28 sons of Eser: Balaan, Zavan and Acan./ The sons of Disan
were Us and Aran.

29 The following are the chiefs of the Horrites: chiefs Lotan,

30 Sobal, Sebeon, Ana,/ Dison, Eser, Disan. These are

the chiefs of the Horrites according to their clans in the land of Seir.

This is the most curious of all the lists; rather, it is two lists, since v. 29 f. is a reprise of v. 20 f. In *14*:6 the Horrites are named as dwelling in the highlands of Seir, and again in Deut. 2:12, 22 it is stated that they inhabited Edom before they were displaced by Esau. There was a well-established tradition, therefore, that the original inhabitants of this land, as far as the Hebrews knew at any rate, were Horrites. This list purports to give the names of their chiefs.

The putative ancestor of these Horrites is given the name Seir, which was that of the region. Several of the names previously mentioned turn up again, e.g. Sebeon, Ana, in v. 20, but they are now Horrites rather than Hevites[2] as in v. 2, and the relationships are different. The list has been tampered with badly. The seven names in v. 20 f. were originally intended to be the seven sons of Seir, and the following verses gave the sons of each of these. Later scribes, however, have tried to make the lists in this chapter agree, and consequently Ana in v. 24 has been made the son of Sebeon as he was in v. 2; other changes have been made for similar reasons.

What is most surprising is that the names in this list are not Hurrian at all but Semitic. The list is, however, wholly artificial. Those names that have not been borrowed from the preceding verses are in general those of the various regions of Edom, which are given the titles by which they were known to the Hebrews. The genealogist did not have the names of the actual Horrite leaders, so he listed them "according to their clans" as best he could. Some of these place-names appeared earlier under a different "ancestry"; e.g. Us (v. 28) in *10*:23.

> *36*:31 The kings who reigned in the land of Edom before they
> 32 had Israelite kings, were the following:/Bala, son of Beor,
> reigned in Edom and the name of his city was Denaba.

---

[2] But see the remarks above on *34*:2. When written with only consonants, Horrite and Hevite in Hebrew are respectively *Hry* and *Hwy*; and since the Hebrew *r* and *w* are easily confused, it is not always possible to tell whether the author's original text had "Horrite" or "Hevite."

33 When Bala died Jobab, son of Zara of Bosra, succeeded
34 him./ When Jobab died, Husam from the land of the
35 Themanites succeeded him./ Husam died and Adad, son
of Badad, succeeded him. He overthrew the Madianites
in the country of Moab, and the name of his city was
36 Avith./ Adad died and Semla of Masreca succeeded him.
37 Semla died and Saul from Rohoboth-Nahar succeeded
38 him./ When Saul died, Baalhanan, son of Achobor suc-
39 ceeded him./ Baalhanan, son of Achobor, died and Adad
succeeded him. The name of his city was Phau, and his
wife's name was Meetebel. She was the daughter of Mat-
red, who was the daughter of Mezaab.

This Edomite namelist of kings is probably an old archival record, dating from the period before David's conquest of Edom.
Eight successive kings are named, each from a different city; this
tells us that there was no hereditary monarchy, and as a matter
of fact the Near East traditionally leaned to elective monarchy.
Those cities which have been identified in the list are known to
have existed in Edom, and the personal names are authentically
Edomite.

36:40 These are the names of the chiefs of Esau, according to
their families or their dwelling places, namely: the chiefs
41 of Thamna, Alva, Jetheth,/ Oholibama, Ela, Phinon,
42.43 Cenez, Theman, Mabsar,/ Magdiel, Iram. These are the
chiefs of Edom, according to their settlements in the land
they occupied. Esau was the father of the Edomites.

Last of all is this final listing of Esau's descendants which partly
agrees and partly disagrees with the earlier lists. Thamna in v. 22
was a daughter of Lotan, son of Seir the Horrite, and in v. 12 (if
the text is original) the concubine of Esau's son Eliphaz. Here
Thamna is a chief or sheikh of Esau, taken as a geographical name
in v. 40. Similarly Oholibama, previously one of Esau's wives.
Cenez and Theman as in v. 11 are Esau's descendants. The rest
of the names are new and seem to be those of districts in Edom,
as the text indicates: "according to their families or their dwelling
places."

This whole chapter has been, as we can see by now, an omnium gatherum. All kinds of traditional sources have been brought together without regard to their variations. The passing of the years and the different streams of tradition had mixed the names up rather thoroughly, though the names themselves were kept with fair accuracy. The author was unwilling to discard the traditions, though he knew they could not be relied on in every detail. We must be grateful that they have been kept, for as our knowledge of the ancient world broadens with increasing discoveries it may be that additional significance will be found in such sources as these to continue our work of piecing together the history of the people of God, which is the history of our salvation.

PART THREE:
ISRAELITE BEGINNINGS

CHAPTER XIII: JOSEPH IN EGYPT

This is the story of Joseph.

Of all the lives of the Hebrew patriarchs, Joseph's is the most thoroughly reported and done in the greatest detail. For one thing, of course, he was the most recent of the patriarchs, and the traditions concerning him were consequently fresher and more abundant. But there were other reasons for this as well. In a sense, Joseph's career was more intimately connected with the Israelites than were any of his predecessors. Because of Joseph the Israelites entered Egypt, where they were to be formed into a people and whence they were to emerge a ransomed people to the glory of God and as a standing testimonial to His grace.

Thus, while no tribe among the Israelites took its name from Joseph, and while Joseph was not the heir of the promise as Isaac and Jacob had been, he receives the lion's share of the author's attention in this last section of his book. This fact itself testifies to the objectivity of Hebrew history and to its emphasis on the aspect of the providential. If Genesis were nothing more than a national saga we would expect to find a collection of glorified exploits of the great men of the dominant Israelite tribes, particularly of Juda, Benjamin, and Ephraim. We do not find this at all. If anything, those persons whom later Israelites might be inclined to regard as important are given a minor or even negative role in Genesis. The stress throughout is on God's action in history, and how through a maze of coinciding and apparently unrelated events He was watching over and preparing the people He had chosen.

During the lifetime of Joseph, and through circumstances of which he was the occasion, the Hebrews of Chanaan began to be welded into the historical phenomenon that is Israel. Genesis does not tell the end of this story, for Genesis is only the introduction to it. Because the purpose of Genesis was to introduce Israel into the world's history, its purpose is concluded in the story of Joseph.

37: 1 Jacob lived in the land of Chanaan, where his father had
2 dwelt as a stranger. / This is his family history. When Joseph was seventeen years old, still a mere youth, he was pasturing the flock with his brothers, the sons of Bala and Zelpha, his father's wives, and he brought a bad report to his father concerning them.
3 Israel loved Joseph best of all his sons because he was
4 born in his old age. He made him a long tunic./ When his brothers saw that their father loved him best of all his sons, they hated him and could not even greet him.
5 Now Joseph had a dream, and when he told it to his
6 brothers, they hated him the more./ He said to them, "Lis-
7 ten to this dream I had./ We were binding sheaves in the field; my sheaf rose up and remained standing, while your sheaves gathered round and bowed down to my sheaf."
8 His brothers answered, "Are you to be our king? Are you to rule over us?" And because of his dreams and words they hated him the more.
9 He had another dream which he also told to his brothers. "I had another dream," he said. "The sun, the moon and
10 eleven stars were worshiping me." When he told that to his father and his brothers, his father reproved him. "What is this dream that you have had?" he said. "Can it be that I and your mother and your brothers will come to bow to
11 the ground before you?"/ So his brothers envied him, while his father pondered the matter.

We meet Joseph still a mere youth, but already with a presage of the future that lies before him. Hated by his brothers because of his closeness to his father, he has the bad taste to dream of a future greatness that will set him above his brothers and even his parents.

There are some curious statements made in this passage which

lead us to suspect that the author is following a tradition which
had chronicled the events of Jacob's life somewhat differently
from the stories we have seen previously. Joseph is described as
though he were the youngest of Jacob's sons (v. 3), and Jacob
speaks as though Rachel was still alive at this time (v. 10). Benjamin is never mentioned, and when he comes into the story much
later on, it is evidently taken for granted that he is a mere child. In
the earlier traditions, however, it appeared that Benjamin was
only a year or two younger than Joseph, and Joseph is presented
here as seventeen years old. From this tradition it would seem
that Benjamin was born only after Joseph went down into Egypt.
We have already remarked on the impossibility of establishing a
hard and fast relative chronology for the patriarchs' lives.

37:12 When his brothers had gone to pasture their father's
13 flocks at Sichem,/ Israel said to Joseph, "Your brothers are
pasturing the flocks at Sichem; get ready, I will send you
14 to them." Joseph answered, "I am ready."/ "Go then," said
Israel, "and see if all is well with your brothers and with
the flocks; and bring back a report to me." So he sent him
15 from the valley of Hebron, and he came to Sichem./ A
man found Joseph wandering about in the fields and
16 asked him, "What are you looking for?"/ "I am looking
for my brothers," he answered. "Tell me, please, where
17 they are pasturing."/ The man said, "They have moved
on from here because I heard them say, 'Let us go to
Dothain.'" So Joseph went after his brothers and found
them in Dothain.

Jacob and his family were living near Hebron where they continued the life they knew best, shepherding flocks. We have seen
before that it was frequently necessary to travel up and down the
land to find suitable pasturage during the various seasons of the
year. When Jacob sends Joseph to the neighborhood of Sichem,
therefore, his brothers had already moved on towards Dothain,
where there was lush pasture land.

Dothain was important for other reasons. It was situated in the
Valley of Jezreel, the mountain pass that has always made this
region significant: who controls Jezreel commands all Palestine

from the north. Through this pass came the caravans which moved from Mesopotamia through Damascus down to the Mediterranean coast and thence into Egypt. We meet one of these caravans below.

To understand properly the story that follows, we must again recognize that our author has combined two traditional accounts. In one story, Joseph's brothers resolve to do away with him, but Ruben forms no part of the conspiracy and persuades the rest, doubtless as the best colorable alternative, to cast their brother into one of the cisterns with which Palestine is still dotted, the reservoirs which catch and hold the precious rainwater. This proposal was followed—luckily the cistern was empty—and then, in the original story, the brothers must have gone away with their flocks. In their absence some Madianite traders passed by, drew Joseph from the cistern, and took him with them to Egypt as a slave. Ruben returned secretly to release Joseph, but found him gone.

In the other story, the beginning of which has not been preserved, it was Juda who intervened once the brothers had decided to kill Joseph. While sitting at their meal debating what to do, they saw a caravan of Ismaelites traversing the trade route from Galaad to Egypt, carrying the aromatics employed so lavishly by the Egyptians in their rituals, in medicine, and, above all, in the embalming for which they have remained famous. Ismaelites and Madianites are, it is true, basically the same Arab people, but Genesis always distinguishes them, deriving the former from Abraham and Agar (chapter *16*) and the latter from Abraham and Cetura (*25*:2). Juda got his brothers to agree to sell Joseph to these traders rather than kill him.

37: 18 They saw him in the distance, and before he drew near
    19 them, they plotted to kill him./ They said to one another,
    20 "Here comes that dreamer!/ Let us therefore kill him and throw him into a cistern; we can say that a wild beast devoured him. Let us see then what becomes of his dreams."
    21 But when Ruben heard of it, he tried to rescue him from
    22 them, saying, "We must not kill him."/ Then he contin-

ued, "Do not shed blood. Throw him into the cistern there in the desert, but do not lay a hand on him." His purpose was to rescue him from them and restore him to his father.

23 When Joseph came to his brothers, they stripped him of
24 the long tunic he had on./ They seized him and threw him into the cistern, which was empty and dry.

25 Then they sat down to eat. Looking up, they saw a caravan of Ismaelites coming from Galaad, their camels laden with gum, balm, and myrrh, with which they were on
26 their way down to Egypt./ Then Juda said to his brothers, "What is to be gained by killing our brother and conceal-
27 ing his blood?/ Let us sell him to the Ismaelites, and let us not lay hands on him; for he is our brother, our own flesh." His brothers agreed.

28 And when some Madianite traders passed by, they[1] drew Joseph up out of the cistern; they sold him to the Ismaelites for twenty pieces of silver. And they took Joseph to Egypt.

29 When Ruben went back to the cistern and saw that Joseph was not in it, he rent his garments, returned to his broth-
30 ers and said,/ "The boy is not there; and I, where shall I turn?"

31 Then they took Joseph's tunic and after killing a goat,
32 dipped the tunic in the blood./ They sent someone who brought the long tunic to their father with the message: "We have found this; see whether it is your son's tunic or
33 not."/ He recognized it and said, "It is my son's tunic. A wild beast has devoured him; Joseph has been torn to
34 pieces!"/ Then Jacob rent his garments, girded himself
35 with sackcloth and mourned his son many days./ Though all his sons and daughters tried to comfort him, he refused to be consoled, and said, "I will go down mourning, to my son in the nether world." So his father wept

---

[1] In the original story, this "they" is the Madianites. This is the first version of the tradition, continuing v. 24. The second half of the sentence, "they sold him . . .," is from the second version, continuing v. 27.

36 over him./ Meanwhile the Madianites sold Joseph in
    Egypt to one of Pharao's officers, Phutiphar, captain of
    the guard.

Thus forewarned, one has little difficulty in picking out the
elements of the "Rubenite" and "Judaite" versions of the history.
There may have been other versions which the author did not
use. He wisely avoided trying to decide who was the hero—or the
least objectionable ruffian—among Joseph's brothers. As for
whether Joseph was kidnaped by Madianites or purchased by
Ismaelites, what did it really matter?

The stories agreed on the substance of the fact, which does not
make a pretty tale. It must have been a sorrowful task for the
Israelites to record this example of their ancestors' perfidy. Their
wickedness is the enduring lesson of this story, for envy and the
hatred of brother for brother have not yet perished in our time.

The stories agree, too, in the conclusion, in what was told the
bereaved father by his faithless sons. Jacob himself provides us
with a lesson that we should not overlook. His unwise display of
affection for Joseph had aggravated family jealousies; shrewd in
so many ways, Jacob was blind to Joseph's danger and to the un-
dercurrents of human passion in those who were nearest to him.
He was capable of dedicated love, but he also loved unwisely.

In v. 35 is one of the few references in Genesis to the life beyond
the grave. *Sheol,* "the nether world," was something the Hebrews
knew little of and mentioned only with reluctance. They had
practically no revelation on the future life, which was providential: since the heavenly beatitude was reopened to man only
through the redemption wrought by Jesus Christ, the full Christian
teaching on the life after death would have been to the Old
Testament Jew at least open to misunderstanding and possibly a
source of despair. If as a result they tended to look for God's re-
wards and punishments almost exclusively in the life of this world,
at the same time they were spared the gross superstition and
magical nonsense with which the Gentiles had surrounded the
whole question. Among the Egyptians the preoccupation with
death approached the stage of monomania. The Hebrew did not
have an enquiring mind for those things that can be known only

by God: he was content to remain in his ignorance with patience and hope.

38: 1 About that time Juda separated from his family and went
2 to tent near an Adullamite named Hiras./ There Juda saw
the daughter of Sue, a Chanaanite. He married her and
3 had relations with her./ She conceived and bore a son,
4 whom he named Her./ Again she conceived and bore a
5 son, whom she named Onan./ She bore still another son
and named him Sela; she was at Chezib when she gave
6 birth to him./ Juda took a wife named Thamar for his first-
7 born, Her./ But Juda's first-born, Her, was wicked in the
sight of the LORD, so the LORD killed him.

Chapter 38 forms a strange interruption in our story, which had just begun on Joseph's career. Why this present narrative has been preserved is evident, because of Juda's later importance, and because of Thamar, ancestress of the great King David (see Ruth 4:18 ff.) and of our Lord Jesus Christ (Matthew 1:3). It is a story that had to be told, and we can conclude that the author inserted it here for want of a better place.

As a matter of fact, it is not at all certain just where else it could have been inserted. The "about that time" of v. 1 is simply transitional and tells us nothing of when "that time" was. We know only that at some period in his life Juda went to live at Adullam, in the Judean hills to the west of the Dead Sea, and there he married the daughter of a Chanaanite by whom he had these three sons. His choice of Thamar, another Chanaanite girl, as the wife of his firstborn son, sets the scene of our story.

38: 8 Then Juda said to Onan, "Go to your brother's wife, perform your duty as brother-in-law, and raise up descend-
9 ants for your brother."/ Onan knew that the descendants
would not be his own, so whenever he had relations with
his brother's wife, he wasted his seed on the ground, in or-
10 der not to raise up descendants for his brother./ What he
did was evil in the sight of the LORD, and he killed him
11 also./ Then Juda said to his daughter-in-law Thamar, "Remain a widow in your father's house until my son Sela

grows up"; for Juda feared that Sela too would die as his brothers had. So she went away and dwelt in her father's house.

For some reason Her died prematurely, without leaving children. "The LORD killed him": the Hebrews believed that an early death could only be a punishment for some sin or other. Since Her had left no heir, Juda told his second son to "perform your duty as brother-in-law." This refers to the so-called levirate marriage law (from the Latin *levir*, "brother-in-law") found in Deut. 25:5 ff., according to which a childless man's next-of-kin was supposed to marry his widow. For various reasons this custom was practised by other peoples besides the Hebrews. In Hebrew law its purpose was to guarantee that a man's name would not perish among his people, since the children of this second union would legally belong to the deceased, and to keep the inheritance of property within the family.

The fierce Semitic desire for children which we have encountered before is the whole point of this story. It dignifies to the extent possible what are some undeniably crude moral lapses.

Onan is selfish and refuses to do his family duty; instead he commits the sin against nature that has been named in his honor. He too dies, leaving Thamar still childless. Social custom now demanded that Juda's third son Sela should become Thamar's husband, but Juda had by now concluded that Thamar was an unlucky match and refused to sanction the union. Accordingly he put Thamar off with excuses, not knowing that she would soon take matters into her own hands.

38:12 After a long time Juda's wife, the daughter of Sue, died. After the time of mourning, Juda went to Thamna with his friend Hiras, the Adullamite, to superintend the shear-
13 ers of his flock./ When Thamar learned her father-in-law
14 was on his way up to Thamna to shear his flock,/ she put off her widow's garments, put on a veil, wrapped herself up and sat at the gateway of Enaim on the road to Thamna; for she was aware that Sela had grown up, yet she had not been given to him in marriage.

15 When Juda saw her, he thought she was a harlot; for she
16 had covered her face./ He went over to her at the roadside and said, "Come, let me have intercourse with you,"
not knowing that she was his daughter-in-law. She asked,
"What will you give me to have intercourse with me?"
17 He answered, "I will send you a kid from the flock." She
responded "Provided you give a pledge until you send it."
18 Juda said, "What pledge shall I give you?" She replied,
"Your signet and cord, with the staff that you are carrying." He gave them to her, and had relations with her,
19 and she conceived by him./ Afterward she arose and
went away. She took off her veil and put on her widow's
garments.
20 When Juda sent the kid by his friend, the Adullamite, to
recover the pledge from the woman, he did not find her.
21 So he asked the men of the place, "Where is the temple-
prostitute who was by the roadside at Enaim?" They answered, "No temple-prostitute has been here."
22 He returned to Juda, saying, "I did not find her; moreover the men of the place told me, 'No temple-prostitute
23 has been here.' "/ Juda replied, "Let her keep the things;
otherwise we shall be ridiculed. I sent this kid, but you
could not find her."

It would be idle to pretend that this is an edifying story. Thamar is guilty of deception, seduction, and adultery—for in Israelite eyes she was Sela's betrothed. Juda commits fornication and
possibly the worse sin of idolatry. Thamar apparently had dis-
guised herself in the veil of a Chanaanite temple-prostitute; union
with one of these women was a religious rite according to the per-
verted morality of the Gentiles. Probably, however, Juda's sin
was simply one of lust and not against faith.

It is a sordid story, but it is honest and true. The ring of truth
is in even its circumstantial details, where the author is striving
for no particular effect. The kid, for example, which Juda offers
seems to have been the standard fee in such transactions. The
signet and cord used as a pledge is the incised cylindrical seal of
which archaeology has unearthed so many examples (see the il-

lustration below). When rolled across the soft surface of a clay tablet it served as a man's signature; hence it was usually worn suspended from the neck as a handy form of identification.

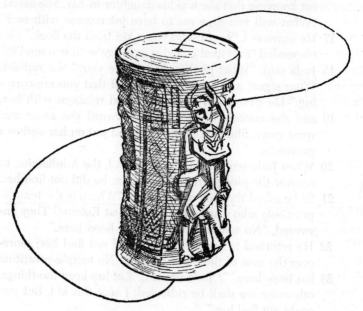

A Cylinder Seal with Cord

The simple honesty of this story is the honesty of the Bible. It would have been easy for the author to gloss over these distasteful events, but he was writing truth. Because he wrote truth, he has taught us a lasting lesson.

38: 24 About three months later Juda was told, "Your daughter-in-law, Thamar, has played the harlot and is pregnant as a
25 result." Juda said, "Bring her out to be burned."/ But as she was being brought, she sent word to her father-in-law, "I am with child by the man to whom these things
26 belong; look whose signet, cord and staff these are."/ Juda recognized them and said, "She is more in the right than I; for I did not give her to my son Sela!" But he had no further relations with her.

The author knew, as Dostoievsky knew when he created the unforgettable Sonia, as every writer has known who has written of human sin with honesty and integrity, that there are greater sins than those of the flesh. He knew that while sin is ugly, the sinner may have lost his way from a very beautiful ideal. Throughout history the fallen woman has been branded "sinner" often by those whose souls are blackened with meannesses of which she is incapable. Thus our Lord also taught in John 8:1 ff. Without condoning Thamar's wrongdoing, the author has taught us to look in our hearts to see whether we are really ready to cast the first stone.

This lesson Juda recognized. Thamar's sin having been found out, he was callously prepared to inflict the punishment which the double standard in morals dictated. But he had the grace to see himself revealed in Thamar's sin: "She is more in the right than I." Juda had sinned against Thamar's natural right, as thousands of respectable people have done since. Juda's sin, and Onan's egoism, were far greater crimes than Thamar's, and the cause of her sin.

Juda's confession is an act of greatness, and our story is great because of it. The rugged individualist would have condemned Thamar and said that Juda was only protecting his own interests. The sentimentalist would excuse Thamar of blame because she was sinned against. The believing Jew and Christian can answer only as Juda did: "She is more in the right than I." That is the wisdom that is the beginning of holiness.

Nor was this lesson lost on the people of the Old Testament. "May your house become like the house of Phares, whom Thamar bore to Juda," is the blessing of God-fearing people in Ruth 4:12. Neither did Matthew hesitate to include Thamar in his list of Jesus' ancestors. Thamar did wrong, but she was more grievously wronged. She had wanted desperately to be what God intended her to be, and those who prevented her were more responsible than she for the wrong path she took.

38: 27 When the time of her delivery came, there were twins
28 in her womb./ During the delivery one put out a hand. The midwife took a scarlet thread, tied it on his hand and
29 said, "This one is born first."/ But as he drew back his

hand, his brother was born. Then the woman said, "How
have you made your way forth?"[2] For this reason he was
30 called Phares./ Afterward his brother with the scarlet
thread on his hand was born, and he was named Zara.[3]

From Thamar were traced two of the most important families
or clans of the tribe of Juda, namely Phares and Zara. This tradition gives the origins of their names from the circumstances of
their birth, somewhat similar to the story of the birth of Esau and
Jacob. The story may indicate that during the course of tribal history the second clan was destined to gain superiority over the first.
This, at least, Father Chaine thinks probable.[4]

39: 1 When Joseph was taken down to Egypt, Phutiphar, an
Egyptian, one of Pharao's officers, the captain of his body-
guard, bought him from the Ismaelites who had taken him
2 down there./ The LORD was with Joseph so that he was
successful. He lived in the house of his master, the Egyp-
3 tian./ When his master saw that the LORD was with him
4 and prospered all his undertakings,/ Joseph found favor
with him and became his attendant. He placed him in
charge of his household, and entrusted all his property to
5 him./ From the time he placed him in charge of his household and over all his property, the LORD blessed the
Egyptian's house on account of Joseph. The LORD's blessing rested on everything that was his, in house and field.
6 He left everything he had in Joseph's charge, and having
him, was concerned about nothing except the food he ate.

The author now turns back to the story of Joseph, and continues
the dual tradition that told of Joseph's going down into Egypt.
As we saw, one story had it that he was abducted by Madianites,
the other that he was sold to Ismaelite traders. The ending of the
first account, the chief source used by our author, stated that "the
Madianites sold Joseph in Egypt to one of Pharao's officers, Phuti-

---

[2] *Mah pharasta aleka phares*, literally, "How have you made a break-
through for yourself?"

[3] Similar to the word *zera*, "seed," "offspring."

[4] *Genèse*, p. 386 f.

phar, captain of the guard" (37:36). It continues in 39:21 ff. and chapter 40, where we see that Phutiphar, called alternately "the warden" and "the captain of the guard" in our text, put Joseph to tending the political prisoners who were lodged in his house.

The other tradition is in this chapter. Here we see that Joseph was sold by the Ismaelites to a man called simply "the Egyptian," who made him his trusted house-servant. In v. 1, however, in order to bring the two stories together, "the Egyptian" has been identified with Phutiphar, and again in v. 20, at the end of this story, mention has been made of "the king's prisoners" so as to introduce the second tradition without breaking the continuity. Originally the traditions were parallel and complementary more than anything else; now they have been made continuous. They harmonize quite nicely, and we read them easily as a unit, but it will be helpful later on to know that they were at one time distinct traditions.

The author had several reasons to keep this account of Joseph's experiences in the house of the Egyptian. For one thing, it contained a fine recollection of Joseph's admirable qualities as administrator, a thing which we shall see stressed later on.

Most important of all, however, is the lesson of the episode that follows. As a happening itself, it is not remarkable. There was an old Egyptian story somewhat similar to it, and the theme occurs again and again in other literatures. It is in accord with observed human conduct. The unsuccessful seducer almost invariably accuses his intended victim of his own crime. The abuse of privileged position to punish the innocent is not new. A husband is reluctant to think that his wife would seek favors other than from him: how much more flattering to believe that she has been the subject of unwelcome advances.

39: 7 Now Joseph was well formed and handsome./ Some time afterward, the wife of his master cast her eyes on
8 Joseph and said, "Lie with me."/ But he refused, saying, "Because of me, my master is not concerned about anything
9 in the house, but has put all that he owns in my care./ He exercises no greater authority in this house than I, nor has he withheld a single thing from me, except yourself, be-

cause you are his wife. How then can I commit this great

10 crime, and sin against God?"/ She urged Joseph day after
day, but he would not consent to lie with her, or to be with

11 her./ On one such day, Joseph went into the house to do
his work, while none of the household servants was at

12 hand./ She seized him by his garment and said, "Lie with
me." But Joseph left his garment in her hand, and fled outdoors.

13 When she saw that he had left his cloak in her hand and

14 had fled outside, she summoned the servants of her house
and said to them, "Look! My husband has brought in a
Hebrew to us to insult us. He came in to lie with me but I

15 screamed./ When he heard me raise my voice and call out,

16 he left his garment beside me, and fled outdoors."/ She
kept the garment beside her until his master came home;

17 then she told him the same story: "The Hebrew slave

18 whom you brought to us came in to insult me,/ but when
I raised my voice and called out, he left his garment beside

19 me and fled outside."/ When the master heard his wife's
story about how his slave had treated her, he became

20 angry./ Then Joseph's master took him and committed
him to the prison where the king's prisoners were kept; so
he remained there in prison.

What is remarkable about this story is the part of it that could
have had no origin other than Hebrew. A pagan could have understood Joseph's refusal on the grounds of the gratitude he owed
his master; he could have understood, too, his second argument,
that the woman was, after all, the master's wife. But only a Hebrew could have said: "How can I commit this great crime, *and
sin against God?*"

The idea that there was a God who called men to account for
moral considerations was unique enough in this ancient world. It
was even more striking, however, in Joseph's case, an alien in a
foreign land, separated from his people. According to the pagan
mind, Joseph in Egypt should have worshipped the gods of Egypt,
just as an Egyptian living among Hebrews would have felt
obliged to worship their God. To each land its own gods. Yet

Joseph pleads a moral law operative in Palestine, in Egypt, and everywhere, the law of a universal God.

We must sometimes pause to remember that if this idea comes naturally to us, it is because of religious truths that we have inherited from the Old Testament.

Thus this story of Joseph's early days in Egypt ends with him committed to prison. The other story, which we shall see in a moment, begins with Joseph in prison, the political prison which was the house of the captain of the guards.

A word on the Egyptians of this period will not be amiss, for a knowledge of their history is essential in understanding some of the events that follow.

Egypt, like Mesopotamia, is one of the cradles of civilization. Man's earliest history in Egypt is considerably obscure, but there was already a thriving civilization there about 5000 B.C.

Historians still divide Egyptian chronology into the twenty dynasties of kings which were counted by the Greco-Egyptian writer Manetho in the third century B.C. The Egypt which Abraham visited was that of the twelfth dynasty (1989–1776 B.C.), also called the Middle Kingdom, when Egyptian culture was at its highest peak. Ruled from Memphis near the modern Cairo, Egypt was then in control of most of Palestine. Mining industries in the Sinai peninsula and control of trade routes made it extremely wealthy.

Long before this, however, Egypt was an important nation. During the period of the Old Kingdom (third to sixth dynasties, or 2700–2200 B.C.) were built the great pyramids, in many ways the most astounding structures created by human ingenuity, and other monumental works that testify to the greatness of this people's imagination and industry.

The Egypt of Joseph's day did not produce such glories. From about 1730 to 1570 B.C., the fifteenth and sixteenth dynasties, occurs what the historians call the Hyksos period, an age of decadence. During this time the capital of Egypt was no longer at Memphis but at Tanis in the Nile delta. The significance of this fact, the meaning of Hyksos, and the relation of this age to the story of Joseph, we shall see later.

39: 21 But the LORD was with Joseph. He showed kindness to
    22 him and gave him favor with the warden,/ who put him
       in charge of all prisoners; and everything that was done
    23 there was done under his management./ The warden did
       not concern himself with anything in Joseph's charge be-
       cause the LORD was with him and prospered all that he
       did.
40: 1 Some time after this the royal butler and baker both of-
    2 fended their lord, the king of Egypt;/ and Pharao became
       angry with his two officials, the chief butler and the chief
    3 baker,/ and had them put in custody in the house of the
       captain of the guard, in the prison where Joseph was con-
    4 fined./ The captain of the guard assigned Joseph to them
       and he became their attendant. They remained in custody
       for some time.

Continuing the story of 37:36, we find Joseph in the political
prison of the house of Phutiphar, captain of the guard. (The word
translated "captain" and "warden" is the same in Hebrew.) As
was stressed before, Joseph soon acquired a position of trust with
his master.

A thing which considerably intrigued the Hebrew author of
Genesis and the other authors who contributed to these traditions,
was the vast difference between the ways of the Egyptians and
their own. We have already remarked how different was the Hebrew notion of religious morality from that of other peoples like
the Egyptians. Here we can almost hear the text voicing its won-
derment at the arbitrary powers of the Egyptian king and the
enslavement of his subjects.

The Hebrews were honest enough to recognize that their culture and living standards were far lower than the Egyptians'. Yet
they had and prized the having of something the Egyptians had
almost forgotten existed—liberty. In Hebrew tribal and family life
democracy and personal freedom were jealously guarded, and
they looked with contempt on the Egyptians' passive acceptance
of tyranny. The text comes back to this subject again and again.
It would have perhaps amused the Egyptians to know that these
rude and uncouth Hebrew nomads looked on their way of life as

inferior. It may amuse some of us today who are secure in the conviction that our way of life is the sum of mankind's aspirations to
learn that the Arab nomads, the modern counterpart of the Old
Testament Hebrews, think of us in the same light and accord
us the pity of free men who are convinced that we have bartered
away our freedom for material security.

With all their civilized ways, the Egyptians were in comparison
with the Hebrews a nation of slaves. A tradition of servility made
the Pharao's slightest whim absolute law, regarded the king as a
god incarnate, and submitted to a social order in which the ruling
class rolled in wealth and the people had the privilege of starving.

The present story is a case in point. The royal butler and
baker had offended the king, and into prison they must go.
Whether they were to come forth alive or dead or not at all, was
up to the royal will. These persons were of course not simply
menials, they were palace officials with political connections. It
was from political motives that they were in disfavor. In this
climate of intrigue and statecraft the Hebrew author wandered
mistrustingly and bewildered.

40: 5 On one and the same night, the royal butler and baker of
Egypt, confined in prison, each had a dream of peculiar
6 significance to himself./ When Joseph came to them in the
7 morning, he saw they were disturbed;/ so he asked Pharao's officials, in custody with him in his master's house,
8 "Why do you look sad today?"/ They answered him, "We
each had a dream, but there is no one to interpret them."
Joseph said to them, "Does not interpretation belong to
God? Tell them to me, please."

How seriously the Egyptians took their dreams and how ear-
nestly they tried to make sense from them, we know from a papyrus
document preserved from this general period. It is a catalogue of
possible subjects that might occur in dreams, together with their
significance. Thus—according to this lore—to dream of white
bread meant good fortune, to dream of a pain in the side meant
the loss of some possession, and so on. Most of these interpretations were based on word-plays.

Joseph, who had before got into trouble because of his dreams, now hoped to turn the dreams of others to his advantage. The favorable interpretation which he proceeded to give to the butler's dream, and the adverse interpretation given the baker, may have been little more than informed guesswork. Through his association with the captain of the guard Joseph must have known as well as anyone which way the political winds were blowing, and he could have surmised what the Pharao's judgment would be in regard to these hapless subjects. On the other hand, we know that Joseph was providentially guided in Egypt, and there may have been more direct divine enlightenment in this matter than Joseph could have obtained by his own unaided resources.

40: 9 So the chief butler told Joseph his dream. "In my dream,"
10 he said, "there was a vine in front of me./ Three branches were on the vine. It budded and blossomed, and its clus-
11 ters ripened into grapes./ Pharao's cup was in my hand and I took the grapes, squeezed them into his cup, and
12 placed it in his hand."/ Joseph said to him, "This is its
13 meaning: the three branches are three days./ Within three days Pharao will take up your case and restore you to your office. You will present Pharao's cup to him as form-
14 erly, when you were his butler./ So if you think of me when good fortune comes to you, do me the favor of men-
15 tioning me to Pharao, and get me out of this house./ I was kidnapped from the land of the Hebrews, and here I have done nothing for which I should have been put into a dungeon."
16 When the chief baker saw that he had given a favorable interpretation, he said to Joseph, "I too had a dream: I
17 had three wicker baskets on my head. In the top basket was every kind of baked food for Pharao, but the birds
18 were eating it out of the basket on my head." Joseph answered, "This is its meaning: the three baskets are three
19 days./ Within three days Pharao will take up your case and hang you on a gibbet; and the birds will eat the flesh off your body."

Birds were almost universally an ill omen in the mind of ancient man. Something of the same idea appears in 15:11 in the description of God's covenant with Abraham, when birds of prey swoop down to try to disturb the covenant sacrifice, but are routed by Abraham.

Joseph's predictions came true.

40: 20 On the third day, which was Pharao's birthday, he made a feast for all his courtiers, and in their presence took up
21 the cases of the chief butler and the chief baker. He reinstated the chief butler in his office of presenting the
22 cup into his hand; but the chief baker he hanged, as
23 Joseph had interpreted to them./ The chief butler did not think of Joseph, but forgot him.

For the present, nothing was to come of this. The butler, no better than other men, forgot the companion of his imprisonment who had predicted good things of him. Eventually, however, the event was to influence Joseph's life.

CHAPTER XIV: THE STUFF OF DREAMS

41:1 Two full years afterward, Pharao had a dream. He was
2 standing by the Nile./ Seven cows, sleek and fat, came up
3 out of the Nile and were browsing in the reed grass./ After
them, seven other cows, ugly and thin, came up out of the
4 Nile, and stood beside those on the bank of the Nile./ The
ugly, thin cows devoured the seven sleek, fat ones. Then
5 Pharao awoke./ But he fell asleep again and had another
dream. Seven ears of grain, fat and fine, were growing on
6 a single stalk./ After them sprouted seven other ears thin
7 and blasted by the east wind./ The thin ears swallowed up
the seven fat, full ears. Then Pharao awoke to find it was a
dream.

8 When morning came he was troubled; so he summoned
all the magicians and wise men of Egypt. Pharao related
his dream to them, but there was no one who could inter-
9 pret it for him./ Then the chief butler said to Pharao, "To-
10 day I must recall my offenses./ When Pharao was angry
with his servants, and put me and the chief baker in cus-
11 tody in the house of the captain of the guard,/ on the one
same night he and I each had a dream of peculiar signifi-
12 cance to himself./ With us there, was a Hebrew youth, a
slave of the captain of the guard. We told him our dreams
and he interpreted them for us. He gave each the proper
13 interpretation of his dream;/ and it turned out just as he
had interpreted to us: I was reinstated in my office, but the
14 other was hanged." Then Pharao sent for Joseph, and they
brought him quickly out of the dungeon. After he had
shaved and changed his clothes, he came into Pharao's
presence.

From this moment of his release from prison Joseph begins to assume the importance that had been foretold of him.

The author of this history was quite familiar with Egyptian customs, as is evident from the last verse above. Joseph's change of clothes was, of course, to don court dress. He was shaved because, unlike the Hebrews, the Egyptians held beards in abhorrence and considered them to be proper to barbarians and serfs.

41:15 Pharao said to Joseph, "I had a dream which no one can interpret; but I have heard it said of you that you know

16 how to interpret a dream." Joseph answered Pharao, "Who but God shall give Pharao a favorable response!"

17 Then Pharao said to Joseph, "I dreamed I was standing

18 on the bank of the Nile,/ when seven cows, fat and sleek, came out of the Nile, and were browsing in the reed grass.

19 After them, seven other cows came up, lean, very ugly and scrawny. I have never seen such poor cows as these in

20 all the land of Egypt./ The scrawny, ugly cows devoured

21 the first seven fat cows./ But when they had consumed them, it was not apparent that they had done so, because

22 they were as ugly as before. Then I awoke./ Again I dreamed I saw seven ears of grain, full and fine, growing

23 on a single stalk./ After them sprouted seven withered,

24 thin ears, blasted by the east wind./ The thin ears swallowed up the seven fine ears. I told the magicians, but no one could explain it to me."

25 Joseph said to Pharao: "Pharao's dream is but one. God

26 has revealed to Pharao what he is about to do./ The seven fine cows are seven years, and the seven fine ears

27 are seven years; it is but one dream./ The seven thin, ugly cows which came up after them are seven years; and the seven empty ears blasted by the east wind are seven years.

28 There will be seven years of famine./ It is as I told Pharao: God has revealed to Pharao what he is about to do.

29 Seven years of great plenty will come through the land of

30 Egypt,/ but there will follow seven years of famine, and then all the plenty will be forgotten in the land of Egypt.

31 The famine will devastate the land,/ and the plenty will

not be discernible in the land, because of the famine
32 which is to follow; for it will be very severe./ The reason
that the dream was sent twice to Pharao is that the matter
is determined by God, and God will soon bring it about.
33 Let Pharao select an intelligent and prudent man, and
34 give him charge of the land of Egypt./ Let Pharao take
action, appoint officials over the land, and prepare the
35 land of Egypt through the seven years of plenty./ And
let them collect all the food of these good years to come,
and store up under the authority of Pharao food in the
36 cities, and preserve it./ The food shall be a reserve for the
land against the seven years of famine which shall be
in the land of Egypt, so that the land will not perish by
the famine."

There is an Egyptian record which purports to date from one of
the very early dynasties, which speaks of just such a seven-year
famine as that which Joseph predicted in interpreting Pharao's
dreams. However, a famine of this length was probably not too
extraordinary.

Herodotus called Egypt "the gift of the Nile." In a sense, Egypt
is the Nile. Egypt extends about five hundred miles north and
south, but the only habitable land is the thin strip a few miles
wide on either side of the river, which at the river's mouth widens
into the famous Delta. All else is desert, separated from the sown
land as though by a knife-edge. The fertility of the Nile valley
and delta is proverbial, the result of the annual flood which
washes in new, rich soil. The Nile originates 2500 miles south of
the Delta in Uganda and winds nearly twice this distance on its
way to the sea. Geographers call this the White Nile. Before it
reaches Egypt the river is joined by the Blue Nile, a mountain
torrent which pours down from the highlands of Abyssinia. It is
the Blue Nile, and the heavy rainfall of Abyssinia, which cause
the flooding in Egypt. If there is no rain, there will be no flood;
and if there is no flood, there will be a famine. (Nowadays the
flood can be turned off and on at will by means of the huge dam
and reservoir constructed at Aswan in the extreme south of Egypt.)

Joseph coupled his interpretation of Pharao's dream with advice probably typical of that which had made him so useful to his master. The advice may not have been entirely disinterested: Pharao and his court, we immediately see, had no difficulty deciding who best qualified as the "intelligent and prudent man" Joseph recommended. To the mind of the Egyptians, if Joseph could explain the dream—and they do not seem to have questioned his interpretation—then he would be best able to do what was necessary to guard against what it portended.

41: 37.38 The advice pleased Pharao and all his courtiers;/ so Pharao said to his court, "Can we find another like him
39 in whom is the spirit of God?"/ Then Pharao said to Joseph, "Since God has made all this known to you,
40 there is no one as intelligent and prudent as you;/ you shall be in charge of my palace and all my people shall obey your commands; only as regards the royal throne
41 will I be greater than you."/ Pharao continued, "I give
42 you charge of the whole land of Egypt."/ Taking the signet-ring from his own hand, he put it on Joseph's. He dressed him in linen robes, and put a chain of gold
43 around his neck./ He had him ride in his second chariot. And they cried out before him, "Bow down." In this way he put him in charge of the whole land of
44 Egypt./ Pharao said to Joseph, "I am Pharao; without your command, no one shall move hand or foot in the whole land of Egypt."
45 Then Pharao changed Joseph's name to Saphanethphanee, and gave to him in marriage Aseneth, daughter of Phutiphare, the priest of On. [Joseph made a
46 tour of the land of Egypt.] Joseph was thirty years old when he entered the service of Pharao, king of Egypt. He left Pharao and traversed the whole land of Egypt.

Thus Joseph came to be viceroy of Egypt. We may think this a suprising change for a Hebrew slave, and perhaps a little incredible. In a moment we will see a few background facts of Egyptian history which can help us understand how all this was possible. Actually, it happened more than once that a mere commoner became Pharao. Egypt has always been a land of violent contrast and surprise.

The chapter continues to evidence Egyptian influence: the author was writing of things he knew. The signet-ring was a characteristic of Egyptian officials, as were the linen robe and gold chain, familiar to us from Egyptian paintings. The chariot we know had only recently been introduced into Egypt. The word which the Hebrew text uses for linen is Egyptian, not Hebrew. So is the word translated above "Bow down."

Joseph's Egyptian name Saphaneth-phanee is now recognized to mean something like "God speaks: He lives" (Father de Vaux's interpretation).[1] Joseph's wife was daughter of one of the priests of On, better known in history as Heliopolis, the city sacred to the sun-god Amun. The priesthood of Amun was very powerful in Egypt, often rivalling the Pharao. The name Aseneth has some reference to the Egyptian goddess Neth. Phutiphare is simply the full form of the Phutiphar we have previously seen, and refers to another name of the Egyptian sun-god, Re or Ra.

> 41: 47 During the seven years of plenty the land produced
> 48 abundant crops./ So he collected all the food of the seven years of plenty in the land of Egypt, and stored it in the cities, placing in each city the food from the neighboring
> 49 fields./ Joseph heaped up grain in great quantities like the sands of the sea until he ceased measuring it, for it could not be measured.
> 50 Before the years of famine came, two sons were born to Joseph by Aseneth, daughter of Phutiphare, the priest of
> 51 On. Joseph named the first born Manasse; "Because," he said, "God has made me forget entirely[2] my sufferings and
> 52 my family."/ He named the second one Ephraim and said, "God has made me fruitful[3] in the land of my affliction."
> 53 When the seven years of plenty in the land of Egypt had
> 54 passed, / the seven years of famine began, as Joseph had foretold. There was famine in all other countries, while
> 55 in all Egypt there was food. But when the whole land of

---

[1] *Genèse*, p. 183.

[2] *Nassani*, "he has made me forget."

[3] *Hiphrani*, "he has made me fruitful."

Egypt also was famished, the people cried to Pharao for food. Pharao said to all the Egyptians, "Go to Joseph
56 and do what he tells you."/ When the famine had spread throughout the land, Joseph opened all the store-houses and sold grain to the Egyptians; for the famine gripped
57 the land of Egypt./ And all peoples came to Egypt to buy grain from Joseph, for the famine was grievous everywhere.

Typically enough, Pharao owned the land's grain, and consequently the people had to buy their food from him when the pinch of the famine came. The final reference, to the other peoples who came to Egypt to buy grain, will introduce the following story, in which we meet Joseph's brothers once again.

Before we see this, what is to be said of the fact that a hitherto unknown Hebrew slave could rise to the place of second man in Egypt? Is there any record of such an astounding thing in Egyptian history?

We must confess with regret that there is no such record. It may yet be found, of course, for the Egyptian sands have yielded up only a trifle of their secrets to the archaeologist's spade. At the same time, we have reason to fear that this obscure period of Egyptian history may never be better known than it is now. It appears that later generations did their best to obliterate these pages from their country's annals. And they had cause.

The high-water mark in Egyptian history, I have remarked, was reached during the twelfth dynasty, when Egypt was in undisputed control of Chanaan and ruled a wealthy empire. Many texts from this period, the nineteenth and twentieth centuries before Christ, have thrown a blaze of light upon the history of Egypt as well as of Chanaan, then undergoing the Amorrite invasions with which Abraham's life must doubtless be associated.[4]

---

[4] Among the many excellent books that deal in a more or less popular way with the lands of the ancient Near East and their relation to the Bible in the light of modern archaeological knowledge, I can highly recommend Mr. Jack Finegan's *Light From the Ancient Past* (Princeton University Press, 1946), Professor Albright's *The Archaeology of Palestine* (1949) in the Penguin series, and the articles in Volume II especially of *Guide to the Bible* by Fathers Robert and Tricot (published in a revised English translation by Desclée and Co., 1955).

Egypt's stake in Chanaan was an ancient one. From as early as the second dynasty (about 2800 B.C.) there is evidence that Byblos, a most important commercial seaport in Phoenicia, was an Egyptian colony. Egyptian utensils from the third dynasty have been found at Ai, and various texts indicate that during the fifth and sixth dynasties (that is, around 2300 B.C.) Egypt already was dominating Palestine.

Egyptian nationalism was severely jolted, however, around 1730 B.C. At this time there came into power in Egypt a dynasty of foreign rulers whose name we know from the historian Manetho as "the Hyksos." The meaning of this word had already been forgotten in Manetho's time, but probably it signified something like "foreign princes." These Hyksos were the ruling class in a wave of invading peoples, Hurrian, Indo-Aryan, and Semitic, the tail-end of the great migration that had come down through Chanaan over a century before. Egypt was thrown into political anarchy, and out of the chaos emerged the rule of these foreigners. They remained the Pharaos of Egypt for another two centuries.

Some of the Hyksos at least were Semites: one of them, for example, had the name Jacob. This can help us understand why Joseph, a foreigner and a Semite, could have risen to power under a king who was likewise a foreigner and, if not a Semite himself, at least favorably disposed to them. Several other aspects of the Joseph story become more understandable when we remember that the Egyptian Pharao of Joseph's day was himself not an Egyptian. The Hyksos cordially detested their Egyptian subjects and were cordially detested in return. Later ages looked back on this one with repugnance.

There seems to be no doubt that we must place Joseph within this Hyksos period. All the indications of the Scripture favor this view. I have already remarked on the chariot which Pharao gave Joseph; it was the Hyksos who introduced the chariot into Egypt. In 47:17 horses are mentioned for the first time in the Bible; it was the Hyksos who introduced the horse into Egypt. We shall see that the Israelites who enter Egypt are given land in the Delta region, near the Pharao. Only during the Hyksos period was the Pharao's capital in the Delta, at Tanis—only then, and then once more about four hundred years later, far too late to be compatible with this stage of Israelite history. Both before and after the rule of these foreign princes the Egyptian capital was further down the Nile, either at Memphis or Thebes.

Therefore, while extra-biblical history has given us no direct evidence of Joseph in Egypt, the biblical traditions harmonize satisfactorily with all the other information that we do have. In a way, this is more interesting than direct evidence. The biblical authors did not write with the intention of proving anything: what indications they have given us of the era of Joseph result simply from their fidelity to their sources. That their material dovetails with the discoveries of disinterested research makes it all the more convincing.[5]

Historians call the Hyksos age a time of decadence, but, as with so many similar periods, largely because we know very little about it. Certainly the Hyksos did a great deal for Egypt, introducing new ideas and techniques which affected the inbred Egyptians despite themselves. How they affected the Israelites, we learn from the remaining chapters of Genesis.

42: 1 When Jacob learned that there was grain for sale in Egypt,
2 he said to his sons,/ "Why do you look at one another? I have heard there is grain for sale in Egypt. Go down there
3 and buy some for us, that we may live and not perish." So ten of Joseph's brothers went down to buy grain in Egypt;/
4 but Benjamin, Joseph's full brother, Jacob did not send with his brothers, for he thought some harm might befall
5 him./ Thus the sons of Israel went with the other purchasers, because of the famine in the land of Chanaan.
6 Now Joseph was the governor of the land; it was he who sold to all the people of the land. Joseph's brothers also
7 came and prostrated themselves before him./ Though Joseph saw his brothers, and recognized them, he acted as a stranger toward them and spoke harshly to them. "Where do you come from?" he asked. They replied, "From the land of Chanaan, to buy food."

[5] There must also be considered the possibility that our popular history of Joseph has understandably exaggerated his importance in Egypt to some extent. Some Egyptologists point out that functions are ascribed to him which would normally have been in the province of several distinct officials.

If there was a famine in fertile Egypt, it is easy to understand why there would have been one in Chanaan too, where they were much more frequent. In fact, "the famine was grievous everywhere" (41:57). Among the neighboring peoples who were coming down to buy grain in Egypt come at length the sons of Israel, to introduce one of the most dramatic stories of the entire Bible.

Previously we saw that there was a "Judaite" and a "Rubenite" tradition about Joseph and his brothers which the author of Genesis skillfully welded together into a single narrative. The threads of these two traditions are picked up again in this and the following chapter. Chapter 42 is composed mostly of the "Rubenite" and chapter 43 mostly of the "Judaite" tradition.

The two stories did not differ a great deal, and the author had little trouble combining them. Both stories agreed that Joseph's brothers, with the exception of Benjamin who was evidently too young to make the journey without danger, came down into Egypt and appeared before Joseph whom they did not recognize. They "prostrated themselves before him" is carefully noted: this is the fulfilment of Joseph's dream of so long ago (37:7 ff.). Joseph knew them immediately, but the years and his changed condition, to say nothing of the fact that they believed him dead and would hardly have expected to find him governor of Egypt, quite concealed him from their eyes. Joseph acted the part of despot handily enough.

42: 8 Joseph knew his brothers, but they did not recognize him.
9 Remembering the dreams he had once had about them, he said, "You are spies; you have come to discover the
10 weak spots of the land."/ But they said to him, "No, my
11 lord; your servants have come to buy food./ We are all sons of the same man. We are honest; your servants are not
12 spies."/ But he said to them, "Not so, but you have come to
13 discover the weak spots of the country."/ They replied, "We, your servants, were twelve brothers, the sons of the same man in the land of Chanaan. The youngest is at pres-
14 ent with our father; another is no more."/ "As for my say-
15 ing you are spies," Joseph rejoined,/ "this shall be your test: as Pharao lives, you shall not leave this place until

16 your youngest brother comes here!/ Send one of your number to bring your brother while you others remain in
bonds. Thus shall your statements be tested for their truth;
17 if they are untrue, as Pharao lives, you are spies!"/ Then he
consigned them to custody for three days.
18 On the third day Joseph said to them, "If you do this, you
19 shall live. I am a God-fearing man./ If you are honest,
let one of your brothers remain confined in your prison,
while the rest go and carry food for the needs of your
20 families./ You shall bring me your youngest brother.
Thus your words will be verified, and you shall not die."
21 And they agreed./ They said to one another, "Alas! we are
guilty regarding our brother, whose anguish of heart we
witnessed when he pleaded with us; we did not heed.
22 Therefore this anguish has come upon us."/ Ruben remarked, "Did I not say to you, 'Do not sin against the boy?
But you would not listen. Now comes the reckoning for his
23 blood!'/ They did not know that Joseph understood them,
24 for an interpreter was employed./ Then Joseph withdrew
from them and wept. When he returned he spoke with
them; and taking Simeon from them, he bound him before
their eyes.

The charge of espionage was a natural enough pretext for
Joseph. The Hyksos rule in Egypt lived in nervous insecurity. As
men will do when unjustly accused, the brothers volunteered
enough information about their family background to give Joseph
the further opening he desired. As we concluded before, the story
of Benjamin's birth in 35:16 ff. is uncertain as to chronology.
Throughout this present episode Joseph acts as though he had
never seen Benjamin before, and it is supposed that Benjamin
was still quite young. Yet in the present chronology Joseph was
over thirty years old and had been in Egypt more than thirteen
years (cf. 37:2). Hence Benjamin could hardly have been born
shortly after Joseph, as the position of the story of Rachel's death
might have previously suggested.

At Ruben's prompting, the brothers are quick to see their
misfortune as a punishment for their sin against Joseph. This is

doubtless what Joseph intended; of course, they could not realize
yet how very right they were. Their consciences must have troubled them frequently during the years when they believed their
brother dead.

42:25 When their bags were filled with grain, Joseph gave orders to put back every man's money in his sack, and to
give them provisions for the journey. After this was done

26 for them,/ they loaded their asses with their grain, and

27 departed./ At the stopping-place, when one of them
opened his sack to give fodder to his ass, he saw his
money in the mouth of his sack, and said to his brothers,

28 "My money has been returned! Here it is in my sack!"
Mystified, they turned to one another trembling and said,
"What has God done to us!"

29 When they came to their father Jacob in the land of
Chanaan, they told him all that had happened to them.

30 "The man who is lord of the land," they said, "spoke

31 harshly to us and regarded us as spies of the country./ But

32 we said to him, 'We are honest men not spies;/ we were
twelve brothers, sons of the same father. One is no more,
and the youngest is at present with our father in the land

33 of Chanaan.'/ Then this man who is lord of the land said
to us, 'Hereby I shall know whether you are honest men:
leave one of your brothers with me, take grain for the

34 needs of your families, and go your way./ Bring your
youngest brother to me, that I may know you are not spies
but honest men. Then I will restore your brother to you,
and you may trade in the land!'"

Joseph amply supplied his brothers with the grain they had
come to buy and also, v. 25 says, gave them provisions for their
journey. This last was so that they would not have to open their
sacks of grain on the way and discover that he had restored their
money. And in fact, in this "Rubenite" version of the story, they
did not discover the money until their return to Jacob, as appears
below. The contrary indication in v. 27 f. has been borrowed
from the "Judaite" version of the story (the first part of which has
not been used in Genesis): in that version, as is seen from 43:21,

they all discovered the money at the stopping-place on the way to Chanaan.

According to this story, then, Simeon remained a hostage in Egypt against the return of all the sons of Israel with Benjamin.

42: 35 When they were emptying their sacks, there in each man's sack was his own purse! At the sight of their purses,
36 they and their father were dismayed./ Their father, Jacob, said to them, "It is I whom you bereave. Joseph is no more, Simeon is no more, and now you would take Benja-
37 min. It is I upon whom all this falls!"/ Ruben said to his father, "Put him in my charge and I will bring him back to you. You may kill my two sons if I do not bring him
38 back to you."/ But Jacob said, "My son shall not go down with you. His brother is dead, and he alone remains. If any harm should befall him on the journey you must make, you would bring down my gray hairs with sorrow to the grave."

The discovery of the money was a source of dismay because it was inexplicable after Joseph's harsh treatment. They could well imagine that it was a trap of some kind.

Ruben is the hero of this version of the story, who now offers to go surety for Benjamin's safety even to the extent of making his own sons hostages: an emphatic, but hardly a useful gesture. Jacob was at first adamantly opposed. We can note that not only Jacob, who after all had been deceived, but the brothers as well believed Joseph to be dead. Whether he had simply disappeared or had been sold under their eyes into slavery, they were convinced that by now he must have perished. The life of an Egyptian slave was probably not one that encouraged longevity.

In the original "Rubenite" story, Jacob without doubt eventually acceded to Ruben's plea, and the return journey of the brothers to Egypt was described probably just about as it is in chapter 43. However, beginning at this point the author has told the rest of the story from the "Judaite" version. He has joined the two halves just where they overlapped, as in this version Juda steps forward to guarantee Benjamin's safety.

43:1.2 Now the famine in the land was severe,/ so when they had eaten all the grain they had brought from Egypt, their father said to them, "Go back and buy us some
3 food."/ But Juda answered, "The man strictly warned us, 'You shall not appear in my presence unless your brother
4 is with you.'/ If you will let our brother accompany us,
5 we will go down to buy food for you./ But if you do not let him, we will not go, because the man said to us, 'You shall not appear in my presence unless your brother is
6 with you.'"/ Israel replied, "Why did you wrong me by
7 telling the man you had another brother?"/ They answered, "The man questioned us in detail about ourselves and our family: 'Is your father still living? Have you another brother?' What we told him was in response to these questions. Could we possibly know that he would say, 'Bring your brother down'?"
8 Then Juda said to his father Israel, "Let the boy go with me, that we may begin our journey and save from
9 death both you and ourselves, as well as our children./ I will be surety for him. Hold me responsible for him. If I do not bring him back to you and place him before you,
10 I shall be guilty of a crime against you all my life./ Had we not delayed, we could by now have made the journey
11 twice."/ Their father Israel said to them, "If it must be so, then do this: take some of the country's best products in your bags and bring them down to the man for a gift: some balsam, syrup, gum, laudanum, pistachio nuts and
12 almonds./ Also take double the money along; for you must return the money placed in the mouths of your
13 sacks, in case a mistake was made./ Take your brother
14 too, and go back to the man./ May Almighty God give you favor with the man so that he will release to you your other brother as well as Benjamin. As for me, if I must be bereft, let me be bereft."

It is evident that no point at all is made in this second half of the story about Simeon's being a hostage back in Egypt. All the discussion concerns Benjamin exclusively. The "Judaite" version apparently had not contained the detail about Simeon; the abrupt

references to him in v. 14 above and later in v. 23 look like inser-
tions that have been taken from the "Rubenite" story after the
two were joined into a unit.

Juda's plea is at length successful, for Jacob realizes he is powerless to refuse. We recognize a few of the differences between the
two versions of the story, chiefly from Juda's speech. He tells Jacob—who is called Israel throughout this part—that Joseph had
questioned them minutely about their family background, while
in the preceding chapter we saw that the brothers themselves
offered this information as a defense. Juda's surety is a powerful
one, for a sin against one's parent was punishable with death.

Jacob tries to do his best to smooth the way for a safe return of
the brothers, by sending gifts and offering signs of friendship.
Jacob had long before perfected the art of getting his way, but
this time he was unaware of the one with whom he was match-
ing wits.

43:15 So the men took their gift, and taking double the money
with them, they went with Benjamin to Egypt and came
16 before Joseph./ When Joseph saw Benjamin with them,
he said to his steward, "Bring the men into the house, and
have an animal slaughtered and made ready, for the men
17 are to dine with me at noon."/ He did as Joseph ordered,
18 bringing the men to Joseph's house./ They became
frightened on being led to Joseph's house, and said, "It is
on account of the money put back in our sacks the first
time that we are brought in, so that he may seek an excuse
19 to enslave us by treachery, and take our asses."/ So they
went to Joseph's steward and spoke to him at the entrance
20 of the house./ "If you please, sir," they said, "once before
21 we came down to buy food;/ but when we reached the
stopping-place and opened our sacks, there in the mouth
of his sack was each one's money in full. But we have
22 brought it back with us,/ and also other money to buy
food. We do not know who put the money in our sacks."
23 "Be calm," he replied; "have no fear. Your God, the God
of your fathers, put treasure in your sacks for you. I
received your money." Then he brought Simeon out to
them.
24 The man brought them into Joseph's house, gave them

25 water to wash their feet, and fodder for their asses./ Then
they set out the present for Joseph's arrival at noon; for
they had heard that they were to dine there.

26 When Joseph came home, they presented him with the
gift they had with them in the house, and prostrated

27 themselves before him./ He inquired about their health,
and said, "Is your father, the old man of whom you spoke,

28 in good health? Is he still living?"/ "Your servant, our
father, is well; he is still living," they said, bowing low to

29 him./ Then Joseph looked up and saw his brother Benjamin, the son of his own mother, and said, "So this is your
youngest brother of whom you spoke to me? God be

30 gracious to you, my son," he continued./ Thereupon Joseph broke off and was on the verge of tears, for his heart
yearned for his brother. He retired to his room and wept.

31 Then he bathed his face and came out. Restraining him-

32 self, he said, "Serve the meal."/ It was served separately
for him, for them, and for his Egyptian guests, because
the Egyptians may not eat with the Hebrews; this is ab-

33 horrent to the Egyptians./ They were seated in his presence in the order of age, from the oldest to the youngest;

34 and at this they looked at one another in amazement./ Joseph had portions brought to them from his own table,
but Benjamin's portion was five times as much as any
other's. They drank and became merry with him.

The friendship of the unpredictable governor of Egypt frightened the brothers more than his previous show of enmity. Whereas in their earlier lives these men had been given to devious ways,
they now felt that absolute candor was their only chance of sur-
vival. Joseph's rather roundabout way of dealing with them was
having its healthy results. They were also realizing probably for
the first time in their lives what it meant to be wholly at the
disposition of someone else's will, even as they had had the boy
Joseph at the disposal of their will and had stifled their pity of
him.

It could only increase their mystification that the viceroy of
Egypt would enquire about their trivial family affairs with a show
of genuine interest. And what could be stranger than that he

should know the proper order of precedence in which to set their places? Upon these things a great deal of importance was put, but it was not expected that a stranger should have found out their customary order of procedure.

The banquet was served separately to Joseph, to the Egyptians, and to the Hebrews. This is very much in keeping with Egyptian folkways, as the text of Genesis points out. Joseph and the Egyptians were separated because of their relative ranks, but the Egyptians were separated from the Hebrews because they scrupled against eating with them and all other foreigners. The Egyptian religion had numerous tabus against certain foods, notably cattle, which were considered sacred. Outlanders who partook of such food could only contaminate a meal.

44: 1 Joseph gave orders to his steward, saying, "Fill the men's sacks with as much food as they will hold, and put each
2 one's money in the mouth of his sack; but in that of the youngest put my cup, the silver cup, together with his
3 money for the grain." The steward carried out Joseph's instructions. At daybreak the men were sent off together
4 with their asses./ They had not gone far out of the city when Joseph said to his steward, "Go, follow the men, and when you overtake them, say to them, 'Why have you re-
5 turned evil for good?/ Why have you stolen the silver cup from me? It is the very one from which my master drinks. He will certainly guess where it is.[6] This is an evil thing
6 that you have done.' "/ When he overtook them he re-
7 peated these words; but they replied, "Why does my lord speak this way? Far be it from your servants to do such a
8 thing!/ We even brought back to you from the land of Chanaan the money we found in the mouths of our sacks. Would we then steal silver or gold from your master's
9 house?/ If it is found with any one of us, he shall die, and
10 we will be my lord's slaves."/ He replied, "Though it ought to be as you suggest, the one with whom it is found shall be my slave; and the rest of you shall go free."

[6] This appears to be an incorrect translation. Better: "It is the very one from which my master drinks, and in which he divines." So the Vulgate and all other translations. See the commentary.

11 Then each one of them quickly lowered his sack to the
12 ground and opened it. A search was made beginning with
   the oldest and ending with the youngest, and the cup was
13 found in Benjamin's sack./ Then they tore their garments,
14 and having reloaded the asses, returned to the city./ Juda
   and his brothers arrived at Joseph's house while he was
15 still there, so they fell to the ground before him./ Joseph
   said to them, "What is this you have done? Did you not
   know that such a man as I would guess correctly?"[7]

Joseph had still not finished the instruction of his brothers. The ruse which he planned worked out to the letter. The brothers were so sure the cup was not with them that they put themselves all in jeopardy of slavery, much as Jacob long ago had rashly sworn when unaware what Rachel had done (*31*:32). This merely afforded Joseph the further opportunity to appear magnanimous, and, apparently, to seal the fate of Benjamin.

The cup which Joseph "planted" in Benjamin's sack was a divining cup. The semi-magical discovery of secrets by divination was common practice among the Egyptians, and a favorite means was by water. The shape of the drops which fell from a divining cup were "read" by those skilled in such things, as a fortune-teller of today reads tea leaves. Joseph would have been expected to use such a device, for was he not skilled in forecasting the future? Joseph had undoubtedly found it convenient to accommodate himself to Egyptian presumptions, just as he found it useful to impress his brothers further as the complete man of mystery.

44: 16 Juda replied, "What can we say to my lord? How can we
   explain matters so as to clear ourselves? God has discovered the guilt of your servants. We are indeed the
   slaves of my lord, both we and the one with whom the
17 cup was found."/ "Far be it from me to act thus," said Joseph. "The one with whom the cup was found shall be my
   slave; as for the rest, go in peace to your father."
18 Then Juda approached him and said, "I beg you, my
   lord, let your servants speak to my lord, and let not
   your anger be aroused against your servant; you are as

[7] "Did you not know that such a man as I would divine it?" Cf. v. 5.

19 Pharao himself./ My lord asked his servants, 'Have you a
20 father or a brother?'/ And we answered my lord, 'We
   have an aged father, and a young brother, a child of his
   old age; his brother is dead, so that he is the only one left
21 of his mother's children, and his father loves him.'/ Then
   you said to your servants, 'Bring him to me that I may
22 look after him.'/ We told my lord, 'The boy cannot leave
   his father; his father would die if he were to leave him.'
23 But you said to your servants, 'Unless your youngest
   brother comes with you, you shall not come into my pres-
24 ence again.'/ When we returned to your servant, my
25 father, we reported to him the words of my lord./ Later
26 our father said, 'Go back and buy some food for us.'/ But
   we answered, 'We cannot go. If our youngest brother is
   with us, we will go down; for we may not see the man un-
27 less our youngest brother is with us.'/ Then your servant,
   my father, said to us, 'You know that my wife bore me two
28 sons;/ one is gone from me, and I said: He has surely
29 been torn to pieces; I have not seen him since./ If you
   take this one also from me, and some harm befalls him,
   you will bring down my gray hairs in sorrow to the grave.'
30 Now if I go to your servant, my father, and the boy is not
   with us—his life is so bound up with the life of the boy—
   he will die as soon as he sees that the boy is not with us;
31 and your servants will bring down the gray hairs of your
32 servant, our father, in sorrow to the grave./ However,
   your servant became surety for the boy to my father, saying, 'If I do not bring him back to you, I will be guilty of a
33 crime against you all my life.'/ Therefore, let your servant
   remain in place of the boy as a slave of my lord, but let
34 the boy return with his brothers./ How can I return to my
   father without the boy? Never could I witness the anguish
   that would come to my father!"

The Judaite character of the present narrative is strongly pronounced. Juda had guaranteed Benjamin's safety, and he was
not slow to honor his word. His eloquent and unselfish plea for
Benjamin's return is one of the most touching scenes in this story.
In his words we have a few more glimpses of the first half of the

"Judaite" tradition for which the "Rubenite" story was substituted.

In Juda's pleading we see the justification of Joseph's education of his brothers through so many tricks and ruses. Juda and his brothers had come a long way since that day when they had heartlessly sought Joseph's life. A regeneration had taken place, which we can see manifested in Juda.

And at this plea Joseph revealed himself. Whether this had been his first plan, or he was now carried away by emotion, we cannot know. This is the climax of our story.

45:1 Joseph could not control himself before all his attendants, so he exclaimed, "Let everyone withdraw from me." No one was with Joseph when he made himself known to his
2 brothers./ He wept aloud so that the Egyptians heard it,
3 and the household of Pharao heard it./ Joseph said to his brothers, "I am Joseph. Is my father still alive?" But his brothers could not answer him because they were terrified
4 in his presence./ Then he said to them, "Come closer to me." When they drew near, he continued, "I am your
5 brother Joseph, whom you sold into Egypt./ Do not be distressed nor angry with yourselves that you sold me here;
6 for God sent me before you to save life./ For two years now the famine has been in the land, and for five more
7 years there will be neither plowing nor reaping./ God sent me before you to preserve a remnant for you in the land,
8 and to deliver you in a striking way./ Not you but God sent me here, and made me a father to Pharao, lord of all his house, and ruler over all the land of Egypt."

Here and in the following chapter the author has drawn together the conclusions of both traditions which he had been using, and had mingled them almost verse by verse. Apparently he took the most dramatic parts of each of the two stories, as appears from v. 3 above. "Is my father still alive?" asks Joseph. This is from the "Rubenite" version; in the Judaite version of the preceding chapter Joseph had been told very thoroughly by Juda that his father still lived.

By all rights Joseph's brothers could fear his vengeance, but Joseph had not played his game with them so long for any petty purpose. He was now in a position to do great things for his family, and there was only love in his heart. We may think, indeed, he was more than generous in minimizing his brothers' sin, attributing all to God's providence in working good despite man's evildoing.

In Acts 7 the New Testament makes much of these details in the life of Joseph which have made him a type and foreshadowing of Christ. Betrayed by his brothers, yet their savior, the magnanimous Joseph is surely one of the most beautiful characters of the Old Testament. It was not for nothing that so much of his life story was preserved.

45: 9 "Go quickly to my father and say to him, 'Your son Joseph sends you this message: God has made me master of all
10 Egypt; come down to me, and do not delay./ You shall live in the land of Gesen and be near me, you, your sons, your grandsons, your flocks, your herds, and all that belongs to
11 you./ Five years of famine are still to come. I will provide for you there, that you, and your household, and all who
12 belong to you may not be impoverished.'/ You yourselves see, and my brother Benjamin sees, that it is I who speak to
13 you./ Tell my father of my splendor in Egypt, and of all that you have seen. Hurry now and bring my father here."
14 Then Joseph fell on the neck of his brother Benjamin and
15 wept; and Benjamin wept on his neck./ Joseph kissed all his brothers, weeping over each, and after that his brothers conversed with him.
16 When the news was received at Pharao's house that Joseph's brothers had arrived, Pharao and his court were
17 pleased./ Pharao said to Joseph, "Say to your brothers, 'Do this: load your animals, be off to the land of Chanaan;
18 then come to me with your father and your families, and I will give you the best of the land of Egypt so that you shall
19 eat the fat of the land.'/ Give them this command also: 'Take carts from the land of Egypt for your little ones and
20 your wives. Bring your father and come./ Do not be concerned about your goods, for the best of the whole land of Egypt is yours.'"

The land of Gesen where Joseph planned to locate his family near himself and Pharao was the eastern part of the Nile delta, around the Hyksos capital of Tanis. Pharao, because of Joseph, was of Joseph's mind in all this. Later we see why, however, apart from Joseph's beneficence, the Israelites were given this "best of the land of Egypt."

45: 21 The sons of Israel did this. Joseph gave them carts as Pharao had commanded, and provisions for the journey.
22 He gave each of them one festal garment, but to Benjamin he gave three hundred pieces of silver and five festal gar-
23 ments./ Likewise to his father he sent ten asses loaded with the good things of Egypt, and ten she-asses loaded with grain, bread and provisions for his father on the
24 journey./ Then he sent his brothers on their way; and as they departed he said to them, "Do not quarrel on the
25 way."/ So they went up from Egypt and came to their fa-
26 ther Jacob in the land of Chanaan./ They told him, "Joseph is still alive, and he is ruler over all the land of Egypt." But he was unmoved because he did not believe
27 them./ However, when they related to him all that Joseph had said to them, and when he saw the carts Joseph had
28 sent to convey him, their father Jacob revived./ "It is enough," said Israel. "My son Joseph is still alive; I will go and see him before I die."

Perhaps it was with delicate irony that Joseph charged his brothers not to quarrel on their way back to Chanaan; he knew by bitter experience what were their possibilities in family strife. But probably these were words of reassurance, telling them not to debate among themselves the responsibility for the deed they had so unjustly done him in the past (similarly 45:5). All was now forgotten and forgiven.

Jacob was understandably unbelieving at first. Apparently it was only when he saw the munificent gifts the brothers had brought back, the strange conduct of the governor of Egypt at last began to make sense.

CHAPTER XV: THE SOWING OF A PEOPLE

And so Israel and his household came down into Egypt. The story is simply told, but it is a great event. They went in a family, and were to emerge centuries later a people, and a chosen people. That is the story of the Book of Exodus.

46: 1 Israel set out with all that belonged to him; and when he arrived at Bersabee he offered sacrifices to the God of
2 his father Isaac. At night in a vision God said to Israel,
3 "Jacob, Jacob." And he answered, "Here I am."/ Then he said, "I am God, the God of your father. Do not fear to go down to Egypt, for there I will make you a great peo-
4 ple./ I will go down to Egypt with you, and will surely bring you up again, after Joseph's hand has closed your eyes."

From Hebron Jacob came down to Bersabee, where long ago the LORD had said to Isaac, "Do not go down into Egypt" (26:2). It is now the fulness of time that God's promise to Abraham should begin to find its realization. Egypt is to be the soil in which Abraham's and Isaac's and Jacob's seed will grow into the mighty nation Israel.

Did all the Israelites go down into Egypt? The Genesis tradition, as we see, speaks as though they did. We have remarked before, however, that some authorities are of the opinion that the Bible has somewhat simplified the complex history of the past, that there were Israelites who remained in Chanaan and who together with those liberated from Egypt under Moses participated in the conquest of the Promised Land. There are various indications and allusions scattered through the Bible which lend support to the view.

It is clear, in any case, that Israel as such did go into Egypt. There is an increasing abundance of historical and archaeological evidence to prove that the story of the Egyptian captivity and the Exodus are every bit as factual as the sojourn of the patriarchs in Chanaan.

Israel went down happy, to live the life of favored guests. It was still many years before their Hyksos protectors would be driven from the land and Egypt, the symbol of bounty, would become the embodiment of oppression.

> 46:5 Jacob departed from Bersabee. The sons of Israel con-
> veyed their father Jacob, their little ones, and their wives
> 6 in the carts Pharao had sent to transport him./ They also
> took their stock and the goods they had got in the land of
> Chanaan; and Jacob and all his descendants migrated to
> 7 Egypt./ With him were his sons and grandsons, his daugh-
> ters and granddaughters; with all his descendants Jacob
> migrated to Egypt.

Whatever was the number of those who went down to Egypt with Jacob, the following list is not to be taken as a precise indication. This list is not part of the preceding story, but has been inserted into the text from another and different source. The author simply did not have an historical list of Jacob's companions; he did have a list of Jacob's descendants, and with this he made do.

How little this list coincides with the story we have just read will be seen from v. 21, where Benjamin appears as the father of ten sons. All along it is presumed that Benjamin is still a young lad, born in his father's old age. The LXX text of this verse, it is true, makes only three of these persons Benjamin's sons, the first three: the rest it names his grandsons except the last, a great-grandson! This only adds to the difficulty. Similarly, v. 12 presupposes the story of chapter 38 and makes Juda a grandfather. We know that the dating of chapter 38 is uncertain, but in the preceding story only twenty years or so have passed since Joseph was a youth among his brothers who were as yet unmarried and part of their father's household (see 37:2, 41:46, 45:6). We must conclude that this is a much later list of Jacob's descent.

46: 8 These are the names of the Israelites, Jacob and his descendants, who migrated to Egypt: Ruben, Jacob's first-
9 born,/ and the sons of Ruben: Henoch, Phallu, Hesron and
10 Charmi;/ the sons of Simeon: Jamuel, Jamin, Ahod, Jachin,
11 Sohar and Saul, the son of a Chanaanite woman;/ the sons
12 of Levi: Gerson, Caath and Merari;/ the sons of Juda: Her,
Onan, Sela, Phares and Zara, of whom Her and Onan, however, died in the land of Chanaan; and the sons of Phares
13 were Hesron and Hamul./ The sons of Issachar: Thola,
14 Phua, Jasub and Semron;/ the sons of Zabulon: Sared,
15 Elon and Jahelel./ These are the sons whom Lia bore to
Jacob in Phaddan-Aram, together with his daughter Dina.
The total number of these descendants, male and female,
was thirty-three.

This list is a good example to illustrate Father Sutcliffe's judgment: "The fact is that the ancient oriental did not set store on
exactness as does the modern western mind."[1] Most of the names
appear elsewhere in the Bible, but with considerable variations.
The list takes Jacob's sons in order by wives, giving the grandchildren. It seems to have been revised at various times. In v. 15
for example the standard concluding formula of vv. 18, 22, 25 has
been revised to "descendants, male and female," in an attempt to
take account of Dina named in the same verse. Yet the number
of descendants was not revised at the same time, for the thirty-
three evidently excludes Dina, who makes a thirty-fourth. Hence
we know that her name was added later. Her and Onan, as is
evident, did not migrate with Jacob to Egypt.

46: 16 The sons of Gad: Sephon, Haggi, Suni, Esebon, Heri,
17 Arodi and Ariel./ The sons of Aser: Jemna, Jesua, Jesui
and Baria, with their sister Sara; and Baria's sons were
18 Heber and Melchiel./ These are the descendants of Zelpha, whom Laban gave to his daughter Lia; these she
bore to Jacob, sixteen persons in all.

[1] *Catholic Commentary,* p. 200.

19 The sons of Jacob's wife Rachel were Joseph and Ben-
20 jamin./ Sons were born to Joseph in the land of Egypt,
   Manasse and Ephraim, whom Aseneth, the daughter of
21 Phutiphare, the priest of On, bore to him./ The sons of
   Benjamin: Bala, Bechor, Asbel, Gera, Naaman, Ehi, Ros,
22 Mopphim, Hoppim and Ared./ These are the descendants of Rachel who were born to Jacob, fourteen persons
   in all.

Besides the difficulty previously noted in Benjamin's case, his
descendants provide other discrepancies with the lists otherwise
given in the Bible. The reader can compare, if he is interested,
the variants in Numbers 26:38 ff., and I Paralipomenon 7:6 ff.
There are differences with the other sons as well, but not to the
degree of Benjamin. Besides passing through different traditions,
the texts have undergone corruption, and it would be impossible
now to decide where accuracy lies.

46: 23.24 The son of Dan: Husim. The sons of Nephthali: Jaseel,
       25 Guni, Jeser and Sellum. These were the descendants
          of Bala, whom Laban gave to his daughter Rachel;
          these she bore to Jacob, seven persons in all.
       26 The total number of persons belonging to Jacob (ex-
          cept his sons' wives) who came to Egypt, his direct
       27 descendants, was sixty-six./ The sons of Joseph who
          were born to him in Egypt were two; the total number
          of Jacob's household who migrated to Egypt was
          seventy.

Seventy was the traditional number of Jacob's descendants
who went down into Egypt (see Deut. 10:22); it is a round number, the sacred seven multiplied tenfold. The figures of this list
in vv. 15, 18, 22, and 25 added together do give seventy. Later on
someone other than the original author of the list inserted v. 26,
for he remembered that Ephraim and Manasse named in v. 20
were born in Egypt, and probably at the same time he noted in
v. 12 that Her and Onan had died in Chanaan. The desire for
mathematical precision is not, however, one of the characteristics
of Genesis.

46: 28 Israel sent Juda ahead of him to Joseph, so that he would
meet him in Gesen. On their arrival in the land of Gesen,/
29 Joseph made ready his chariot and rode to meet his father Israel in Gesen. When he met him he fell on his neck,
30 weeping long in his arms./ Israel said to Joseph, "Now I
can die, after seeing you still alive."
31 Joseph said to his brothers and to his father's household,
"I shall go and inform Pharao, and say to him, 'My brothers and my father's household, who lived in the land of
32 Chanaan, have come to me./ The men are shepherds, for
they breed livestock. They have brought their flocks and
33 herds and all their possessions.'/ Accordingly, when he
34 summons you and asks, 'What is your occupation?'/ you
must answer, 'We your servants have bred livestock from
our youth until now, both we and our ancestors,' in order
that you may sojourn in the land of Gesen." For shepherds
are all repugnant to the Egyptians.
47: 1 Joseph came and told Pharao, "My father and brothers
have come from the land of Chanaan with their flocks
and herds and all their possessions, and they are now in
2 the land of Gesen."/ He had selected five of his brothers,
3 whom he presented to Pharao./ When Pharao asked them,
"What is your occupation?" they answered, "Your servants,
4 both we and our ancestors, are shepherds./ We have come
to sojourn in your land, for there is no pasture for your
servants' flocks, and the famine is severe in the land of
Chanaan. Permit your servants to settle in the land of
Gesen."

This is the final bit of the "Judaite" narrative which the author
has included in his history of Israel's coming to Egypt. It includes
a touching description of Jacob's meeting with Joseph. According
to this tradition Joseph took the initiative throughout with Pharao,
going out to meet his people and bringing a delegation of five
of his brothers before the king. Five seems to have been a number
dear to Egyptian hearts as seven was to Hebrew. We remember
that the Egyptianized Joseph sent a fivefold portion of food from
his table to Benjamin (43:34), gave him five festal garments

(45:22), and we shall see in a moment that income taxes in Egypt were counted by fifths.

It sounds curious that Joseph should insist that his brothers tell Pharao that they were shepherds (which of course was perfectly true), when the text notes that "shepherds are all repugnant to the Egyptians." It makes sense, however, when we remind ourselves that Pharao was not an Egyptian but a Hyksos foreigner, even as the Hebrews were foreigners in Egypt. Joseph did not want his family to be settled among the Egyptians but near himself and Pharao in the delta-land of Gesen, the best part of the country. Here they would live among their own kind, not with a hostile populace which would resent their presence.

Just why the Egyptians abominated shepherds is not too clear. Probably it had to do with more of their religious tabus. The likes and dislikes of a people who deified cows will not invariably strike us as logical or reasoned.

47:5 Pharao said to Joseph, "Your father and your brothers have
6 come to you./ The land of Egypt is at your disposal. Settle your father and your brothers in the choicest section of the land. Let them live in the land of Gesen, and if you know of any able men among them, place them in charge of my own stock."
7 Then Joseph brought his father Jacob, and presented him
8 to Pharao. Jacob greeted Pharao,/ who said to him, "How
9 old are you?"/ Jacob answered Pharao, "The length of my pilgrimage has been one hundred and thirty years; short and wretched has been my life, nor does it compare with
10 the years my fathers lived during their pilgrimage."/ Then Jacob blessed Pharao and withdrew from his presence.
11 Joseph settled his father and brothers in the land of Egypt, giving them property in the choicest section of the land,
12 in the district of Rameses, as Pharao had ordered. Joseph provided his father and brothers and all his father's household with food, according to the number of their dependents.

Now Pharao takes the initiative. The district of Rameses in which he orders Jacob and his relatives to be settled is the same

as the land of Gesen. This name is given by anticipation by the
author, for it was not called Rameses until many years later, when
it was rebuilt by Hebrew slave labor, probably under the Pharao
Ramses II. Rameses is Tanis.

47:13 There was no food in the entire land, for the famine was
very severe; Egypt and Chanaan were languishing be-
14 cause of the famine./ Joseph collected all the money he
found in Egypt and in Chanaan as payment for the grain
that was bought, and he brought it to Pharao's palace.
15 When there was no more money in Egypt and Chanaan,
all the Egyptians came to Joseph clamoring, "Give us
food lest we die in your presence; we have no money."
16 Joseph replied, "If you have no money bring me your
17 livestock, and I will give you food in exchange for it./ So
they brought their stock to Joseph, who bartered food
for horses, flocks, herds and asses; and he supplied them
18 with food in exchange for all their stock that year./ The
year ended, and they came again the next year and said:
"We cannot hide from my lord that our money is gone,
and our livestock has come into the possession of my lord.
There is nothing left for my lord but our bodies and our
19 land. Why should we and our land perish before your
eyes? Buy us and our land in exchange for food, and we
and our land will be the property of Pharao. Give us seed
that we may live and not perish, and the land may not
become a waste."
20 Joseph therefore bought all the land of Egypt for Pharao,
for every one of the Egyptians sold his field because the
famine was unbearable for them. Thus the land became
21 Pharao's,/ and from one end of Egypt to the other, Jo-
22 seph made the people slaves./ But the priests' lands he
did not buy, because they had a stated allowance from
Pharao, and lived on the allowance which Pharao granted
them. Therefore they did not sell their land.
23 Joseph said to all the people: "Today, indeed, I have
bought you and your land for Pharao. Here is your seed
24 to sow the land./ Of the produce you must give a fifth

part of the crops to Pharao; four fifths are for yourselves
for seeding and for food for yourselves, your families and
25 your dependents."/ They answered, "You have kept us
alive; let us win the favor of my lord, and we will be
26 slaves of Pharao."/ So Joseph made it an ordinance for
the land of Egypt, which holds to this day, that one fifth
is Pharao's. Only the land of the priests did not become
Pharao's.

This story, virtually the last which the author has to tell of
Joseph, again shows the keen interest the Hebrews had in com-
paring their way of life with the Egyptians'. In Egypt, as long as
the Israelites had known the Egyptians, all property was technically at least crown possession. It was not simply that the Pharao
exercised a right of eminent domain: theoretically he owned
Egypt personally, and the tenure of land was after the manner of
a fief. This was entirely in keeping with the notion that he was
a god incarnate, that it was at his bidding that the sun rose in
the morning and set at night, and that he was absolute master
of his subjects. In keeping with this, too, the Egyptians were
Pharao's property. One Egyptian might own another as his slave,
but every Egyptian possessed his freedom at the Pharao's good
pleasure. He ruled as absolute despot, could conscript any of his
subjects for public works or other services. In the Cairo Museum,
among the treasures recovered from the Pharaos' tombs, are two
very revealing objects. One is a footstool made of the carved
figures of typical Egyptians: all Egypt lay beneath Pharao's foot.
The other is a walking stick whose handle represents entwined
Egyptians: all Egypt lay in the Pharao's hand. There was more
fact than symbolism in these; probably the craftsman who fashioned them did so with grim humor.

All this was foreign to the Israelites. In Israel property was
private and jealously safeguarded by law. The most ancient legislation of this people positively forbade the alienation of a man's
patrimony, to prevent the possibility of monopoly of any com-
modity, and not even the king, when the Israelites finally had
one, could set aside these laws. The Israelites, prided themselves
on being free men, slaves to no one. The slavery of one Israelite to

another was, in fact, at first unknown, was later tolerated, but only as a kind of indenture for payment of debt, and strictly limited as to duration. One of the chief grievances of the people against King Solomon, and a cause of schism after his death when his son threatened to continue his policies, was his forcing the Israelites to labor at public works as the Egyptians did.

The Israelites were amazed that a people could submit to such an order of society as the Egyptians took for granted. They concluded, however, after bitter experiences at their hands, that this sort of thing served the Egyptians quite right. The Egyptians were just the people who should be slaves. Hence this tradition which attributed the existing Egyptian economy to Joseph. We do not fancy it as putting Joseph in a very gracious light, perhaps, but the Israelites would have considered it another jewel in his crown that he was responsible for making the Egyptians the contemptible spectacle that they were.

And the story is not unhistorical. The Egyptian system which vested all rights in Pharao was the result of an innovation, which came into being sometime during this general period. Historians usually assign it to the seventeenth dynasty, which expelled the Hyksos; however, the origins may well be earlier.

Historical, too, is the careful notation that the priesthood was exempt from this policy. The powerful theocracy ruled by the priests of On was Pharao's one rival in Egypt, able at times to unseat kings and make new ones. It was untouchable. One Pharao alone tried to divest it of its influence, and signally failed; and he was a madman.

47: 27   Now Israel dwelt in Egypt, in the land of Gesen. They acquired property there, were fruitful, and became very
   28 numerous. Jacob lived seventeen years in the land of Egypt, and the length of his life was one hundred and
   29 forty-seven years. As the time approached for him to die, he summoned his son Joseph and said to him, "If I find favor with you, put your hand under my thigh, and act kindly and faithfully toward me. Do not bury me
   30 in Egypt,/ but let me rest with my fathers; carry me
   31 out of Egypt and bury me in their sepulchre." He an-

swered, "I will do as you say." Then Jacob said, "Swear to me"; and Joseph swore to him. Then Israel bowed toward the head of the bed.

Seemingly the author had at least three stories relating to Jacob on his deathbed, or at least near death. This first is the simplest, Jacob's request and Joseph's oath, sworn after a form that was apparently common with the patriarchs (cf. *24*:2 f.), that Jacob should be buried in the Land of Promise rather than in Egypt. The sequel to this story is in *50*:4 ff.

The second story has to do with Joseph's sons, Ephraim and Manasse. All the sons of Israel were the traditional ancestors of Israelite tribes except Joseph. No tribe was named after Joseph, but instead two tribes derived their names from his two sons. This story accounts for that fact: Ephraim and Manasse were adopted by Jacob as his own sons.

48: 1 After these events it was reported to Joseph, "Your father is ill." So he came to see Jacob, bringing along his two
2 sons, Manasse and Ephraim. When Jacob was told, "Your son Joseph has come to see you," Israel rallied his strength
3 and sat up in bed. Jacob said to Joseph, "God Almighty appeared to me at Luza in the land of Chanaan. He blessed
4 me/ and said, 'I will make you fruitful and numerous; I will make you many nations, and I will give this land to your descendants after you as a possession for all time.'
5 Therefore I adopt your two sons who were born to you in the land of Egypt before I joined you here. Ephraim and
6 Manasse shall be mine even as Ruben and Simeon. The children born to you after them shall be yours, and they shall be named after their brothers and included in their
7 inheritance./ And as for me, when I was returning from Phaddan, to my sorrow Rachel died during the journey in the land of Chanaan, a short distance from the environs of Ephratha. And I buried her there on the road to Ephratha, that is, Bethlehem."[2]

---

[2] "Bethlehem," cf. the commentary on *35*:19. This passage also follows the same tradition, which placed Benjamin's birth shortly after the return from Phaddan-Aram.

8 When Israel saw Joseph's sons and asked, "Who are
9 these?",/ Joseph said to his father, "They are my sons,
whom God has given me here." Then he said, "Bring them
10 to me that I may bless them."/ Now Israel's eyes were dim
from old age so that he could not see. Joseph brought them
11 near him, and he kissed and embraced them./ Then Israel
said to Joseph, "I had no hope of ever seeing you, and now
God has allowed me to see your children as well."

12 Joseph took them away from his knees, and prostrated
13 himself before him with his face to the ground./ Afterward
Joseph took the two of them, Ephraim on his right at
Israel's left, Manasse on his left at Israel's right, and led
14 them to him./ But Israel stretched out his right hand and
placed it on the head of Ephraim, though he was the
younger, and his left hand on Manasse's head—thus cross-
15 ing his hands—although Manasse was the first-born./ Blessing Joseph, he said,

"May the God in whose presence my fathers Abraham
    and Isaac lived,
the God who has been my shepherd all my life
    until this day,
16   the angel who has delivered me from all evil,
        bless the boys;
That my name and the name of my fathers Abraham
    and Isaac be preserved through them;
And may they grow in numbers on the earth."

17 When Joseph saw that his father had placed his right
hand on Ephraim's head, he was displeased, so he took
hold of his father's hand to remove it from Ephraim's
18 head to that of Manasse./ He said to his father, "That is not
right, father, for this one is the first-born; put your right
19 hand on his head."/ But his father refused. "I know, my
son, I know," he said. "He too shall become a people; he
too shall be great; but his younger brother shall be greater
than he, and his descendants shall become a multitude of
20 nations."/ So he blessed them that day and said, "By you
shall the people of Israel pronounce blessings, saying, 'God

make you like Ephraim and Manasse' "; thus placing Ephraim ahead of Manasse.

It was only fitting that Ephraim and Manasse, born in Egypt which was to become the Israelites' oppression, should be put on a level with Jacob's sons by his specific act that they might become ancestors of free Israelites.

This beautiful account likewise was intended to explain why the tribe of Ephraim, though descended from Joseph's younger son, should have become by far more important than the tribe of Manasse. God's providence made it so, said the Hebrew poet, expressed through their father's blessing, even as Noe's blessing accounted for the varied careers of Sem, Ham, and Japheth. During Israel's first days in Chanaan after the conquest, it was the tribe of Ephraim which held undisputed primacy. Not until the establishment of the monarchy, about two hundred years later, did Ephraim's strength begin to wane, and even afterward it was a power to be reckoned with.

48:21 Then Israel said to Joseph, "I am about to die. But God will be with you, and will lead you back to the land of
22 your fathers;/ I give you one more portion than your brothers, which I captured from the Amorrites with my sword and bow."

These last two verses are mysterious. Jacob is still speaking to Joseph in the person of his sons, as the fathers of Israelite tribes. Joseph was not to return to Egypt, neither were his sons, but the tribes of Ephraim and Manasse were to be outstanding in the conquest of the Promised Land.

This prediction seems to refer to the tribe of Ephraim. Both Ephraim and Manasse will be bywords for good fortune in days to come, Jacob has said, but Ephraim whom he has given the blessing of the firstborn has the customary right to a double portion. The word translated "portion" is the same as Sichem. Sichem was, in fact, allotted to the tribe of Ephraim in the division of Palestine after the conquest. Here once again we seem to have an allusion to a prior Israelite capture of Sichem, as we suggested in the commentary on chapter 34. Here Jacob himself asserts the conquest to himself, which is related nowhere else in the Genesis traditions. The Sichemites are in this passage called Amorrites, previously Hevites (or Horrites); but "Amorrite" is often the general equivalent of "Chanaanite," which in turn can refer to any of the varied peoples of Chanaan.

That Ephraim possessed Sichem did indeed entail a double portion. Sichem was for many years the most important Israelite political and religious centre before the days of the monarchy.

49: 1 Then Jacob summoned his sons and said:
    "Come together, I will tell you,
      what shall befall you in days to come.
  2   Gather together and listen, you sons of Jacob,
      listen to Israel your father."

This last deathbed scene is the most interesting of all, and by far the most important. It contains some of the oldest sustained poetry in Genesis: so old, in fact, that some of it is quite obscure and the translation is accordingly not certain. We must first of all carefully understand its literary form.

It is traditionally called "the blessings of Jacob" because of the title given it in v. 28. The blessings of a dying father were conventional, and to this extent the scene is taken from life. Actually, however, hardly any of the parts of this poem deserve the name of a blessing, except the one addressed to Joseph. It is in the form of predictions, historical descriptions of the state of the Israelite tribes at a time far removed from Jacob.

As Father Sutcliffe comments, "The language of the blessings is elaborate and poetic, and it is agreed that they cannot have been pronounced by the aged and dying Jacob in their present form."[3] Further, they descend to considerable meticulous detail in some instances, detail of a political or geographical nature. "God could, of course, reveal the future to Jacob in all its details, but it is not in accord with God's ordinary providence to reveal in advance the geographical location of the territory to be allotted to a tribe, as is the case here with Zabulon, 13."[4] It is generally conceded

3 *Catholic Commentary*, p. 203.
4 Loc. cit.

among commentators, therefore, that in their present form the utterances placed on Jacob's lips are poems which date from the early Israelite times in Chanaan after the conquest: for the most part probably the period of the Judges, that is, the first two centuries of Israelite Palestine, and somewhat later, probably David's time, in the case of the blessing of Juda in v. 8 ff. The literary form of the similar "blessings of Moses" in Deut. 33 is very much the same; together these series provide a precious font of primitive Israelite history, though the blessings of Deuteronomy are somewhat more recent.

We are thus afforded a real look into the future of Jacob's descendants from the standpoint of the period of Genesis.

> 49: 3 "Ruben, you are my first-born,
> my strength, the first-fruit of my manhood,
> exceedingly proud, exceedingly fierce.
>
> 4 Unstable as water, never first shall you be,
> for your father's bed you did ascend;
> him have I degraded who went up to my couch."

Ruben, Jacob's firstborn son, had committed an unpardonable crime against his father (35:22). To that fact is attributed Ruben's repudiation, and the subsequent decline of that tribe. The Song of Debora in Judges 5:15 f. shows that in the period of the Judges Ruben was still an important tribe; by the time Deut. 33:6 was written, however, the vicissitudes of history had made it virtually extinct.

Theologically, we also see an explanation why Ruben was passed over as the recipient of the promise which had descended to Jacob through Isaac from Abraham. Not in the tribe of Ruben was the promise to have its fulfilment.

> 49: 5 "Simeon and Levi, brothers indeed,
> weapons of violence are their swords.
>
> 6 My soul, never enter their company,
> never be in their assembly, my spirit!
> Because in their fury they slew men,
> in their willfulness they hamstrung oxen.

7   Cursed be their fury because it is violent,
        their rage because it is cruel.
    I will disperse them in Jacob,
        I will scatter them in Israel."

Simeon and Levi, the next in order of birth, are likewise passed
over, and the reason given is without doubt their cruelty and wan-
ton destruction at Sichem as related in chapter 34.

They were indeed as tribes "dispersed in Jacob, scattered in
Israel," though with vastly different fates. It is interesting to compare the poetry of Deut. 33:8 ff., where Levi is extravagantly
praised but Simeon is not mentioned at all. Simeon apparently
passed out of history rather early and its remnants became assimi-
lated into the powerful tribe of Juda. In Josue 19:1 ff. the territory
in Chanaan assigned to Simeon is actually Judaite, and v. 9 makes
it clear that Simeon had by now become nothing more than an
adjunct of Juda.

The Levites never obtained any distinctive territory of their
own: they were to live forever as Abraham, Isaac, and Jacob had
lived in Chanaan, residents and inhabitants, but not owners of
the land. Through the Law of Moses, however, the priestly functions of Israel were vested in the Levites, and it is this that is
celebrated in Deuteronomy.

49: 8   "Juda, your brothers shall praise you;
        your hand shall be on the neck of your enemies;
        the sons of your father shall bow down to you.
9   A lion's whelp is Juda;
        from the prey you have gone up, my son.
    He crouches and couches as a lion;
        as a lioness, and who will disturb him?
10 The sceptre shall not depart from Juda,
        nor the staff from between his feet,
    Until he comes to whom it belongs.
        To him shall be the obedience of nations.
11 He tethers his ass to the vine;
        his ass's colt to the choicest vine.
    He washes his garment in wine,
        his robe in the blood of grapes.

12   His eyes are darker than wine,
        his teeth whiter than milk."[5]

With the first three of Jacob's sons disqualified, the choice falls at last on Juda. With the monarchy, the tribe of Juda came into its own. David the first king of the Judaite line became the ideal type of Israelite ruler; he made the united kingdom of Israel into a real empire and established precedents of government that were to remain standard among his people. Juda was in every sense at this time the most important of the tribes, and even when its political leadership was later challenged, it maintained a prestige despite all that was possessed by no other.

This passage does not refer, however, simply to political domination. It is also messianic, the last statement in Genesis concerning the future Messias and Redeemer. The promise is to be fulfilled from the tribe of Juda.

Though some of the language is obscure, the general sense of v. 10 ff. is plain enough, and the passage has traditionally by both Jewish and Christian authors been taken as a reference to the Messias. Juda's power will not be broken, for at the end, in the fulness of time, will come the one who will rule by divine right over the nations. It is probably true that the author of this poem was thinking of David, the great king, but this does not weaken its messianic sense. David was by divine intention, and frequently as well by the intention of the biblical authors, a type and prefigure of the Messias. The imagery of these verses is very like the prophetic descriptions of the messianic age, when vines will be so plentiful that even the best can be used to tether a beast of burden, when wine will be so common it can be used to wash clothing, when there will be an abundance of all good things.

And it was from the tribe of Juda, the house and family of David, that Christ our Lord came into the world. The promise so dimly outlined in 3:15, reiterated and determined to the descendants of Abraham, Isaac, and Jacob, is now narrowed to the tribe of Juda and to the Davidic line.

[5] A probably better translation is, "His eyes are dark with wine,/ his teeth are white with milk." This fits in with the theme of abundance stressed in the verse above.

49: 13 "Zabulon shall dwell by the seashore;
   and he shall be by the shore of ships,
   with his flank toward Sidon."

Not much is said of Zabulon. It was to all appearances never a very important tribe. Its geographical location in Chanaan is given here, which does not agree with Josue *19*:10 ff., which confines Zabulon to inland territory, near but not on the Phoenician seashore. Nevertheless Deut. *33*:19 insists on the same kind of description for Zabulon as does this verse of Genesis, and probably, therefore, we see here an historical allusion recorded nowhere else which tells us that either before or after the boundaries of the tribes were fixed according to the lines drawn in Josue, Zabulon's territory was much larger.

49: 14 "Issachar is a sturdy ass,
   among the stock-pens he lies.
 15 He saw that settled life was good,
   and that the land was pleasant;
   He bowed his shoulder to bear burdens,
   and became a slave under taskwork."

It is hard to decide whether this is meant as a condemnation or a commendation. The tribe of Issachar obtained some of the best farmland in Palestine, and settled down quickly to the sedentary life. It seems as though Issachar's diligence is being praised, yet the author in the same breath speaks rather slightingly of one who would bow his head like an ox or an ass to tie himself down to the land. Possibly both elements of praise and disapproval are contained in this passage. The early Israelites were the natural children of the desert, and even when they were all becoming farmers they felt an instinctive contempt for the peasantry.

49: 16 "Dan shall achieve justice for his people,
   like any tribe of Israel.
 17 Dan shall be a serpent by the road,
   a viper by the path;
   Biting at the hoofs of the horse,
   so that the rider tumbles backward."
 18 ["Thy salvation, O LORD, I wait for!"]

The career of the tribe of Dan was exceedingly chequered. After the conquest they first settled between the two giants Juda and Ephraim; then, to make matters worse, they were continually harassed by the Philistines who had invaded the coastlands about the same time the Israelites entered Chanaan from the east and were now attempting to expand their territory. The Danites eventually migrated to the north, at least a great part of them, and carved out a territory for themselves between Sidon and the Lake of Galilee. All this is told us in the Book of Judges, and it is doubtless to this that v. 16 has reference.

Once they had acquired their new land, the Danites discovered that it had distinct advantages. The trade routes from the Phoenician ports of Tyre and Sidon had to pass through it on their way south. Control of the trade routes meant taxes and tolls which often, it is true, had to be collected forcibly. This seems to be the meaning of v. 17: the taxgatherer has never been a remarkably popular person. The prayer in v. 18 is a later addition to the text.

49: 19 "Gad, raiders shall raid him;
　　　　but he shall raid their rear."

The tribe of Gad settled in the Transjordan region, north of the Dead Sea. The land of Transjordan is bleak and bare, not at all suited to farming. Of all the tribes, Gad probably maintained the longest the old nomadic structure of society, and enjoyed an existence very little different from the Bedawin Arabs who inhabit this land today. A great part of the life and love of the Bedawin consists in the *razzia*, the raids carried out on neighboring tribes. These take the place of productive labor, provide forage, wives, entertainment and recreation, slaves. The incursion of the kings in chapter *14* is an example of a *razzia*, on perhaps a more grandiose scale than ordinary. Most of the early invasions of Chanaan by foreign peoples like the Assyrians were simply raiding expeditions, hit-and-run affairs for quick profit and a speedy withdrawal. It was into this give-and-take life that Gad entered, apparently with gusto.

49: 20 "Aser, his food shall be rich;
               he shall provide dainties for kings.
      21 Nephthali is a deer set free,
                . . . ."

About Aser and Nephthali there was not much to say. Aser's territory was the coastland in the extreme north of Chanaan, from the hook of Carmel as far as Tyre. This rocky seacoast is not fertile land, but it was immediately adjacent to Phoenicia, whose wealth was gained chiefly by trading and other commerce. Into Aser, therefore, came the exotic produce in which the Phoenicians traded, and it is probable that even as early as this in history there were combined commercial ventures of Phoenicians and Israelites as later the Bible tells us were carried out under Solomon.

Nephthali was in the same general area, to the east. What was said of it in this poem, however, we do not know. The text is partly corrupt, and what is not corrupt is unintelligible.

49: 22 "Joseph is a young fruit tree,
               a young fruit tree near the spring,
               with branches climbing over the wall.
      23 Against him in bitterness they fought;
               archers assailed him,
      24 But his bow remained firm,
               his strong arms supple,
           By the strength of the Mighty One of Jacob;
               by the name of the Shepherd, the Rock of Israel;
      25 By the God of your father, may he help you;
               by the God, the Omnipotent, may he bless you,
           With the blessings of the skies above,
               the blessings of the abyss couching beneath,
               the blessings of the breasts and womb;
      26 The blessings of your father surpass
               the blessings of my forebears
               to the limit of the timeless hills.
           May they rest on the head of Joseph,
               and on the brow of the prince among his brothers."

This blessing glorifies the tribe of Ephraim; Manasse apparently goes unmentioned. The word translated "fruit tree" in v. 22, *pharath,* is a play on words with Ephratha, which was originally the name given to the territory of Ephraim. Though there is considerable obscurity in much of the text, it is evident that only good is said of this Joseph tribe. Despite bitter opposition the tribe will flourish and be the recipient of all divine blessings. As indeed it was with Ephraim. There is perhaps an indication of the changing times in which these poems were composed, when we note that both Joseph in v. 26 and Juda in v. 8 are hailed as supreme among the sons of Israel. Juda's, however, would be the ultimate triumph.

> 49: 27 "Benjamin is a ravenous wolf;
> devouring prey in the morning,
> and at evening dividing spoil."

All that we have seen of Benjamin, the youngest of Jacob's sons, has hardly prepared us for this formidable description. The tribe of Benjamin, however, was noted for its fierceness, so much so that it had to be severely disciplined by a coalition of the other tribes. During the latter period of the Judges it assumed importance, and Israel's first king, Saul, was a Benjaminite. A latter-day Saul, himself not the meekest of men, better known in our history as Paul of Tarsus, was likewise of the tribe of Benjamin.

49: 28 All these are the twelve tribes of Israel, and this is what their father said to them. He blessed them, and gave each
29 his proper blessing./ He gave them this charge, "I am about to be gathered to my people. Bury me with my fathers in the cave which is in the field of Ephron, the
30 Hethite,/ the cave in the field of Machphela, facing Mamre in the land of Chanaan. Abraham bought it from Ephron, the Hethite, together with the field, for use as a
31 burial ground./ There Abraham and his wife Sara are buried; there Isaac and his wife Rebecca are buried;
32 and it was there I buried Lia."/ [The field with its cave was purchased from the Hethites.]
33 When Jacob had finished giving directions to his sons, he drew up his feet into the bed and expired. And he was gathered to his people.

50:1 Joseph fell on his father's face, weeping over him and
2 kissing him. Then he ordered the physicians among his
servants to embalm his father. They embalmed Israel,/
3 spending forty days at it, for it takes that much time
to embalm. And the Egyptians mourned Israel for seventy
days.

So are we brought to the end of Jacob's life. Before, in 48:7
when Jacob was speaking of his coming death with Joseph, he
mentioned the site of Rachel's tomb, as he does here Lia's. This
has led some to think that perhaps the former source recorded a
tradition that Jacob was buried with Rachel in Ephratha. At least,
there was more than one tradition of his burial place, as we shall
see below. Of these, however, the author has selected only the
one which set it in Mamre.

It has been remarked that such a speech as is credited to Jacob
in v. 29 ff., relating in detail what was as well known to his hearers
as to himself, was to impress upon the Israelites that their home
was in Chanaan, the land of their fathers, and not in Egypt. When
Moses led the Israelites from Egypt there were those among them,
as there have always been men through history, who preferred
security with slavery to the uncertainties of freedom. The allure
of Egypt was to be a real temptation to Jacob's descendants.

The author describes briefly for his readers the unfamiliar practice of embalming, the mummification which seems to have been
almost peculiar to the Egyptians. Other peoples besides the Hebrews were fascinated by this queer custom. In his *History,* Herodotus gives the details of the process, explaining the three rather
gruesome ways in which it was done, depending on the rank and
wealth of the person involved. None of the ways according to
Herodotus required less than seventy days. The Hebrew author's
estimate, therefore, seems to be a conservative one.

The Egyptians mummified animals as well as men. Behind the
practice of course lies the belief in immortality: primitive though
many of ancient man's ideas may have been, it has been reserved
for modern man to conclude that life is but smoke and the human body once dead only a piece of garbage. Israel too believed
in immortality, but Israel also believed in a God who gives life

to the dead. From Israel's belief developed the doctrine of the resurrection; they never resorted to this somewhat childish Egyptian practice, and the embalming of crocodiles and bulls must have seemed to them preposterous.

50: 4 When the days of mourning him had passed, Joseph said to Pharao's household, "If I find favor with you, say to
5 Pharao/ that my father at the point of death made me promise an oath to bury him in the sepulchre that he dug for himself in the land of Chanaan. Now therefore I beg to
6 go up to bury my father, and I will return." Pharao replied, "Go up, and bury your father as he made you swear."
7 So Joseph went up to bury his father, and all Pharao's servants, the elders of his household and all the elders of
8 the land of Egypt went with him, together with all of Joseph's household, his brothers, and all his father's household. They left only their children, their flocks and their
9 herds in the land of Gesen. Chariots and charioteers too went up with him, so that there was a very large caravan.
10 When they arrived at Goren-Atad, which is beyond the Jordan, they held an exceedingly great lamentation there.
11 And Joseph mourned his father for seven days./ When the inhabitants of the land, the Chanaanites, noticed the mourning at Goren-Atad, they said, "That is a solemn mourning the Egyptians are observing." Therefore it was named Abel-Mesraim, which is beyond the Jordan.

This account follows directly on the episode of 47:29 ff., the oath which Joseph swore to return his father's body to the sepulchre of his ancestors.

It is curious that as important a person as Joseph approaches Pharao on this matter only through Pharao's courtiers. Evidently it was difficult for Egyptian subjects to leave the country, though Joseph had no intention of departing permanently and he and his companions left their families and possessions behind in pledge of good faith. Perhaps the Egyptians who accompanied the Israelites were sent as much for security reasons as to honor the dead. Egypt, particularly during these times, was always suspicious of foreigners and their intentions.

Even more curious is the route they followed, if Jacob was to be buried at Machphela near Hebron. A casual glance at the map tells us that they had to pass directly by Hebron in order to reach Transjordan. As a matter of fact, v. 12 f. which immediately follow are from a different tradition, the one consistently adopted by the author of Genesis, who always places Jacob's burial in the tomb at Machphela. It seems to be an inevitable conclusion that this story about Transjordan is the beginning of an alternate tradition, rejected by the author, which located the tomb elsewhere, in the Transjordan region. Otherwise there would hardly be any point to the story at all, which carefully identifies a site which we do not know but which was known to the readers by the names Goren-Atad and Abel-Mesraim. Goren-Atad means "the threshing floor of the thorn-bush," or, possibly as a proper name, "Atad's threshing floor." Abel-Mesraim is "the field of the Egyptians," which sounds like Ebel-Mesraim, "the mourning of the Egyptians," with which it is associated in v. 11.

On the other hand, the inhabitants of the land are called Chanaanites, a name ordinarily reserved for the hither side of the Jordan, the traditional Palestine. It is possible, then, that the "which is beyond the Jordan" tacked to these names in vv. 10 and 11 is a later addition to the text. Whatever the explanation, the tradition favored by the author is in the following verses.

50: 12 Jacob's sons did for him what he had commanded them.
13 They carried him into the land of Chanaan, and buried him in the cave in the field of Machphela, facing Mamre. Both the cave and the field Abraham had bought from Ephron, the Hethite, for use as a burial ground.

These verses follow logically on 49:33, the conclusion of Jacob's instructions to his sons about his burial. They share the prolixity characteristic of this series of traditions, which loves to repeat set formulas and to leave very little to the reader's imagination.

Only one short episode remained for the author to tell of Joseph's life, a vignette in keeping with the figure thus far drawn of the great patriarch.

50:14 After Joseph had buried his father, he returned to Egypt
with his brothers and all who had gone up with him to
15 bury his father./ Joseph's brothers were fearful after their
father's death, and said, "What if Joseph should hate us,
16 and pay us back for all the harm we did him!"/ So they
sent this message to Joseph, "Before he died, your father
17 gave us this command,/ 'Thus shall you say to Joseph:
Jacob begs you to forgive your brothers' crime, and the
sin they committed in doing you harm.' Now we also pray
that you forgive the crime of the servants of the God of
your father." Joseph wept over their message to him.
18 Then his brothers came to him in person and prostrated
19 themselves before him, saying, "We are your slaves."/ But
Joseph said to them, "Do not fear; can I take the place of
20 God?/ You intended evil against me, but God intended
it for good, to do as he has done today, namely, to save
21 the lives of many people./ Therefore do not fear. I will
provide for you and your dependents." Thus he reassured
them, speaking kindly to them.

One of the punishments of ungenerous men is that they must
live in constant fear that others are as mean-spirited as themselves.
The thief trusts no man with his money and the traitor who
would sell his country for a price is precisely the one who regards every innocent act as potential treason. The man whose
own word is worth nothing considers every other man a liar. To
this extent at least it is true that sin is its own penalty.

Joseph's brothers could not feel sure that Joseph had really forgiven them. Perhaps they never felt sure and Joseph could never
make them sure. Whether or not he believed in this dying wish
of his father, however, he did all he could to convince them that
he was a far bigger man than they. This is a pleasant last glimpse
that we have of this man whose character and personality are
the most finely drawn in Genesis.

50:22 Joseph remained in Egypt with all his father's household.
23 He lived one hundred and ten years./ He saw Ephraim's
children to the third generation. The sons of Machir too,
the son of Manasse, were born on Joseph's knees.

24 Joseph said to his brothers, "I am about to die, but God
   will certainly come to you and lead you up from this land
   to the land which he promised on oath to Abraham, Isaac
25 and Jacob." Joseph made the sons of Israel swear that,
   when God should come to them, they would carry his
26 bones with them from that place./ Joseph died at the age
   of one hundred and ten years. He was embalmed and
   placed in a coffin in Egypt.

Already, as Genesis comes to a close, the sons of Israel as distinct individuals, his brothers, begin to merge into the sons of
Israel the Israelites who will be brought out of Egypt by God's
hand and given the inheritance of the Promised Land. When
that day came, we read that "Moses also took Joseph's bones
along, for Joseph had made the Israelites swear solemnly that,
when God should come to them, they would carry his bones away
with them" (Ex. *13*:19). And appropriately enough, it was in the
added portion of Ephraim that Joseph's mortality found its resting
place. "The bones of Joseph, which the Israelites had brought up
from Egypt, were buried in Sichem in the plot of ground Jacob
had bought from the sons of Hemor, father of Sichem, for a hundred pieces of money" (Josue *24*:32).

A final Egyptian note is struck in the age that is assigned to
Joseph. The Egyptians, who probably kept no real records of
their ages, repeatedly in their documents that have come down
to us use the number of one hundred and ten years to stand
for a full, well-rounded lifespan, a complete life. So it was with
the Egyptianized Joseph, whose body was embalmed and placed
in a coffin, that is, the Egyptian sarcophagus, likewise unfamiliar
to the later Israelites.

EPILOGUE

The Book of Genesis is now ended, but the Bible has only begun. The Book of Exodus will tell the wonderful story of Moses, how the Israelites were oppressed by a Pharao who knew nothing of Joseph, and how God brought His people out of this land and bore them up on eagle's wings through the desert for forty years until there was a worthy remnant to enter the Land of Promise. It will tell of the great Covenant of Sinai and the delivery of the Law to Israel. Leviticus, Numbers, and Deuteronomy are a treasury of the precious traditions of history and law which stem from the Mosaic age, completed by the story of the conquest in Josue and of Palestine under the federated tribes in Judges. How Israel took a king and how it fared under the monarchy through a half millennium will be the theme of the books of Samuel, Kings, and Paralipomenon. The divine punishment and purification of the Babylonian Exile is told in Esdras and Nehemias; and how Israel was restored through suffering and from a nation became a church. The Books of the Maccabees recount the last proud defiance of Judaism to political and religious tyranny, and the Church has not hesitated to enroll its martyrs in her calendar of saints. "Worthy are they of all honor," said St. Gregory Nazianzen, "who were brave and kept faith with the laws and uses of their fathers." Standing outside the historical books for the most part, but forming a complement without which they would be unintelligible, are the oracles of the prophets. Israel was the only nation in the ancient world that wrote into its laws the conditions under which it would accept a king and held its king to these conditions. Israel alone produced the phenomenon of prophetism, whose rep-

306

resentatives arose in the name of the LORD to denounce both king and people, priest and prophet alike, who dared to compromise with God's law. Israel alone produced the climate of social consciousness utterly lacking in every other religion save Christianity. Through the prophets God continually spoke to His people and "last of all in these days has spoken to us by his Son, whom he appointed heir of all things" (Hebrews *1*:2). The *Heilsgeschichte* of Israel and its prophetic tradition are together the beginning of Christianity.

So too are those books which the Israelites called Wisdom. When all our fathers worshipped stocks and stones the restless, misnamed patient Job called, and not in vain, on God to reply to man's perplexities. It is in him and in the unillusioned Coheleth, in the psalmists and the wise of Israel, that we must find the roots of Christian theology. The Fathers of the Church and the mediaeval Scholastics went to school with the Greek philosophers and learned a mastery of thought unknown to the Old Testament Jew, but the questions they asked and solved were those of the Jew, not of the Greek.

Finis quaestionis non finis quaerendi. The Old Testament was not the end of all wisdom, nor is the New Testament. Christianity is not buried in a book. The Church which perpetuates sacramentally the life of Christ's grace has also the prophetic ministry of His word. The word of God is living, always able to be better known, always capable of inspiring new life. The written word is not all of God's revelation, nor was its inspired writers' comprehension of the word definitive for all time. To think otherwise, to make Christianity a book religion in this sense as some have tried to do, is anthropomorphism with a vengeance, of which the authors of the Bible were never guilty; it is to confine the eternal God in a point of time which is His creation.

The end of the Bible must be our beginning. This is why there must be no shrinking from a truly scientific study of the Bible; for if we are to begin with the Bible, we must be sure that it is the Bible and not, as Pius XII has deplored, some clever use that we may make of the Bible. This scientific study by the Church's scholars, which I have tried to summarize in respect to Genesis, is vital to the Church's prophetic activity. The Church does not

create new dogmas, it defines them. The Church's definitions are
the authoritative pronouncements of the arbiter of divine truth
upon the patient probings of Christian thinkers. Without Duns
Scotus there would perhaps have been no definition of the Im-
maculate Conception. The Fathers of the Council of Trent had
laid before them the open Bible and the *Summa theologica* of
Thomas Aquinas.

Every commentator on the Bible must feel, when he has done,
that he has done inadequately. What equation is there between
his poor words and those of the quickening Spirit? In truth, only
the Spirit can unlock the fulness of the Bible's meaning, since He
is its final Author. "No prophecy of Scripture is made by private
interpretation. For not by will of man was prophecy brought at
any time; but holy men of God spoke as they were moved by
the Holy Spirit" (2 Peter *1*:20 f.). The Spirit has been given to the
Church to guide and lead it into all truth. If we are in communion
with the Church and read the Scripture in a spirit of faith, we can
hope to share in the fruits of the Holy Spirit given by means of
His word. To this extent only a commentary can have meaning
and validity.

And chiefly thou, O Spirit, that dost prefer
Before all temples the upright heart and pure,
Instruct me, for thou know'st; thou from the first
Wast present, and with mighty wings outspread
Dove-like sat'st brooding on the vast abyss,
And mad'st it pregnant: what in me is dark
Illumine, what is low raise and support;
That to the height of this great argument
I may assert eternal Providence,
And justify the ways of God to men.